NATURE
COMPANION

The National Trust

The National Trust

NATURE
COMPANION

JOHN HARVEY
KEITH ALEXANDER
& DAVID RUSSELL

With illustrations by
SANDRA FERNANDEZ

Published in association with
THE NATIONAL TRUST

DORLING KINDERSLEY
LONDON

A Dorling Kindersley Book

**Edited and designed for Dorling Kindersley
by David Burnie and Peter Luff**

MANAGING EDITOR Daphne Razazan
MANAGING ART EDITOR Anne-Marie Bulat

First published in Britain in 1990
by Dorling Kindersley Limited
9 Henrietta Street, London WC2E 8PS
in association with The National Trust
36 Queen Anne's Gate, London SW1H 9AS

British Library Cataloguing in Publication Data

The National Trust nature companion.
    1. Great Britain. Rural regions. Natural history.
    I. Title
    508.41

    ISBN 0-86318-414-6

Typeset by Tradespools Limited, Frome, Somerset
Printed by William Collins Sons & Co. Limited, Glasgow

CONTENTS

INTRODUCTION

. . .

ANCIENT WOODLANDS 10

. . .

FIELDS & HEDGEROWS 24

. . .

CHALK & LIMESTONE GRASSLANDS 38

. . .

PARKLAND 52

. . .

LOWLAND HEATHS 64

. . .

MOUNTAINS & MOORLANDS 76

. . .

LAKES & RIVERS 86

. . .

BOGS & FENS 98

. . .

DUNES, SALTMARSHES & MUDFLATS 110

. . .

CLIFFS & ROCKY SHORES 122

. . .

GAZETTEER 134

. . .

INDEX 188

. . .

ACKNOWLEDGMENTS 192

INTRODUCTION

. . .

The National Trust is the largest private land-owner and conservation society in Britain. It owns or manages more than 550,000 acres of land in England, Wales and Northern Ireland, including over 500 miles of coastline. Much of the land owned by the Trust is protected against sale or compulsory purchase by Act of Parliament.

Since it was founded in 1895, the Trust has acquired many areas of countryside in order to safeguard wild plants, animals and natural habitats. The first of these was Wicken Fen in Cambridgeshire, part of which the Trust has owned since 1899. During this century many other sites have been added to the list. They range from large expanses of heathland to small meadows and tracts of semi-natural woodland. Whatever their size, all play a vital part in preserving the wildlife of the countryside.

The two tasks of protecting the landscape and its wildlife are often inextricably mixed. For example, many parks have a special value for wildlife. Their ancient trees form a habitat that is a living relic of the days when Britain was covered by forest. They harbour a great variety of lichens, and also insects and other small animals that can only live in dead wood. So, by protecting parks and their trees, the Trust safeguards both unique communities of plants and animals and historic landscapes.

In the same way, scenic beauty and wildlife interest often go hand in hand. Nowhere is this more so than on upland moorland, where heather and bracken create a mosaic of contrasting colours and shades, and also provide the

BOG ASPHODEL

AMPHIBIOUS
BISTORT

LEAF BEETLES

habitat for a range of animals, from birds to insects. Similarly, in Lake District valleys, the woods that are such a delightful feature of the landscape are also essential for the area's wildlife. Without them, far fewer species of plants and animals would be found.

The shores around these islands have a remarkable variety of scenery and habitats, from the dramatic cliffs at Fair Head in Northern Ireland to the shifting dunes of the north Norfolk coast. Each habitat has its own characteristic wildlife. Through its ownership of key sites, such as the bird-packed Farne Islands or lichen-rich woods of the north coast of Cornwall, the Trust ensures that distinctive communities of plants and animals continue to thrive.

Some of the Trust's most spectacular coastal land has been acquired through *Enterprise Neptune*, which was launched in 1965 to preserve the best of our coastline. As well as outstandingly scenic coastline, the Trust also owns large amounts of farmland and woodland. These, too, can act as important refuges for the more common plants and animals that contribute so much to the countryside.

JOINTED RUSH

SMOOTH MEADOW-GRASS

CONSERVATION IN ACTION

· · ·

Nature conservation is not a matter of leaving the countryside to look after itself. Throughout the land owned by the National Trust, visitors will often see signs of management to protect wildlife.

In many cases, this consists of helping particular species to survive – for example, by cutting down encroaching scrub that would otherwise smother grassland plants. Grazing animals are sometimes used to control scrub

EARWIG

seedlings and to keep the grass short.

At Box Hill in Surrey, sheep have been reintroduced after a gap of between 60 and 70 years. Thanks to their grazing, grassland that had become tall and rank is once again rich in wild flowers and butterflies.

Grazing has also been reintroduced on some cliff-tops, again with the aim of controlling vigorous tall-growing grasses and invading scrub. At Predannack on the Lizard in Cornwall, for example, this has helped to recreate the conditions needed by a wealth of low-growing plants. Many of these are species rare in these islands, and are characteristic of this southernmost part of Britain.

At Kinder in the Peak District, one object of management has been to reduce grazing by sheep, which over many years has led to the decline of heather and its replacement by grass. Walls have been repaired and fences erected to keep the sheep off the hill, and straying sheep have been rounded up. Within five years, the amount of heather has increased dramatically, and there has been a parallel increase in the number of red grouse and other upland birds.

The control of grazing by sheep has been only part of this major scheme. Various factors, possibly including fires and acid rain, have destroyed all the vegetation in some areas, leaving many acres of bare peat. In an attempt to bring the vegetation back, lime and fertilizer have been spread by helicopter, and seeds of grasses and heather sown over the moor. Special fencing around these areas protects young plants by keeping out stray sheep.

These are just three of the many conservation projects that the National Trust carries out. To manage so much land, the Trust relies on

HAREBELL

MUSCID FLY

SELF-HEAL

ADONIS BLUE

both a skilled and committed staff, and detailed knowledge of the plants and animals that require protection. About 280 wardens and 150 foresters look after the National Trust countryside, while a Biological Survey Team, formed in 1979, has assembled detailed information on almost all the Trust's holdings. Between 1979 and 1988, the Team surveyed almost 450,000 acres in England and Wales. The results of the field survey were combined with information from other sources, such as the Nature Conservancy Council and county wildlife trusts, to produce reports identifying key features of biological interest at each site. Much of this book is based on these reports.

ENJOYING THE NATIONAL TRUST COUNTRYSIDE
. . .

THE LAND IN the National Trust's care is so extensive and varied that no single book could hope to describe all the wildlife to be found in it. However, all this countryside is made up of a range of distinct habitats, from woodland and heathland to cliffs and mudflats. These habitats, and some of the fascinating plants and animals that can be found in them, are described and illustrated in the first part of this book. To help you plan your exploration of the countryside, the second part of the book – the gazetteer – is a detailed guide to over 150 National Trust sites throughout England, Wales and Northern Ireland. Each has been selected for its natural history interest, and the special features of its wildlife are described.

CROSS-LEAVED HEATH

The National Trust countryside is renowned for its beauty and variety. It is the aim of this book to help you enjoy its wildlife to the full.

Ancient Woodlands
· · ·

IN MYTHS and fairy tales, woods and forests are mysterious places that conceal nameless terrors, and their depths are shunned by all except hunters, poachers, outlaws and those who work with trees and timber. Today, woodlands have lost this sinister reputation. In our modern, domesticated countryside, they are among the few places where an apparently timeless stillness can be found, and where the possibility is ever present of an exciting glimpse of the unusual or shy.

Although dominated by trees, woodlands are complete communities of plants and animals. Healthy, mature trees carry a huge area of leaves, and this makes them highly successful gatherers of light. Because nearly all flowering plants need light in order to survive and grow, the pattern of shade that trees produce, and the way this changes throughout the seasons, are crucial in determining which plants can live under them and on them.

FROM FOREST TO COPSE
· · ·

Britain's woodland cover – 10 percent of the total land area – is small compared with that of many continental countries. However, the varied geology and climate of these islands, together with centuries of management, have produced many different kinds of woodland. Throughout lowland Britain, there are great woods dominated by a single species of tree, often oak, while in the south, majestic hangers

THE BURSTING OF A BUD

Although the first truly warm days of spring often occur in early March, the buds of most of our deciduous trees, such as the wych elm (above), do not burst until late April or May. This delay is crucial to many woodland plants, because it allows them a chance to grow before the trees shut off much of the light.

A WORKING WOOD

Like many of our woods, Littleworth Wood in the Cotswolds (right) was once intensively worked. The hazels were regularly cut, or coppiced, to provide a crop of poles.

WAYFARING TREE *shoot*
with clasped leaves

WAYFARING
TREE *flower*
buds

SIGNS OF SPRING
In years with mild winters, alder catkins (above) can start to open in early February. Catkin-bearing trees, which include hazel and the poplars, are pollinated by the wind. A single catkin sheds millions of pollen grains into the air.

UNDER ATTACK
From the moment it appears in spring, a hazel leaf (below) provides food for large numbers of insects. By the time it falls in autumn, it bears the scars of many months of attack.

of beech cling to rolling hillsides, with little growing beneath them in the dense shade. As well as these there are extensive woodlands made up of oak, ash, lime, willow, yew, beech, hazel and many other species. The exact mixture reflects the different soils and different levels of exposure to wind and light. Some of these woods are dark and tangled, while others, such as the Caledonian Forest in Scotland or the New Forest in Hampshire, have vast boggy glades or stretches of open grassland, kept clear of saplings by grazing animals.

Only about three dozen species of tree are native to these islands. Over the centuries, many more have been introduced, some for ornament, others for timber. Many of our largest forests are now made up not of native trees but of introduced species – trees such as the North American sitka spruce whose prodigious powers of growth are well demonstrated in upland Britain.

Alongside these large woods and forests are the numerous small woods that are equally important in our landscape – spinneys, rues, shaws, copses, groves, dingles, friths, holts and coverts. Ancient local names such as these reflect the need in earlier times to distinguish them according to their size and use.

All these different types of woodland have their characteristic plants and animals. But invariably the richest and most interesting are the ancient woods, those known to have been in existence before 1600, and especially those made

SPINDLE TREE *shoot*

LIME-LOVING TREES
Spindle and wayfaring trees often grow on limestone or chalk. Although neither of them grows more than 6m (20 feet) high, they once played an important part in rural life. The wayfaring tree's supple young shoots were used to bind bundles of sticks, while the spindle tree's very hard wood was used in the forerunner of the spinning-wheel.

Empty beech mast case

up of native trees, growing much as they would have done before the advent of forestry.

THE END OF THE WILDWOOD
. . .

For the last 5,000 years, the natural and gentle changes that occur in all woodlands as trees grow and decay, and as one species replaces another, have taken place within a higher and generally less patient order of change – that created by man. Around 3000 BC Neolithic settlers brought arable agriculture to a Britain of vast and sometimes impenetrable forest. The "wildwood", as it is known, covered nearly all of mainland Britain with the exception of the highest ground, and inhospitable stretches of coastal dune and saltmarsh.

The Neolithic settlers began to clear the woodland and cultivate the soil. This process accelerated so that one thousand years ago there was scarcely more woodland in Britain than we see today. Much of that, far from being remnants of the wildwood, was probably woodland that had sprung up on cleared or partially felled sites, which had subsequently been abandoned.

Quite early on as the area of woodland shrank, techniques were developed to manage it to provide basic necessities. These included fuel, animal food, building materials, tannin for use in leather manufacture, and later the less basic but

Slender, pointed BEECH *bud*

DOG'S MERCURY

LADYBIRD

HAWTHORN

Old GALL *formed by insects on hawthorn*

A WOODLAND AWAKES

In a wood, the advancing spring sets in motion an almost changeless programme of events as plants and animals stir into life. One of the first signs to watch out for is the sprouting of dog's mercury, which creates a continuous green carpet on the floor of some woods. Dog's mercury flowers from February onwards, and it is at this time that the leaves of hawthorn begin to appear. By the time the buds of trees such as beech and oak begin to burst, the hawthorn may be in full leaf.

important luxury of deer
for the Saxon and Norman
kings. Of these forestry techniques
two in particular – pollarding and
coppicing – were of great importance in the
development of today's woodland wildlife.

Flowers of
DOG VIOLET

PRIMROSE

POLLARDS AND COPPICES
. . .

Several of our native trees, notably oak,
ash, hazel, alder and hornbeam will, if
severed, produce new shoots from
dormant buds around the wound. As early
as 3000 BC this was found to produce useful
and easily harvested wood. If the cut is made

. . .

CUTTING A COPPICE

A working hazel coppice (left) is cut at intervals of about four to six years, while the young shoots are still straight and slender. Coppice woods of sweet chestnut are cut about every eight years, while those of oak are cut about every 30 years. The stumps left behind after coppicing are known as "stools". In an ancient coppice wood, these stools can be hundreds of years old and as much as 1m (3 feet) across.

LETTING IN THE LIGHT

Violets (left) and primroses (below) thrive in hazel coppice woods. The regular cutting of the trees around them gives the plants a chance to develop lush and vigorous foliage.

at ground level the practice is known as coppicing, while if the cut is made a few metres above the ground – thereby keeping the succulent shoots out of the reach of grazing animals – the practice is known as pollarding. Coppices can be seen throughout Britain, while the oldest examples of pollards are generally found in parkland (*see pp. 58–9*).

When a coppice wood is cut, light floods onto the woodland floor, and the flowers that grow there may be briefly but dramatically prolific, creating a beautiful swathe of colour. But this burst of brilliance is short-lived. Gradually, over a year or two, brambles and coarse grasses spread over the ground and swamp the flowers. As the coppice grows it in turn suppresses the brambles and grasses. But even in the deep shade, the flowers of the woodland floor do survive, and when the coppice is cut again, they once more burgeon and bloom.

THE ANIMAL LIFE OF A COPPICE WOOD
. . .

It is not only plants that benefit from traditional coppicing. Invertebrates too, notably butterflies that feed on spring flowers, are especially well suited to this cycle of cutting and growth. Four species of fritillary, including the rare high brown fritillary, which is found in scattered woods in southern England and Wales, rely upon the violet. Their caterpillars particularly appreciate the lush and leafy violet plants that grow in coppice woods. The ever-rarer heath fritillary, a southern species bordering on extinction,

TREMBLING IN THE WIND

The wood anemone gets its name from the Greek for "wind", an allusion to the way that the flowers tremble in the slightest breeze. Wood anemones spread by underground stems that can form large mats in fertile woodland soil. In early spring, the tip of the stem produces a single flower, and after flowering grows forwards to produce one or two leaves.

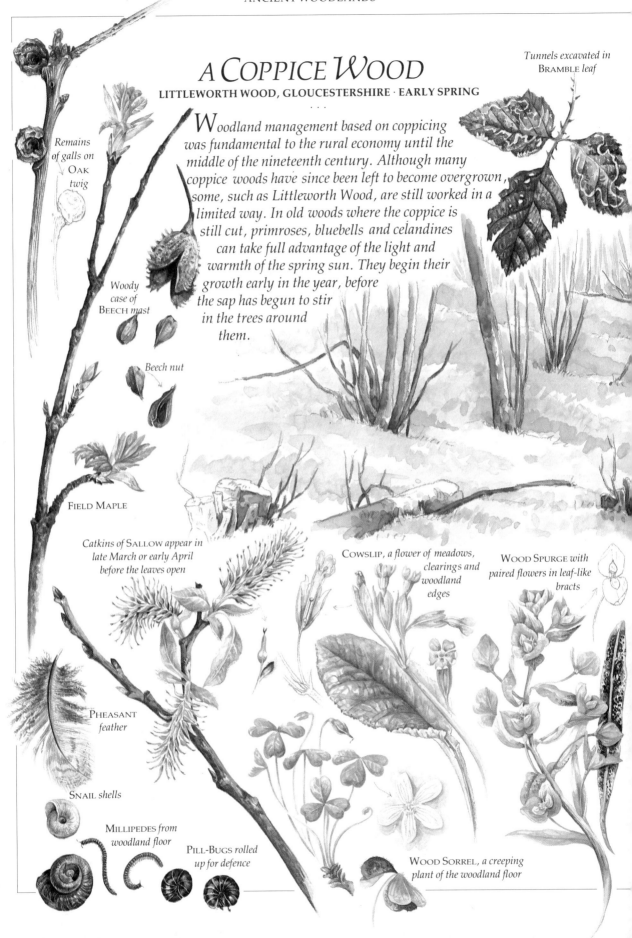

A Coppice Wood
LITTLEWORTH WOOD, GLOUCESTERSHIRE · EARLY SPRING

Woodland management based on coppicing was fundamental to the rural economy until the middle of the nineteenth century. Although many coppice woods have since been left to become overgrown, some, such as Littleworth Wood, are still worked in a limited way. In old woods where the coppice is still cut, primroses, bluebells and celandines can take full advantage of the light and warmth of the spring sun. They begin their growth early in the year, before the sap has begun to stir in the trees around them.

Remains of galls on Oak *twig*

Woody case of Beech *mast*

Beech nut

Field Maple

Tunnels excavated in Bramble *leaf*

Catkins of Sallow *appear in late March or early April before the leaves open*

Pheasant *feather*

Snail *shells*

Millipedes *from woodland floor*

Pill-Bugs *rolled up for defence*

Cowslip, *a flower of meadows, clearings and woodland edges*

Wood Spurge *with paired flowers in leaf-like bracts*

Wood Sorrel, *a creeping plant of the woodland floor*

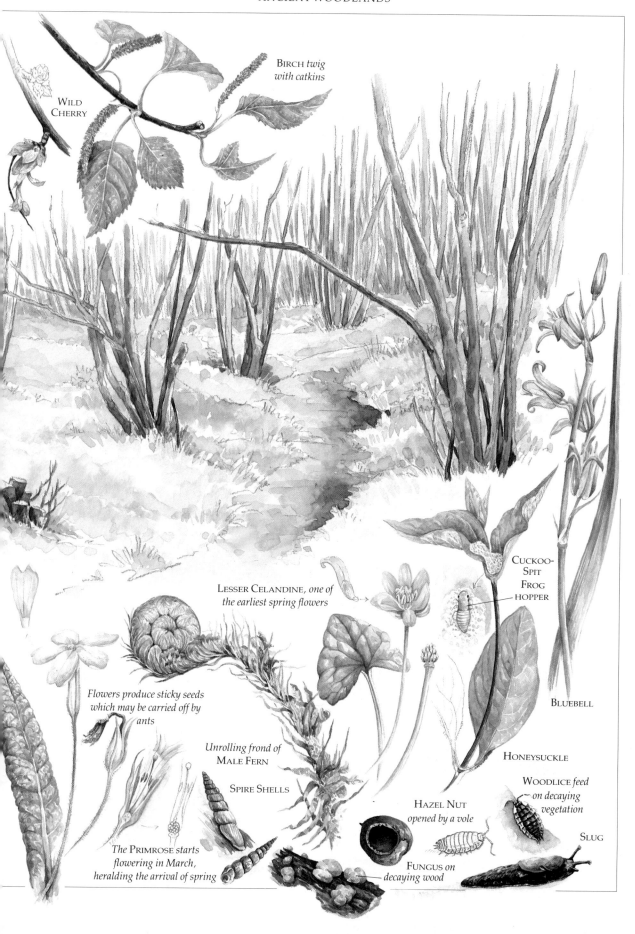

WILD
CHERRY

BIRCH *twig
with catkins*

CUCKOO-
SPIT
FROG
HOPPER

LESSER CELANDINE, *one of
the earliest spring flowers*

BLUEBELL

*Flowers produce sticky seeds
which may be carried off by
ants*

Unrolling frond of
MALE FERN

HONEYSUCKLE

SPIRE SHELLS

*Woodlice feed
on decaying
vegetation*

HAZEL NUT
opened by a vole

SLUG

The PRIMROSE *starts
flowering in March,
heralding the arrival of spring*

FUNGUS *on
decaying wood*

requires cow-wheat which, while not an early spring-flowering plant, thrives in coppice woods.

As the coppice grows after cutting, it forms a thicket providing cover for many species of birds of which the blackcap, garden warbler and nightingale are especially characteristic. These three birds are not always easy to see, the nightingale being particularly good at concealing itself. However, with practice, each can be identified by its song alone. The blackcap has a strong, clear song, broken up into bursts rather like a musical conversation. The garden warbler's song is similar, but more subdued and drawn out. The easiest way to recognize the nightingale's song is by its introduction, which often consists of a single note repeated a number of times, becoming gradually louder, which is then followed by a series of fluting trills. Despite its reputation as a strictly nocturnal songster, the nightingale can be heard throughout the day in spring.

The thickets may also conceal deer, which enjoy the privacy, warmth and shelter within coppice woods. The native roe deer, a russet-coloured animal, is the smallest deer native to Britain, and is characteristic of lowland coppices. It is often seen in threes, consisting of two adults and a youngster that stays with the parents for a year. The introduced fallow deer (see pp. 52–3), which was once restricted to royal forests and deer parks, is also found in these woods. It moves in herds of up to 30 or 40 animals. Older coppice may be inhabited by

WOODLAND STRAWBERRY

The wild strawberry flowers from April to July. From June to August it produces a crop of tiny but delicious fruit, which look like miniature versions of the garden strawberry. A similar plant – the barren strawberry – also grows in woodland. Its fruit is small, dry and inedible.

CLAIMING A STAKE

The wren and robin are year-round birds of woodland. Throughout their brief lives – only one or occasionally two years long – male wrens and robins are strongly territorial. Both use loud songs to announce their ownership of a small piece of woodland. Competing robins are very aggressive towards each other, and will attack anything that resembles the red breast of a rival.

squirrels, foxes, badgers and also by a much smaller and rarer mammal, the dormouse. Dormice are largely tree-dwelling. They benefit from coppicing only because it ensures the survival of a dense shrub layer in the hazel woods they favour. Dormice use this layer as an aerial pathway for collecting nuts and fruit. They rarely come to the ground.

THE BANK VOLE
Voles, mice and shrews are the smallest woodland mammals. The bank vole (above) feeds entirely on plants and their seeds, and moves through covered runs among the plants and decomposing leaves of the woodland floor. Voles can be distinguished from mice by their blunt noses. Shrews are two-thirds to one half the length of voles and mice. They have tiny eyes, and rely almost entirely on their sense of smell to guide them to food.

COPPICE-AND-STANDARD WOODLANDS
· · ·

ANCESTRAL HOMES
Although badgers are not the easiest of animals to see in a wood, evidence of their presence is often all around. Badgers' burrows, known as setts, are handed down from one generation to the next. A sett may have a dozen or more entrances, each at least 20cm (8 inches) across, and will often be surrounded by large piles of excavated earth and well-worn paths. A close look at the ground near a sett usually reveals the badgers' black and white bristles, which are shed as the animals scratch or walk through the undergrowth.

For several hundred years coppice woods have been modified by allowing some of the trees to grow tall to supply timber. These "standards" are usually oaks, and not more than about 25 or 30 per hectare (10 to 12 per acre) are grown. The tall trees create a more diverse habitat than coppice alone, and are particularly good for insect-eating birds such as the tree pipit, treecreeper and the woodpeckers.

During the heyday of coppice-and-standard woodlands, the standards would have been harvested while still relatively young. By contrast, many of the long-neglected woods of southern England today have large spreading oak, beech or ash trees, often growing over hazel coppice. They weaken the coppice by intercepting light and taking a large share of the soil nutrients and moisture. In more advanced stages of neglect, the hazel becomes little more than an occasional shrub in the understorey, and the character of the wood is changed – but not necessarily for the worse.

WINTER MOTH

SCATHOPHAGID FLY

The presence of many old trees has an inter-esting effect on woodland wildlife. The tawny owl nests in holes in old trees, and spends the daytime roosting either in holes, or among branches close to the trunk, where it looks from below like a piece of dead wood. Old trees also encourage bats to roost. The species found in woodland include the noctule and serotine, two large bats, and the smaller common long-eared bat, which has ears half as long as its body. Noctules and serotines take to the air in the early evening, but the long-eared bat waits until it is fully dark before emerging from its roost to feed.

EMPERORS AND MICROMOTHS
. . .

Neglect in a coppice also allows sallow, or pussy willow, to flourish. Although it is often regarded as a weed, it is the foodplant of one of Britain's largest, most spectacular and certainly most elusive butterflies, the purple emperor. Purple emperors are found only in the woods of central southern England. The adults emerge in July and the males congregate in the crowns of particular tall trees which are used every year by successive generations. They soar and battle high up in the canopy, displaying to attract females with their rich purple colour that flashes in the sunlight. It is a sight that few people are privileged to witness. The females are rarely seen.

Another "weed" tree is the aspen, which flourishes in unmanaged woods. It provides a rich source of food for moth caterpillars. Many of the adult moths are brightly coloured, but they are often so tiny – some are smaller

REVIVING A COPPICE

In Littleworth Wood, a revival in the practice of coppicing allows the woodland plants to benefit from increased light. The greater the diversity of plants, the more insects and other animals will be able to live there.

than a housefly – that they go unnoticed. Old coppice woods often throng with these "micromoths", fluttering around leaves and bark.

WOODLAND ORCHID

The early purple orchid is common in woodlands, especially those on chalk and limestone. The dark splashes on its leaves make it easy to recognize when not in flower.

A RELIC FROM THE PAST

Perhaps the least diverse of all coppice woods are the oak coppices of the mainly acid soils of western Britain. These consist almost entirely of small, twisted sessile oaks, because other naturally occurring tree species like rowan and

birch have been excluded by past management. Many of these woods originate from seventeenth- or eighteenth-century plantings. The coppices were managed to provide charcoal for the iron industry and bark for tannin, which is used in the preparation of leather. Most were abandoned before the Great War as the demand for charcoal fell.

The flowering plants of these woods are not so striking as those of other coppices, but what they often do have is an abundance of primitive plants – water-loving mosses and liverworts – and also lichens. All these need at least some shade or the presence of old trees. They survive despite coppicing, often living in deep gullies or on inaccessible slopes within the coppices where extraction of timber has always been impractical or impossible.

Sheep now graze through many of these oakwoods, and they keep down the ground vegetation and prevent the growth of saplings.

WOODLAND MOSS

Moss is quick to cover rotting branches in damp woodlands. A moss's rootlets extract all the minerals and moisture that the plant needs from the wood. Capsules on slender stalks produce spores that enable the moss to spread.

SCAVENGERS AND RECYCLERS

The leaves and dead branches that fall onto the woodland floor shelter and nourish many different forms of life. Some are visible to the naked eye, others are microscopic.

Fungi feed on the dead wood, breaking it down into a crumbly material which becomes part of the soil. Woodlice feed on decaying leaves and wood, while some slugs feed both on living plants and small animals, occasionally eating other slugs.

Woods grazed in this way provide an ideal habitat for four birds in particular, all summer visitors. The pied flycatcher, which has bold black and white plumage, nests in holes in ageing coppice, or more often perhaps in nest boxes where the coppice is still too young to be rotten, while the wood warbler nests on the ground in sparse vegetation. Like them, the redstart and tree pipit also cross the Sahara every year to reach these woods. These birds are all insect-eaters, feeding on the moth caterpillars that live on the oak leaves.

Among the most notable of these woods of the many owned by the Trust are those on the Helford River in Cornwall, where the oaks come down right to the water's edge, dipping their branches into the saline water of the creeks, Horner Wood on Exmoor, which has well over 150 species of lichens, Dolmelyllyn Woods in Gwynedd and the Borrowdale Woods of the Lake District. In Borrowdale the oakwoods are spread out from the relatively dry northern end near Keswick to the very wet Seathwaite end where the rainfall is nearly 500cm (200 inches) every year. Johnny's Wood, at the wet end, is of international importance for its plant life. Human visitors may not appreciate these soaking conditions, but mosses and liverworts thrive in them.

Moss

Woodlouse

Slug

Fungus *on rotting wood*

KING ALFRED'S CAKES
The dark, rounded swellings seen on the branches of ash trees are known as King Alfred's cakes, or cramp balls. They are the fruiting bodies of a fungus, and develop in autumn, persisting on the tree throughout the winter. To begin with, the swellings are reddish-brown, but as winter approaches they become black.

FIELDS &
HEDGEROWS

. . .

FIELDS, MORE than any feature, are the essence of the British landscape. Whether bounded by hedges, marked out by walls or by fencing, they dominate every scene. At one time, all fields, especially the permanent grassland meadows and pastures, abounded with wild flowers and animals. Today, the picture is very different. The widespread use of fertilizers, herbicides and pesticides, together with more efficient drainage and deep ploughing, has destroyed much of the wild abundance of former years.

Despite the advance of modern farming, there are still some small pockets of land that have managed to escape the onslaught of farming's twentieth-century efficiency. Here and there, either through accidents of geography or of ownership, fields survive unaffected. The ground is perhaps too wet to drain, the land too steep to plough, or the field simply too small and too distant from the farmhouse. It is in old pastures and meadows such as these that it is possible to see at first hand the flowers, birds, butterflies and other insects that were once such an integral part of our countryside.

OUT OF THE WOODS
. . .

Although fields have existed in Britain for many centuries, they are nevertheless a relatively new habitat for wildlife. They first appeared when early farmers began to cut

FALSE EYES

The meadow brown (above) is one of Britain's commonest butterflies. To a bird pursuing it, its eyespots may act like targets, diverting attention from the much more vulnerable body. The loss of part of a wing seems to have little effect on a butterfly, as can be seen from the many tattered specimens in the air in late summer.

**POLLEN
ON THE WIND**

As many hay-fever sufferers know to their cost, grasses rely on the wind to carry their pollen from one plant to another. A typical grass flower is enclosed by a pair of scales, and when it "blooms", it simply sheds its pollen into the air.

Coiled flower buds

WATER FORGET-ME-NOT

down Britain's original woodland cover (*see p. 13*) to make way for crops, sheep and pigs. Gradually, these small clearings merged so that today we have a landscape in which tracts of woodland are scattered in almost continuous fields, rather than the other way around.

Most of today's wild plants and animals of farmland must have been those that once lived in open areas within the woodland. As well as these, others probably came from cliff-tops, riverbanks and similar places. Here, exposure to wind or water suppressed the trees and shrubs that would otherwise have smothered them. When farmers began to fell the woodland, many of these species were able to flourish on the newly cleared ground.

GRAZED MEADOWS AND PASTURES
· · ·

Damp meadows and the pastures of drier ground are kept free from shrubs and trees in two ways – either by grazing or by cutting for hay. Without this, they gradually revert to woodland as saplings spring up and eventually shade the plants beneath them.

MEADOW BLOOMS

Until herbicides entered widespread use in the middle of this century, the plants shown below would have been common in almost any damp meadow. Today they are more often confined to roadside verges and the sides of ditches, where they have some protection from agricultural sprays. These are all flowers of middle to late spring. The cuckoo flower is so named because it traditionally blooms when the cuckoo arrives in April.

HUGGING THE GROUND

The daisy is one wild flower that has very much benefited from man-made changes to the landscape. A plant of short grass, it has managed to spread very successfully into lawns, where its flat rosettes of leaves survive the closest cutting.

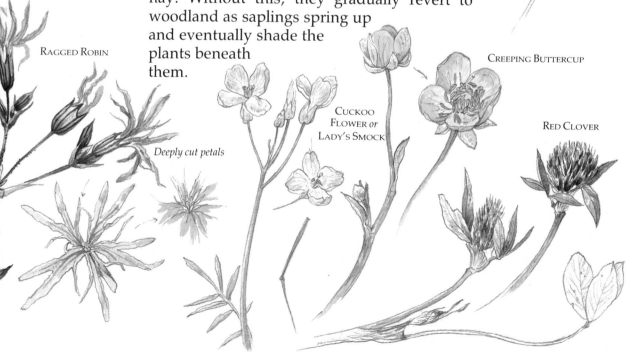

RAGGED ROBIN

Deeply cut petals

CUCKOO FLOWER *or* LADY'S SMOCK

CREEPING BUTTERCUP

RED CLOVER

To survive being grazed, a plant has to be able to tolerate the constant nibbling back of its leaves. Grasses are well adapted to this, because they grow not at the tips of their leaves, like most flowering plants, but at their bases, near where they meet the ground. Even if a grass blade is almost wholly bitten off, it still continues to grow.

Unless grazing is very severe, the wild flowers in a meadow, such as cowslips, speedwells and forget-me-nots, can usually survive by producing new plantlets or setting seed. Together with the grasses, they form a thick carpet of vegetation. Insects, spiders, slugs, snails and other invertebrates live in, over and beneath this cover, feeding on the plants or on each other.

THE WILDLIFE
OF GRAZED MEADOWS
. . .

The wild flowers of grazed meadows provide food for insects, such as butterflies and bees, that depend on nectar and pollen. The flowers often harbour thrips, tiny sap-feeding insects also known as "thunder bugs". The seeds are food for many species of weevil.

Large anthills are a special feature of old grazed fields. Each hill slowly increases in size year by year, and the biggest can be of a great age, possibly hundreds of years old. Considerable numbers of anthills dotted over the surface of a field are a sign that it has not been ploughed for a very long period.

Because an anthill is raised, the soil that makes it up is warmed by the sun more than the surrounding turf. This heat incubates the eggs within the nest. As well as having its own

WATERCRESS
Like many members of the cabbage family, watercress (above) has a sharp-tasting oil in its leaves. Wild watercress grows in shallow rivers and ditches, but it is also grown commercially in flooded beds. In the wild, tiny snails feeding on the plant may harbour the liver fluke, a parasite which can be passed on to humans.

GROWING ON WET GROUND
Rushes (right) are common in badly drained fields. Their stems are filled with pith and are solid, unlike those of grasses which are hollow.

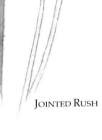

JOINTED RUSH

COMPACT RUSH

microclimate, an ant-hill even has its own plant life. The sun-facing sides are visibly different to the more shaded sides, which are often mossier. Wild thyme frequently grows on the top of anthills, flourishing in the freely draining soil.

The animals that spend all their lives in permanent grassland are joined by others that need woods, hedges or walls as well as the grassland itself. Fields are a feeding place for animals such as the hedgehog and blackbird, but both need a habitat with more cover for breeding and resting. Green woodpeckers also delight in eating ant pupae from anthills, but need hedgerow or

MARSH MARIGOLD
With its tall clusters of glossy blooms, the marsh marigold or kingcup is one of our most striking spring flowers. It grows in wet meadows and damp woodlands, often in standing water. When the flowers wither, they are followed by rosettes of curved seed-pods.

woodland trees for nesting in the spring.

Among larger animals, the true grassland species are found more in extensive, rough fields that are less heavily grazed. Long-tailed mice and short-tailed field voles both need the cover of thick, lank grass, although not even this is guaranteed protection against their great enemies, the owls. The skylark and partridge are two birds that are found where the grass is long, but rarely where it is closely cropped.

STRIKING A BALANCE
· · ·

The dung produced by farm animals acts as a natural fertilizer. Not only does it return nutrients to the soil, it also creates a habitat for some insects with very specialized lifestyles. The furry yellow dung-fly and the slow, cumbersome droning flights of the dor beetle are very much features of any pasture. The dung-fly lays it eggs directly on dung, while the dor beetle excavates holes in the ground, burying the dung which provides food for its larvae. Grazing animals have other beneficial effects. The trampling of the ground by sheep, cattle and horses prevents the build-up of litter from dead plants. This litter can otherwise smother the small plants and invertebrates which live on the soil surface. Trampling hooves also break the sward, creating the bare ground so

Ripe seed-pods

SOUTHERN
MARSH ORCHID

MEADOW ORCHIDS

About 50 species of orchid grow in the British Isles. The southern marsh orchid (left) and the heath spotted orchid (below) are two species sometimes found in damp fields. Orchids are unusual plants. Their flowers are extraordinarily complex, many having evolved a shape or scent that attracts just a single species of insect. Their seeds are among the smallest in the plant world, and a single flower-head may release hundreds of thousands into the wind. Each seed can only germinate and develop through a close partnership with a particular species of fungus.

important for many insects and spiders that need open areas for hunting and chasing prey. This bare ground also give new plants an opportunity to establish themselves.

Taken to extremes, grazing can sometimes be damaging to wildlife. If it is too heavy, it may destroy the more delicate plants, and when these disappear, so too do the insects and spiders that rely on them. Clumps of creeping thistle, docks or nettles are sure signs of an overgrazed field, because these are often the plants that take over when others die.

THE WILDLIFE OF HAY MEADOWS
. . .

The ecology of a hay meadow is quite different from that of a grazed field. Grazing is a slow and steady business, gentle on flora and fauna alike. In hay meadows, on the other hand, the year is punctuated by a sudden and dramatic change – the summer cut.

During spring, the grass of a hay meadow is allowed to grow thick, tall and flowery, providing cover and food for animals from insects to rabbits. But once this growth reaches its peak in summer, everything is cut down and the dried hay is carried away. Animals that need cover must run for the adjoining hedges and woods or perish, while the insects that need late-season flowers, seeds or tall plants are deprived of their means of survival.

The life-cycles of hay-meadow plants

PLUNDERING PARTNER

Yellow rattle is named after the noise made by the ripe seeds when the plant is shaken. It is a hemiparasite of grass, meaning that it extracts minerals and water from the roots of grass plants. Unlike fully parasitic plants, it has normal leaves which make food from sunlight. Yellow rattle often grows in open groups. The grass around these becomes stunted, showing the effect of supporting an unwelcome guest.

HEATH SPOTTED ORCHID

Old Meadows

BLICKLING, NORFOLK · EARLY SUMMER

. . .

The meadows that form part of the great estate surrounding Blickling Hall are managed in a traditional way, one that maintains their value as grazing land without the use of harmful chemicals. Spring and summer see meadows such as these at their most beautiful and fascinating. Dozens of species of flowers bloom in the damp grass, attended by feeding butterflies, while above them, the seed-parachutes of goatsbeard are borne away by the gentle summer breeze.

SMALL TORTOISESHELL *butterflies*

Seed parachutes of GOATSBEARD *or* JACK-GO-TO-BED-AT-NOON

CLICK BEETLE

CRESTED DOG'S-TAIL *grass*

Stem of HORSETAIL *with concentric "leaves"*

DAISY

Central florets

RED CLOVER

Unopened flowers

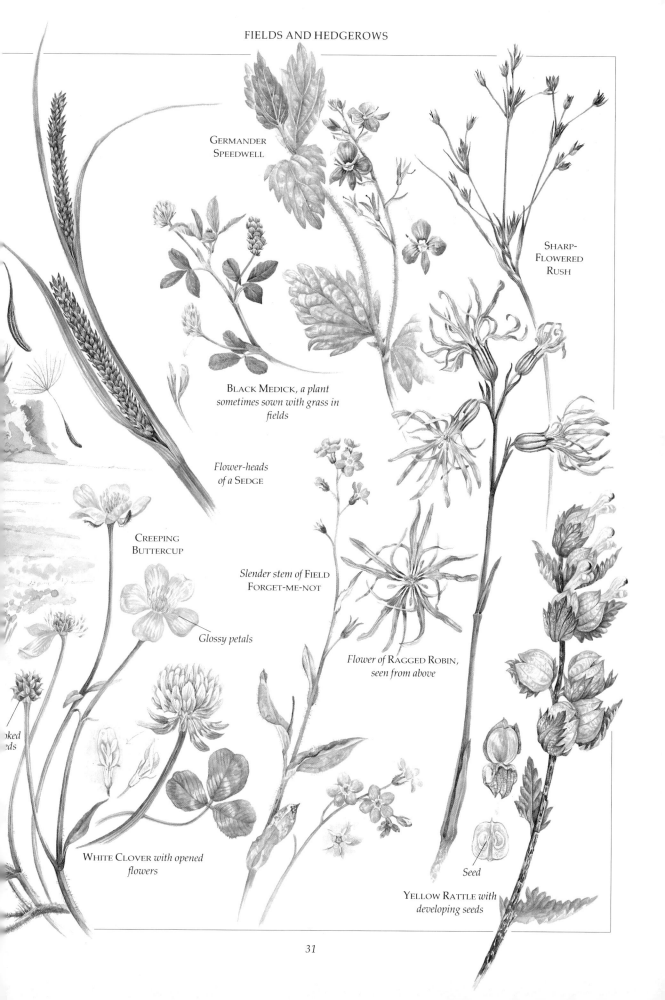

GERMANDER
SPEEDWELL

SHARP-
FLOWERED
RUSH

BLACK MEDICK, *a plant
sometimes sown with grass in
fields*

*Flower-heads
of a* SEDGE

CREEPING
BUTTERCUP

Slender stem of FIELD
FORGET-ME-NOT

Glossy petals

Flower of RAGGED ROBIN,
seen from above

oked
eds

Seed

WHITE CLOVER *with opened
flowers*

YELLOW RATTLE *with
developing seeds*

have to fit this annual pattern of growth and cutting. The green-winged orchid and globeflower grow up early and have flowered and set seed well before cutting. Yellow rattle flowers later, but it has largely seeded by the time of cutting, and the cut actually helps to ripen and disperse its seeds. A few plants, such as the fritillary, which is now a rarity, suffer under spring and summer grazing but thrive in fields that are cut for hay. Hay meadows therefore have a very special kind of plant life.

NORTH AND SOUTH
. . .

As with other wildlife habitats, old meadows and pastures vary very much across the country, depending on local conditions such as the nature of the soil and the history of land use. Even adjoining fields can have quite different plants and animals.

These regional variations in character always make visiting "unimproved" farmland an interesting experience. In the northern hay meadows of the Lake District and the Yorkshire Dales, some specialities include the mauve-petalled flowers of the wood cranesbill, the pink bell-shaped flowers of water avens, the tiny yellow flowers of lady's mantle, and the pink or red club-shaped flower-heads of great burnet and common bistort. In their wetter areas, pastures in northern England also have mountain pansy, grass of Parnassus (not a grass, but a plant with white flowers and heart-shaped leaves), northern marsh orchid, and the delicate birdseye primrose. Southern meadows often have

A DUAL DIET
Dance flies (above) feed on nectar and on other insects, which they catch in flight. As a prelude to mating, a male dance fly will offer his partner a captured insect. This gift is thought to distract her from eating her suitor.

PASTURE INSECTS
The caterpillars of the bloodvein moth (below) feed on docks in rough pastures. Dung-flies lay their eggs in dung, helping to break it down so that it fertilizes the soil.

FEEDING AT FLOWERS
All bees (below) feed on nectar and pollen. The familiar honey bee comes originally from Asia. It lives in colonies of tens of thousands of individuals, housed either in man-made hives or in holes in trees. Bumble bees form much smaller colonies, while many other bees are solitary.

HONEY BEES

BUMBLE BEES

quite different plants, including meadow-rue, which has foam-like flowers, pepper saxifrage, fritillary, green-winged orchid and autumn crocus, which flowers in September or October when most other plants have long since set seed. Spiny rest-harrow is another southern species, together with corky-fruited water drop-wort (a member of the carrot family), meadow thistle and, in the southwest, the low and spreading ivy-leaved bellflower.

SURVIVING IN A CHANGING HABITAT

The majority of plants in fields are hosts to a profuse but almost hidden wildlife. They have insects or mites feeding on their roots, in their stems, and on their leaves, flowers and seed-heads. Dyer's greenweed, for example, has more than 30 species of insect that feed primarily on it, devilsbit scabious at least 13 and ox-eye daisy at least 25.

These animals are not automatically present with their host plants, but only when conditions are exactly right. The caterpillars of the marsh fritillary butterfly, for example, feed in communal webs spun on the leaves of devilsbit scabious where grazing is moderate or light. Increased grazing, if only for a season or two, can easily destroy the butterfly colony, even though the plant itself may persist and recover when the grazing eases. If another colony nearby survives the butterfly may return, but often a colony is isolated and once it disappears, the butterfly vanishes completely.

Another very striking inhabitant of wet meadows, the scarlet tiger moth, can be just as sensitive to subtle changes. Its caterpillars feed mainly on the leaves of comfrey, spending the

**THE
SMALL SKIPPER**
Skipper butterflies get their name from their agile, darting flight. The small skipper is common throughout southern Britain, especially among flowers in tall grass.

winter and pupating at ground level, generally on banks within the meadow. Winter flooding can kill the caterpillars, while spring flooding can do the same to the pupae. A slight change in rainfall can make all the difference between survival and failure.

Many grassland invertebrates share this need for precise conditions. Plants are generally much more tolerant, and can persist for longer periods in unfavourable conditions. Fields, meadows and pastures rich in butterflies and other insects are therefore much rarer than those rich in wild flowers.

BIRDS AND MAMMALS OF FARMLAND
· · ·

The bird life of fields and permanent pastures depends very much on the degree of drainage and the presence of standing water. Dry fields may often be the home of little else apart from the skylark, a bird often heard high above the

A SLY SURVIVOR
Unlike many of Britain's larger mammals, the fox has managed to adapt and thrive in our changing countryside. This is mainly due to its very varied diet. In the country, foxes will eat anything from earthworms and beetles to rabbits and pheasants, while in towns, they can survive on the contents of dustbins. Although they are largely nocturnal, foxes can also be seen during the day. Even at a distance, a fox can easily be distinguished from a dog by its light, trotting gait and its bushy tail or "brush", which is held almost horizontally.

NESTING IN THE GRASS
When seen in the air, or across a field, lapwings or peewits (above) seem to be marked entirely in black and white. It is only at close quarters in good light that their plumage reveals its beautiful green and blue iridescence. Lapwings have an unusual and quite characteristic way of flying. Their heavy wing-beats are interrupted by sudden twists and tumbles – almost as if they have lost control – and in spring, they perform spectacular turns and dives. Lapwings nest in shallow hollows on the ground. In the past, their eggs were collected in large numbers for food.

grass long before it is seen. The
skylark nests on the ground, and
therefore needs freedom from disturbance, especially from farm machinery.

Damp fields bring in wading birds such
as the redshank, lapwing, snipe and curlew,
all of which are attracted by the abundance of
small animals in early summer. Reed buntings
and sedge warblers also live in this kind of
farmland if the field margins are lined with
taller plants. In summer, when flying insects
abound, swallows and house martins swoop
low over the grass to collect their share. They
are easy to tell apart as the martin has a white
rump, while the swallow's is dark.

Grassland insects and earthworms are
also a great attraction to many flocks
of birds during winter months, providing the grass is short enough for them
to be able to probe the soil with their bills.
Waders such as the lapwing and golden plover,
various species of gulls, crows, starlings and
wintering thrushes such as the redwing, will
all gather on farmland for this winter feast.
Golden plovers are known to have traditional
winter feeding areas, and black-headed gulls
– ever ready to exploit an opportunity – often
get their food by stealing it from the more timid
plovers around them.

HEDGEROW WILDLIFE
· · ·

A field's size and the nature of its boundaries
depend very much on its history, location
and current use. Many of the fields we
see today were originally marked
out in the eighteenth
and nineteenth

PRESERVING THE LIVING PAST

Since 1939, more than 90 percent of Britain's old, unimproved pastures have been ploughed up and replaced by cereals or new strains of grass. The few traditional grasslands that do remain, like those at Blickling, are important refuges for wildlife and poignant reminders of a former landscape. Low-intensity farming is the key to their survival.

centuries, as a result of the passing of the many Enclosure Acts, which obliged farmers to make boundaries around their land. Others are much older, and may date back as far as pre-Roman times.

Before the invention of barbed wire, the simplest way to make a stock-proof boundary in lowland Britain was to plant a hedge. The hedgerows around fields are now habitats in their own right, with a large number of animals spending their entire lives within them and not using the adjacent fields at all.

The least interesting hedges, in terms of

their wildlife, are those that consist of a single species of tree or shrub. Hedges planted solely with hawthorn or beech, for example, attract fewer animals than those containing a mixture of species, such as elder, blackthorn, hawthorn, hazel, wild cherry, wayfaring tree and field maple.

In a mixed hedge, the different trees and shrubs attract their own insect life, and so the variety within the hedge is even greater than that suggested by the diverse flowers, foliage and berries. A typical mixed hedge may include plants from woodland and scrub, while its edges may harbour flowers that are found in grassland.

Hedges act like long corridors for woodland animals. Birds such as the long-tailed tit, which rarely ventures into the open, travel along them, picking insects from the branches, while the wren scuttles mouse-like within their cover, emerging only to emit a surprisingly loud song for such a small bird. Great and lesser spotted woodpeckers also use hedges as an extension of their habitat.

The way a hedge is managed also affects what lives within it. A layered hedge – one that is periodically cut through almost to ground level and then woven to form a dense barrier – provides better cover for birds. Irregular trimming helps animals that either feed or nest in the outer foliage, but an annual cut, especially if it is carried out by machine, produces a hedge that is poorer in its wildlife.

BUTTERCUP LOOKALIKE
Tormentil's four petals readily distinguish it from the buttercups, which have five. A common plant of meadows, heaths and marshes, tormentil was once much used by herbalists.

MARSH SPEEDWELL
Marsh speedwell is one of about 20 speedwells which grow wild in Britain. Quite how they get their name is unclear. Their small but cheery flowers were certainly thought lucky, and it may be that travellers used them to preserve their good fortune on journeys. The colour of speedwell flowers ranges from intense light blue to pale pink and white.

CHALK & LIMESTONE GRASSLANDS

. . .

THE GRASSLANDS of Britain's chalk and limestone country are justly famous for their scenic beauty. But the appeal of their scenery is more than matched by that of their wildlife. Their springy turf harbours some of our most colourful and delicate flowers, and in summer, butterflies flutter among them in search of nectar and suitable places in which to lay their eggs. These grasslands make up a very special habitat, because so many of their plants and animals are found nowhere else.

Chalk and limestone are both sedimentary rocks, laid down over a hundred million years ago and composed of the hard remains of small marine animals. Chalk is the softer of the two rocks and, because it is so readily worn away by rain and streams, it produces much more gentle landscapes, such as the Downs of southeast England.

Chalk is confined to an area south of a line from Flamborough Head in Yorkshire to southeast Devon. Limestone occurs more widely, reaching as far west as Devon and Anglesey, and north to the apex of Scotland. Because it is more resistant to weathering than chalk, rocky outcrops and gorges are common in limestone country. So too are caves, which are created by water slowly percolating through the porous rock. There are many different types of limestones. The hardest occur

SCENTLESS MAYWEED

COMMON ROCK-ROSE

WILD THYME

SELF-HEAL

Self-heal (right) is a plant of short grass. Its creeping stems spread to form large patches on sunny ground. Self-heal gets its name from its traditional use as a treatment for wounds and inflammations.

PLANTS OF THE TURF

The grasses of south-facing chalk and limestone slopes are not as vigorous as those on cultivated ground, so flowers such as wild thyme are able to survive in the turf without being swamped.

COMMON BENT

QUAKING GRASS

in the north Midlands and north-west England, and here the rock has produced dramatic landscapes such as the gorge of Dovedale on the Derbyshire-Staffordshire border, and the extensive rock-strewn terrain of the Malham Estate in the Yorkshire Dales. By contrast, the oolitic limestone of the Cotswolds is relatively soft, and it has created a largely gentle, rolling plateau that is deeply cut by steep-sided valleys.

A LIKING FOR LIME

The special wildlife of chalk and limestone grasslands is due, either directly or indirectly, to the high lime content of their soils. Lime, or calcium carbonate, is derived from the underlying chalk or limestone rock, and it makes the soil alkaline. This alkalinity suits a great variety of plants. Animals also benefit from the lime. Some use it directly – snails, for example, use it to build their shells – while others rely on it indirectly because they depend on lime-loving plants.

On gentler ground, the soil tends to be deep, and acts as a barrier to the lime beneath. Some lime is drawn upwards, helped by burrowing animals such as earthworms and moles, and also by the roots of plants. But, in general, these flatter areas are poorer in the plants, butterflies and other animals that make chalk and limestone areas unique. The best places to find these species are

GRASSLAND FUNGI
Although many species of fungi (below) prefer damp, shady conditions, there are plenty that thrive in open grassland. Puffballs are often encountered in this habitat. They sometimes grow to great sizes – a diameter of up to 30cm (1 foot) is not unusual. When a puffball reaches maturity, its top splits open and releases millions of tiny spores.

PUFFBALL

STORING WATER
A plant of well-drained rocky slopes, orpine (above) has fleshy, water-storing leaves. Its flowers are tiny and star-shaped. This specimen has finished flowering, and is about to shed its seeds.

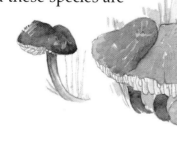

Gilled TOADSTOOL

A LIMESTONE DALE

Dovedale (opposite), a deep valley on the Derbyshire-Staffordshire border, has been carved out of the limestone plateau of the Peak District by the River Dove. The dale is famous not only for its spectacular scenery but also for its plant life. The grass is kept short by sheep and rabbits and, in spring and summer, is studded with wild flowers. Dovedale Wood is a good example of a large wood dominated by ash trees.

GRASSLAND COUSINS

The hare (above) is a much bigger animal than the rabbit (right). Both feed on grass – the rabbit usually in groups, the hare on its own. Unlike the rabbit, the hare lives entirely above ground, and brings up its young, known as leverets, in thick cover.

on steep slopes where the soil is thin, where animals and plants live closer to the lime-bearing bedrock, and where the plough cannot easily reach.

THE ROLE OF THE RABBIT

Like most of Britain's grasslands, those over chalk and limestone were created by the systematic clearance of trees and shrubs. They are maintained as grassland only because they are constantly grazed by animals such as sheep and rabbits. Chewing, biting and trampling all prevent coarser grasses and young trees from becoming established, and so the plants that grow in a particular area of turf depend very much on the animals that feed on them.

The traditional rough grazing that in the past has preserved this habitat has gradually fallen from favour as an economical way to use land. In some places, the most accessible areas have been ploughed up, while in others, grazing farm animals have disappeared, to be replaced by wild rabbits.

The rabbit was introduced into Britain by the Normans for its

LIMESTONE GRASSLAND

DOVEDALE, DERBYSHIRE · MIDSUMMER

In winter, the upper reaches of Dovedale can be bleak and windswept, but on a warm summer's day, even the highest ground is enlivened by wild flowers, especially where walls or outcrops of rock provide shelter. The flowering season shortens with increasing altitude, and by August most of the plants, even on the highest slopes, have flowered and set seed. The seeds of thistles are carried through the air on feathery parachutes, those of rock-rose and harebell are scattered directly onto the ground, while the hooked seeds of agrimony attach themselves to passing animals and walkers.

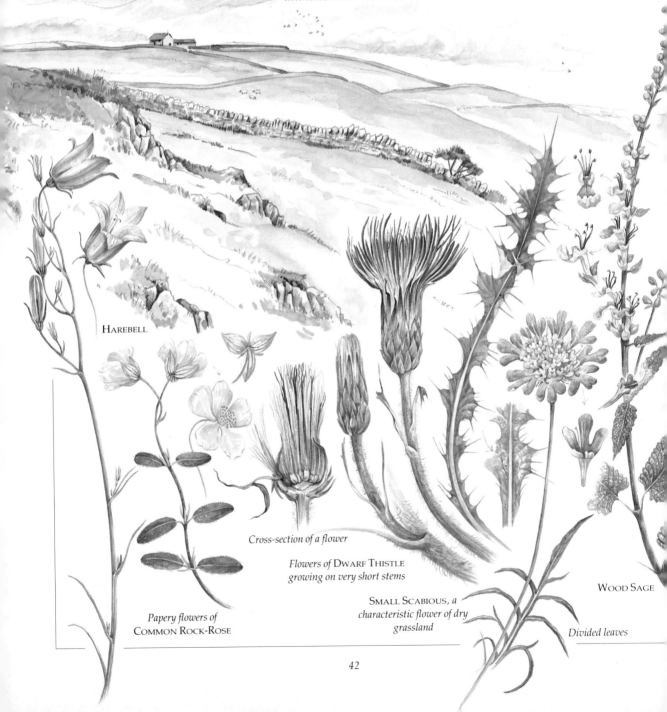

HAREBELL

Cross-section of a flower

Flowers of DWARF THISTLE *growing on very short stems*

SMALL SCABIOUS, *a characteristic flower of dry grassland*

Papery flowers of COMMON ROCK-ROSE

WOOD SAGE

Divided leaves

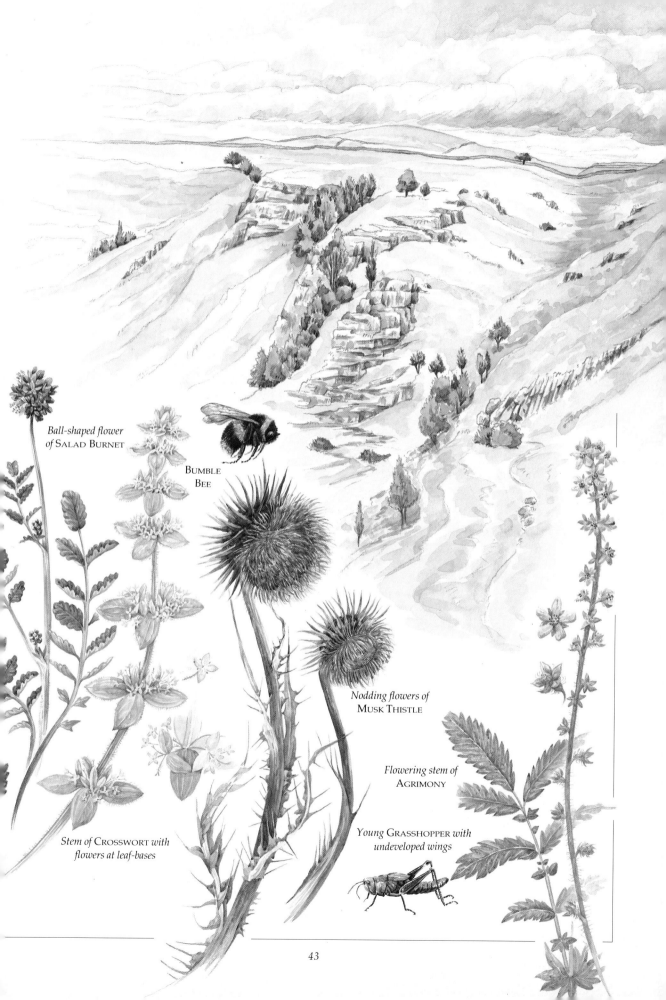

Ball-shaped flower of SALAD BURNET

BUMBLE BEE

Nodding flowers of MUSK THISTLE

Flowering stem of AGRIMONY

Stem of CROSSWORT *with flowers at leaf-bases*

Young GRASSHOPPER *with undeveloped wings*

43

PYRAMIDAL ORCHID

The pyramidal orchid (below) flowers in July, after most other orchids. It is named after the triangular shape of the developing flower-head.

meat and fur, and was originally kept in enclosed warrens and farmed. It was only during the eighteenth century that it became established in the wild, but from that time, its numbers increased hugely. In the 1950s, the disease myxomatosis was deliberately introduced in an attempt to control the rabbit's spread on farmland. This had drastic effects on many chalk and limestone grasslands. Because they were no longer grazed by livestock, their turf was often kept in good condition only by rabbits. As rabbit numbers plummeted, so many of our most beautiful grasslands became overgrown and poorer in flowers, eventually developing into scrub and woodland.

Many wild flowers have very durable seeds, and so can recover after a long period of bad

CHALKLAND SLOPES

Box Hill in Surrey (above) is a well-wooded example of chalk downland. The woods and scrub on the hill's sides contain box – the evergreen shrub which gives the hill its name – as well as yew and whitebeam, two more trees that thrive on chalk. The hill's flower-studded slopes abound with orchids.

conditions. Animals, unlike plants, do not have a stage in their life-cycles that can survive difficult times. So, as the scrub moved in, many animals dwindled or died out. One of the most celebrated casualties was the large blue butterfly, a species that feeds on the wild thyme that grows only in short grass. It became extinct in Britain in the 1970s. Attempts are being made to re-establish it using Scandinavian stock.

THE GRASSLAND TURF
· · ·

Where the grass is still grazed, chalk and limestone turf makes up a unique habitat. On south-facing hillsides, there can be up to thirty or more species of flowering plant in a square metre of turf – two or three times as many as you would expect to find in an equivalent piece of grass in a woodland clearing, for example, or on a roadside verge.

Although rich in lime, which favours a great variety of wild flowers, the soil beneath the turf often lacks other minerals, such as nitrates and phosphates. This acts as a brake on the growth of plants,

A BOX HILL FLORA
The open grassy spaces on Box Hill are the result of grazing by sheep, reintroduced by the Trust after a long absence. Grazing prevents saplings from becoming established and allows smaller wild flowers to grow in open, sunny conditions. The plants shown here all flower from early summer onwards.

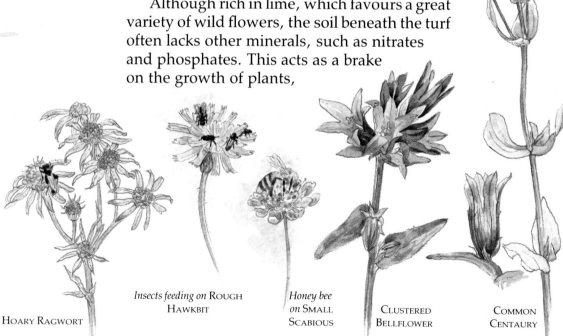

HOARY RAGWORT

Insects feeding on ROUGH HAWKBIT

Honey bee on SMALL SCABIOUS

CLUSTERED BELLFLOWER

COMMON CENTAURY

CISTUS FORESTER MOTH

SOLDIER BEETLES
feeding at flowers

GREENBOTTLE FLIES

HOVERFLIES
feeding on nectar

DADDY-LONG-LEGS SPIDER

suppressing common species such as docks and dandelions that otherwise would become dominant, and allowing less vigorous plants a chance to grow, flower and set seed.

The soil's depth, its steepness and the direction that it faces all have a great influence on the wild flowers of the turf. Because chalk and limestone are both porous, the soil above them tends to be well-aerated and dry. On a sunny slope in southern England, this produces conditions more like those on the Continent than in other parts of Britain. Grassy hillsides like this are a foothold for plants and animals more common on the opposite side of the Channel. They include the rare bastard toadflax, a low plant with small leaves that lives parasitically on the roots of other grassland species.

On the dry, warm slopes, conserving water is a priority. Plants like common rock-rose are low-growing, and have small leaves with thick surfaces to reduce evaporation. Some species flower early and so avoid the heat of the summer, as well as the threat of being smothered by the later developers. These plants include the pasque flower, which has downy leaves and a deep purple flower, and the green-winged orchid, which has a hooded pink flower that appears from May onwards. Other plants, such as thyme and wild carrot, have woody stems or deep tap-roots that enable them to survive dry conditions.

Further north and west, the climate is less sunny and wetter,

GRASSLAND INSECTS AND SPIDERS

In spring and summer, the grassy slopes on chalk or limestone are alive with insects and other invertebrates, some scuttling through the grass in search of food and others jostling for space at open flowers. By day, bees, beetles, butterflies and hoverflies visit the flowers, and burnet moths fly slowly between plants, their bright colours perhaps warning birds that they have an unpleasant taste. After dark in spring, cockchafers fly noisily over the turf and, later in summer, female glow-worms use their pale green light to attract males flying overhead.

ORB-WEB SPIDER

HARVESTMEN
with parasitic mites

BURNET MOTHS

Flowerhead of
HOARY
PLANTAIN

but this does not mean that the chalk and limestone grassland is poorer for wildlife. Instead, it has its own specialities. These include Jacob's ladder, a pretty blue-flowered plant, grown in cottage gardens, that is common in the wild in the Derbyshire Dales. Thistle broomrape is another curiosity, a parasitic plant that grows on the roots of thistles, found in grasslands in the northeast. The birds-eye primrose, which has beautiful clusters of carmine-coloured flowers, grows only as far south as the Craven district of Yorkshire.

CHALKLAND BUTTERFLIES
· · ·

In high summer, the air above chalk and limestone grasslands throngs with insects. Many of the species that breed in this habitat depend on a few, or even one, species of plant, and cannot survive without them. The purple clustered bellflower, for example, which blooms in June and July, almost invariably has *Miarus* weevils in its flower-heads. It is also visited by a very small species of bee, and sometimes as many as a dozen of these tiny black insects can be seen flying around each flower or settling on its petals.

CHAFER BEETLE

Wingless female
GLOW-WORM

EARWIG

But of all these insects, the most conspicuous are butterflies. On the whole, they are not large species, but what they lack in size, they often make up for in colour. Among butterflies, the grassland specialities are the ''blues'' – small, very active butterflies that have grub-like caterpillars. Most male blues have iridescent blue upper-wings, the colour of the sky on a clear summer's day. The underwings

LADYBIRD

JACOB'S LADDER
Although widespread in parts of Europe, wild Jacob's ladder is a very localized plant in Britain, growing only in Derbyshire, parts of the Pennines and a few places in Scotland. It is much more often seen in gardens, where it seeds itself very successfully.

LATE SUMMER COLOUR

On southern hillsides, marjoram, black knapweed and hedge bedstraw (below) continue flowering until the end of August. At this time of the year, traveller's joy seeds begin to develop the long "tails" that will turn white and fluffy before winter.

of both sexes are marked with an intricate and colourful pattern of streaks and spots.

The horseshoe vetch, which carpets the ground with yellow flowers in the early summer, plays an important part in the lives of some of these butterflies. Its flowers are a nectar source for many insects, while its leaves are the food of caterpillars of the Adonis blue and chalkhill blue.

The Adonis blue – the most brilliant of the British blues – is found on the Downs and the Chilterns, while the chalkhill blue, which is also restricted to southern England, is slightly more widespread. Although the two butterflies share the same foodplant, they prefer it in different forms. The Adonis blue lays its eggs singly on the leaves of horseshoe vetch in grazed turf. Here the soil is warm, providing the right conditions for ants that nurture the caterpillars. The caterpillar secretes a sugary fluid, known as honeydew, which the ants feed on, while in return, the ants guard the caterpillar. The chalkhill blue lays its eggs in taller turf, where the vetch is more lank and bushy.

The caterpillars of another downland butterfly, the small blue, feed in the flattened flower-heads

ADONIS BLUE

CHALKHILL BLUE

Winged seed of TRAVELLER'S JOY

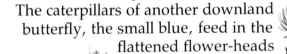

BLACK KNAPWEED

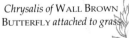

Chrysalis of WALL BROWN BUTTERFLY *attached to grass*

MARJORAM

TRAVELLER'S JOY, *also known as* OLD MAN'S BEARD

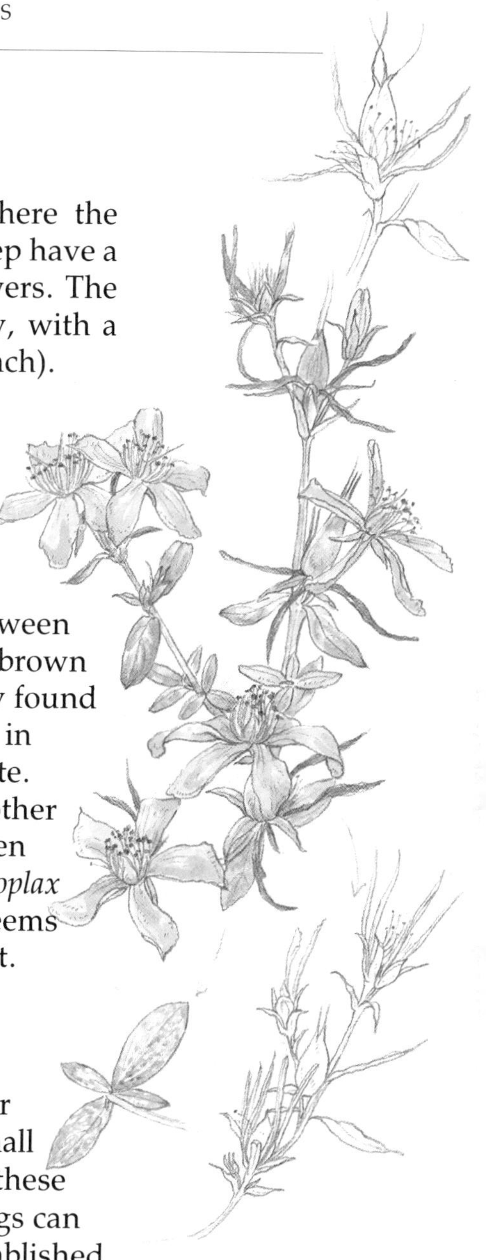

GRASSLAND BLUES
The Adonis and chalkhill blues (left) *produce different numbers of generations or "flights" in a year. The Adonis blue has two generations annually. Butterflies in the first generation take to the air in May and June, and it is from their eggs that the second generation appears in August and September. The chalkhill blue has just one generation, with the current year's butterflies taking to the air in July and August. The Adonis blue spends the winter as a caterpillar, the chalkhill blue as an egg.*

of the kidney vetch. They suffer where the grass is grazed by sheep, because sheep have a particular liking for kidney vetch flowers. The small blue is Britain's tiniest butterfly, with a wingspan of just 22 mm (less than 1 inch).

Common rock-rose is another important caterpillar foodplant, in this case for the brown argus. This butterfly belongs to the family that includes the blues, but both male and female are brown in colour. They can often be seen in groups, fluttering between flowers on sunny days. The northern brown argus, a closely related species, is only found north of the Midlands, with Dovedale in Derbyshire being its most southerly site.

Common rock-rose also nurtures other invertebrates, such as the metallic green cistus forester moth and the bug *Macroplax preysleri*. In Britain, this rare species seems to be confined to limestone in the west.

MINERS AND BURROWERS

Trampling by cattle, sheep or horses creates paths and small breaks in the turf, and in these openings seedlings can become established. These warm, dry clearings are also places where hunting insects and spiders can pursue their prey without the obstacle of plants. Rabbit scrapes and burrows too provide patches of open ground, and these are often used by solitary bees and wasps.

PERFORATED LEAVES
Perforate St. John's wort gets its name from translucent glands in its leaves. When the leaves are held up to the light, the glands look like tiny perforations in the leaves' surface.

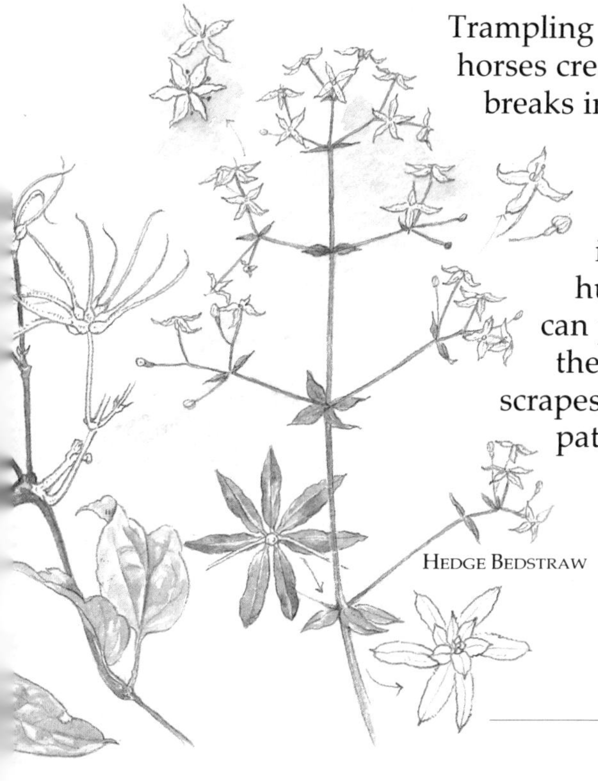

HEDGE BEDSTRAW

Unlike those bees and wasps that make communal nests, these insects live alone. The females excavate tunnels in which they lay their eggs, and these are incubated by the warm soil. A close look at one of these dry banks will often reveal a number of tiny holes, each an entrance to a nest. Sometimes the hole is sealed with a plug of earth to prevent predatory insects entering the tunnel.

GRASSLAND TREES AND SHRUBS

· · ·

As many conservation workers will know, trees and shrubs can be a problem in grassland when they spread too quickly. However, if kept in check by regular cutting, they do have a value for insects and birds.

Bushes often provide a roost for butterflies such as the green hairstreak and the Duke of Burgundy fritillary, a species that lays its eggs on cowslips. Dry, open grassland is not a particularly good habitat for birds, but where it is partly covered by scrub, it provides food, cover, shelter and nest-sites for warblers, finches, tits and thrushes. If there are taller trees, birds such as the green woodpecker

ESCAPING THE PLOUGH

Box Hill in Surrey (below) has over 400 species of flowering plant. One of the reasons for this great variety is that its steep slopes have never been ploughed. By contrast, many similar areas of chalk downland, from the Marlborough Downs in Wiltshire to the South Downs in Sussex, are now used for growing cereals instead of for raising flocks of sheep. Where this happens, the original wild flowers have retreated to the hedgerows – if they still exist – or vanished altogether.

SNAILS AND SHELLS

Snails thrive on chalk and limestone, because the calcium in the soil is the raw material that they use to make their shells. These are banded snails, one of the larger species found in this habitat.

. . .

SPRING ARRIVAL

In spring, a harsh weet-chak-chak *call heralds the arrival of the wheatear, a summer visitor from Africa. Wheatears live on high ground, including limestone hills, and are easy to see as they fly about restlessly over the ground, perching on fenceposts, walls and outcrops of rock.*

and kestrel can nest. Both of these birds forage over grassland, the woodpecker mainly for ants that it collects on the ground with its long tongue, and the kestrel for small mammals that give themselves away by moving while the bird hovers silently high above.

Britain has only three native conifers. Of these, two – yew and juniper – are found in this habitat. Wild yews can be seen clinging to rocky slopes in places like Cheddar Gorge in Somerset, while juniper is a special feature of chalk and limestone in the south. This rare shrub supports an interesting wildlife of its own, with particular insects feeding within its fruits, buds, foliage and even leaf litter.

Where grassland is grazed, native trees and shrubs are prevented from spreading too rapidly, and so a balance between scrub and open grass is maintained. However, many trees and shrubs have been brought into Britain to decorate our parks and gardens, and some of these thrive in open grasslands, turning them into dense thickets. Species such as holm and Turkey oaks, pine and larch, cotoneaster and sycamore may look attractive, but they often squeeze out our grassland wildlife. Preserving the grasslands often involves cutting down and clearing away these trees – an apparently destructive act that actually helps the native wildlife rather than harming it.

HANGING IN THE AIR

The kestrel is the only British bird of prey capable of hovering for sustained periods. From its vantage point above the ground, it can drop noiselessly onto mice, voles and shrews below. Small mammals are not its only food – it also eats earthworms, grasshoppers and beetles, and chases insects on the wing .

PARKLAND

. . .

**PARKLAND
PUFFBALL**

*The stump puffball fungus
lives on decaying wood.
Its fruiting bodies emerge
near affected trees in the
autumn, and when ripe
they release their spores in
smoke-like clouds through
a central hole. The flesh of
young puffballs has a firm
texture and can be
very tasty.*

WITH THEIR ancient trees, tranquil lakes and sweeping grassy slopes, landscaped parks are designed to be a distillation of all that is perfect in our countryside. Their open, tree-studded expanses set them apart from the land around them, and in them the eye is drawn to far-off vistas – to herds of deer grazing on the turf, to bridges spanning broad streams, to distant lakes rippling in the wind, or to sombre woods silhouetted against the skyline. At the focal point of every landscaped park is a great house, an imposing seat for a wealthy family, resplendent in a sea of green luxuriance.

But parks were not always like this. Indeed, the landscaped parks that now surround so many of the National Trust's grandest properties often date back no earlier than the eighteenth and nineteenth centuries. They were fashioned under the guiding hands of men like "Capability" Brown and Humphry Repton, who created rolling contours with the help of armies of labourers. Before this kind of landscaping became so popular, many of these great parks already had a long and fascinating history, one which has a bearing on the plants and animals within them today.

UTILITY AND ORNAMENT

One of the earliest references to a park in the Western world comes from the writings of the Roman author, Columella. He describes woodland being enclosed within walls or a fence of wooden stakes. Such a park, with its constant supply of water,

THE FALLOW DEER
*The beautiful fallow deer
is the most common deer
kept in parklands. In the
past large parks supported
herds hundreds strong,
and today these handsome
animals still breed in large
numbers in places such as
Richmond Park in
London. The fallow deer's
rich, spotted coat and its
flat, palm-shaped antlers
easily distinguish it from
the red deer, which is
larger. Its spots, which are
thought to camouflage the
deer in dappled sunlight,
grow and fade with the
seasons. In summer, they
are at their most
pronounced, while in
winter they can disappear
completely. Individual*

animals also vary in colour. The "white hart" seen on inn signs is not a mythical animal but a white variant of the fallow deer; dark grey animals are also sometimes seen. Fallow deer are well suited to life in open parkland because they thrive on a diet that includes large amounts of grass. In winter when grass is in short supply, they will feed on acorns, sweet chestnuts and beech mast, all of which are produced by parkland trees. One of the problems of keeping deer is that in winter they will also feed on bark, and so young trees need to be protected to prevent the deer killing them.

nut-bearing trees, deer, wild pigs and aurochs (the ancestors of modern cattle), combined practicality with decoration. This epitomized parks from the earliest years, for the animals were not only ornamental, they were also a source of food. Such parks were luxuries, but apparently not uncommon in Italy and Gaul 2,000 years ago.

In Britain there is no evidence of Roman parks of this type. The earliest indications of the use of parks in Britain comes from an Anglo-Saxon will dating from 1045, while the earliest certain record is from the Domesday Survey of 1086. This lists 35 parks, eight of which belonged to the King. It has been estimated that by 1300, over 3,000 parks were in existence, together occupying perhaps two percent of the area of England.

These medieval deer parks were enclosures made chiefly for the management and protection of deer, especially after 1086 when the fallow deer was introduced to Britain by the Normans. The Normans considered deer to be woodland animals, and accordingly parks normally contained woods and scattered trees, but were doubtless quite as variable in composition as they were in size. Being expensive to maintain, many of these medieval parks had only the shortest of lives.

It is possible, with a practised eye, to pick out the outlines of long-lost medieval parks from the field patterns of the modern countryside. Sometimes, as in the Great Wood at Slindon in Sussex,

ARRIVAL FROM ASIA
This discarded feather comes from a pheasant – a bird traditionally reared in copses and on rough ground in parks. The ring-necked pheasant comes originally from southeast Asia, where wild birds still live in their natural habitat of damp reed-beds. Reared pheasants often feed on open ground, but if allowed to, they roost in trees like their wild relatives.

SITTING ON STALKS

There are two kinds of oak common in Britain – the sessile oak, which has acorns that grow directly from the twigs, and the pedunculate or English oak, which has acorns that sit on long stalks (below).

The English oak is the more common species in fertile lowlands. Although they have a bitter taste, the acorns of parkland oaks are eagerly eaten by deer, birds (particularly jays) and insects. Squirrels collect acorns and bury them to provide food during the winter.

the bank upon which the old stake fence was constructed is still clearly visible.

During the sixteenth and seventeenth centuries, a new prestige development became fashionable with the wealthy. This was the enhancement of the land surrounding the house with formal landscapes of immense and geometric complexity – nature tamed by art. Briefly, the balance between utility and ornament was lost. But, in the eighteenth and nineteenth centuries, changing tastes combined beauty and utility in a new but artificial naturalness, on the grand scale favoured by Brown and Repton.

Many parks of medieval origin were embraced within these designs. Because of this, they have been protected from the even more radical changes that have taken place in the surrounding countryside.

ANCIENT TREES
. . .

The great age of their trees makes parks of special significance for nature conservation. Ancient trees are even now only rarely found in woodland. They were not, certainly, a common feature of medieval woods, but they did occur in parks and park-like areas of the royal forests, the hunting preserves of medieval kings. In many places, it is likely that they had replaced ancient trees before them, just as we are planting to replace them today. This succession of ancient trees over many centuries has created an unusually stable habitat for plants and animals.

Invariably the oldest and most venerable of these surviving ancient trees are the great oaks, whose crowns of massive branches,

SPANGLE GALLS

The curious red discs (left) found on the underside of oak leaves in the summer are galls produced by a tiny wasp. A single wasp larva lives in each of these ''spangle'' galls. The galls fall from the leaves in autumn, and adult wasps emerge from these in spring.

both alive and dead, are supported on short, gnarled and deeply furrowed trunks. Park oaks have tremendous lifespans. One, still flourishing at Calke Abbey in Derbyshire, has been dated back at least 650 years and the oldest still alive today may have begun life at the time of the Norman conquest.

Although old oaks frequently carry large amounts of dead wood, this is not necessarily a sign that they have reached the end of their lives. Indeed oak, almost more than any other native tree, has a great ability to reconstruct a new crown of branches if old ones die back. These new branches grow from long-dormant buds that

LIVING IN DEAD WOOD

Dead trees (below) are used by a host of animals, from owls to insects. Hollow trunks are the home of creatures such as beetles and flies whose larvae feed on the wood itself or the fungi that infest it. Some, such as the stag beetle, are large and spectacular, while others are tiny.

AN HISTORIC PARK
CALKE ABBEY, DERBYSHIRE · AUTUMN

With its magnificent stag-head oaks, Calke Abbey still retains very strongly the atmosphere of ancient woodland. The trees form a dramatic backdrop to lakes and grassy slopes, and every autumn, their falling leaves add a rich layer of leaf mould to the ground. This fertile layer of decaying leaves and rotting wood harbours many different kinds of fungi. On a damp still day, the pungent smell of toadstools pervades the parkland woods while newly bare branches herald the approach of winter.

Twig of
SPINDLE TREE
*with empty
seed capsules*

BRACKEN *frond*

Decayed skeleton of an
OAK *leaf*

BEECH *twig with dead leaves
and next year's buds*

Young WOOD BLEWIT

HAIRY STEREUM, *a fungus
of dead and dying trees*

MYCENA *fungus growing in
decomposing leaves*

Old WOOD BLEWIT *with
upward-sloping gills*

56

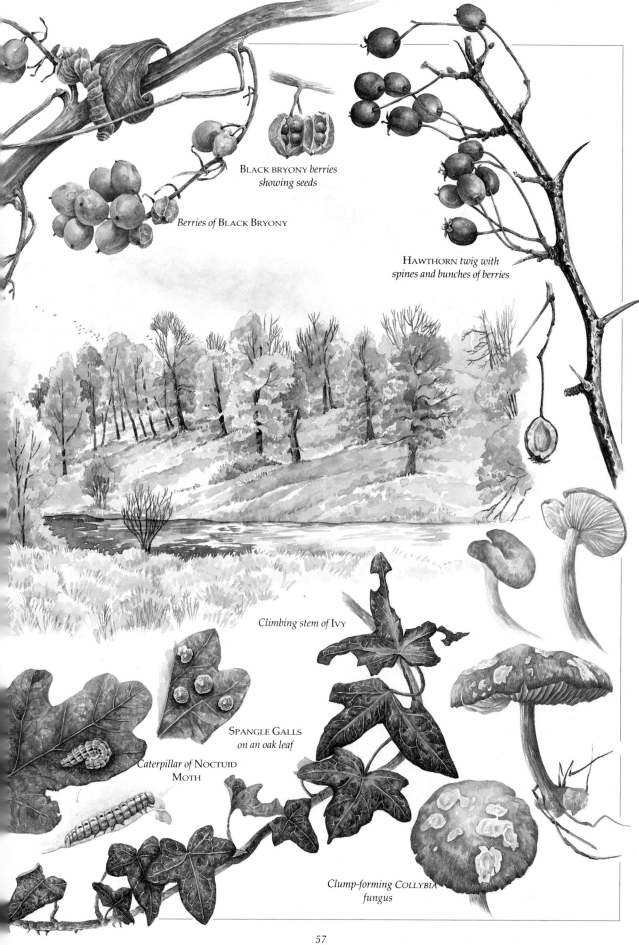

Black bryony *berries showing seeds*

Berries of Black Bryony

Hawthorn *twig with spines and bunches of berries*

Climbing stem of Ivy

Spangle Galls
on an oak leaf

Caterpillar of Noctuid
Moth

Clump-forming Collybia
fungus

Winged seed of Sycamore

Sweet Chestnuts
in spiny case

SPREADING SEEDS
The winged seeds of the sycamore spin through the air like helicopters, and are carried away from the parent tree by the wind.
The nuts of the sweet chestnut fall straight to the ground and are carried away by feeding animals, some surviving to germinate. This, at least, is what happens in warmer climates. But the sweet chestnut is originally a tree of the Mediterranean region, and in some years the British summer is not warm enough for the nuts to mature fully.

lie beneath the bark of branches that are otherwise almost totally dead.

The specimen trees of open parkland also include limes, beech, cedar of Lebanon, horse chestnut and sweet chestnut. Although the patterns in which they were planted sometimes had symbolic meanings, these are often more imaginary than real. At Croft Castle in Hereford and Worcester, for example, ancient English oaks and sweet chestnuts are said to be laid out to represent the English and Spanish fleets when Drake confronted the Armada. Sadly, this theory does not bear close examination.

While horse chestnut and sweet chestnut were commonly planted during the seventeenth century or earlier, most of the limes planted in parks date back to the eighteenth or nineteenth centuries. For reasons which are still not clear, landscape planters largely ignored the native species of lime. Instead, they went to Holland to obtain a hybrid form, which was a cross between the small-leaved lime and the large-leaved lime. This hybrid was largely propagated from cuttings. These were often from the same stock, and consequently many of the limes we see in parks today have a similar characteristic outline and appearance.

Early-flowering trees like the hawthorn may be less prominent than the tall and spreading specimen trees, but for insects at least, they are outstandingly important. The larvae live and feed on the rotting wood and fungi of ancient trees, while many of the adults feed on the nectar produced by the flowers of hawthorn.

The longest-lived of parkland trees are often those that have been pollarded, or cut through 2.5–4.5m (8–15 feet) above ground level. This

THE ASH'S BRIEF SUMMER
The ash tree's smooth grey twigs and paired black buds (below) make it one of the easier trees to identify in the winter. Traditionally, the ash vies with the oak in being one of the last of our native trees to come into leaf. Unlike the oak, it sheds its leaves early in autumn, and so it often spends a longer part of the year without leaves than with them.

ancient practice was carried out in parks to produce a regular crop of new shoots beyond the reach of cattle or deer. The new shoots sprouting from the trunk (known as the "bolling") would be harvested in a continuous system of production, with the leaves being used for fodder and the wood to make faggots for fuel.

Pollarded trees are especially long-lived, a lifespan of 600 years not being unusual. One reason for this is that the new, light and flexible shoots put no significant strain on the often weak and rotten stem of an old tree. Often it is the weight of the crown that pulls a tree apart in a severe storm.

In many parks, pollarding ceased long ago. Even so, ancient pollards can be identified by their very stout trunks, which are often hollow, and their branches, all of a similar age, which sprout at the same height above the ground.

PLANTS THAT LIVE ON BARK
. . .

Old and ancient trees have their own particular plants and animals. The most important plants are "epiphytes", those that use the bark of trees as a base upon which to grow. They do not damage the tree because they take no nutrients from it, but on the other hand, they do not help it either.

The most noticeable of these plants are lichens and mosses. A lichen is a compound organism, comprising a fungus, which provides the physical structure of the lichen, and an alga. The alga provides the green pigment that harnesses the energy in sunlight to generate food.

ROSE-HIPS

The berry-like hips of wild roses (above) are fleshy cases containing the plant's seeds. Wild rose-hips provide food for birds and small mammals. Finches peck away at the flesh to reach the seeds inside, while mice eat both the flesh and the seeds. Rose-hips are rich in vitamin C, and are used as the main ingredient of rose-hip syrup.

YEAR-ROUND PROVIDER

Standing only a few metres tall, the hawthorn may not be an imposing tree, but what it lacks in stature it more than makes up for in value to animals. The creamy-white flowers attract huge numbers of bees and hoverflies, while its berries are a staple food for many birds – particularly thrushes – until late in the winter. The leaves are also eaten by caterpillars, which in turn attract insect-eating birds.

PERMANENT PARTNERS

The cups of this Cladonia *lichen (below) are its reproductive structures.*

Different mixes of lichens and mosses are found on the bark of trees, depending on the light level and position. The side of a tree facing southwest, for example, will normally be wetter than the opposite side, favouring species that need more moisture. As a tree ages, the character of its bark changes, and the mix of plants changes as well. In light shade on the bark of mature trees – usually oak and ash – one particular mix of lichens and mosses may be found. This is called the "lobarion", after its most conspicuous lichen, *Lobaria pulmonaria*. This is large and fleshy, and because it is so distinctive it is one of the few lichens to have an English name – the tree lungwort.

In time, as the tree continues to age, other lichens become dominant. Then, as the tree approaches death, the bark

DEATH AND DECAY

In nearly all cases, the death of a tree (above) is brought about by its arch-enemies – fungi. A tree may battle against fungi for decades or centuries before it finally succumbs. The contest is not entirely one-sided, because trees are able to contain the development of fungi by "shutting off" old wood, preventing the fungal threads from spreading to new growth. However, eventually the fungi win. After the tree dies, yet more fungi feed on the dead wood.

flakes away, exposing the wood to attack by many different kinds of fungi.

For most of their lives, the fungi that infest trees consist of minute filaments or threads that spread through the wood, yielding few outward signs of their presence. But when conditions are right, the threads combine to form fruiting bodies. These vary greatly in shape and size. Some are microscopic, while others, such as toadstools and "brackets", can weigh a kilogram or more.

Different species of fungus live on both living and dead wood. The dryad's saddle – named after the shape of its stalked, saddle-shaped brackets – causes white rot in living elm, beech and sycamore trees. The beefsteak fungus, an edible species, causes brown rot in living oaks. The discolouration it produces in the wood is much sought after by furniture makers if caught in the early stages of infestation. By contrast, the brackets of the many-zoned polypore are only found on dead wood.

THE BIRD LIFE OF PARKS

The wild birds of parkland are quite elusive. Several species live in parkland, although not exclusively so. A number of these feed on insects. They depend on old large

BRACKET FUNGI
The many-zoned polypore (above and below) is a bracket-forming fungus that lives on wood that is already dead. The small semicircular brackets can be seen all through the year. They are soft and pliable to begin with, but as they age they become hard and dry. Many other fungi form brackets on living trees, and their sudden appearance at the base of a trunk is often the first sign that a tree is fatally infested.

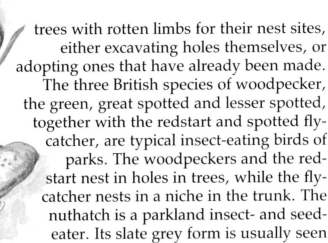

trees with rotten limbs for their nest sites, either excavating holes themselves, or adopting ones that have already been made. The three British species of woodpecker, the green, great spotted and lesser spotted, together with the redstart and spotted fly-catcher, are typical insect-eating birds of parks. The woodpeckers and the red-start nest in holes in trees, while the fly-catcher nests in a niche in the trunk. The nuthatch is a parkland insect- and seed-eater. Its slate grey form is usually seen lurching down tree-trunks, a characteristic that distinguishes it from the tree-creeper, a brown-backed bird that usually moves up the trunk when searching for insects.

Larger birds, too, nest in holes in old trees. Of these, the tawny owl and the kestrel are the most characteristic predatory birds of parkland. In Windsor Great Park, and the surrounding areas of Berkshire and Surrey, the mandarin duck, introduced in 1747 as an ornamental fowl, is now naturalized. It nests in holes in trees and feeds on acorns, sweet chestnuts and beech mast. The most unusual and exotic hole-nesting bird, breeding only rarely in Britain but favouring old parks and pollards, is the hoo-poe. It is unmistakable, with black, white and brick-coloured plumage and a crest that it flicks up on landing.

NATURE CONSERVATION IN PARKS

. . .

Because they contain large, old trees of ancient lineage, parks are a special habitat for wildlife. Several National Trust parks are of outstanding

HONEY FUNGUS

Dreaded by foresters, park managers and gardeners, an outbreak of honey fungus spells almost certain death for any tree affected by it. Honey fungus spreads not only by spores, but also by long, flattened threads. These threads travel through the ground and up tree trunks, forming a layer between the bark and the wood. The fungus's deceptively pretty toadstools appear in thick clumps on trees or in small clusters on the ground.

FOOD AND FEATHERS

Parkland birds leave evidence of their presence in the form of feeding remains and moulted feathers (right). Owl feathers have soft surfaces which silence their flight.

PROTECTION FROM THE RAIN

The fungus Mycena galericulata *is one of the many species that produces small gilled toadstools (below) on dead wood. The domed cap prevents rainwater reaching the gills, keeping the spores dry so that they can be carried away by the wind.*

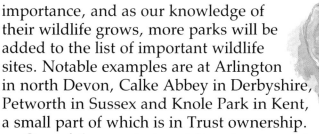

importance, and as our knowledge of their wildlife grows, more parks will be added to the list of important wildlife sites. Notable examples are at Arlington in north Devon, Calke Abbey in Derbyshire, Petworth in Sussex and Knole Park in Kent, a small part of which is in Trust ownership.

One of the greatest problems in preserving parkland wildlife is that there may be a big age gap between the old trees and the young ones, particularly in parks where planting was neglected during the later nineteenth or early twentieth centuries. Mature trees are becoming ancient, but young trees are only slowly heading towards maturity. To correct this, much care has to be taken over choosing species and sites when planting. Ash, for example, grows quickly and matures faster than oak, producing old wood in less time.

Equally important is maintaining the old trees and their fallen debris as long as possible. The old practice of pollarding can be revived to provide dead wood in living trees for parkland insects. This was a particular priority in planning the parkland restoration in southeast England following the great storm of 1987. On the whole parks suffered less severely than woodlands, but large-crowned trees in full leaf, bearing heavy seed crops, were particularly vulnerable. Some of these blown trees have been "tidied up", but apart from this are being left on the ground to rot. Here they will supply shelter for deer and food for insects and fungi for many years.

Parkland itself is not under threat. With sensitive management, its hidden wildlife can be catered for without seriously compromising the beauty and elegance of the surroundings.

LAST REMAINS
This skull is all that remains of a rabbit that has been caught and eaten by a fox. Foxes chew their prey, breaking most of the smaller bones into pieces. Owls do not digest bones, feathers or fur, but instead regurgitate them in pellets.

LOWLAND HEATHS

. . .

Iₙ ᴛʜᴇ ᴏʀɢᴀɴɪᴢᴇᴅ and productive landscape of lowland Britain, heathlands seem a natural wilderness. For many, the appeal of these unkempt stretches of heather, gorse and bracken is that of something ancient and untamed. But appearances can be deceptive. We can discover how natural and how ancient the heathland is by pollen analysis, and the results of this kind of investigation tell a quite different story.

The minute grains of pollen produced by flowering plants have distinctive shapes. Pollen is also immensely durable, and survives intact for thousands of years in the right sort of soil. By identifying pollen deposited in peat bogs over many centuries, it is possible to reconstruct the pattern of development and change in Britain's vegetation back as far as the last Ice Age. There is evidence from this that the majority of heaths are not ancient natural habitats, but owe their existence to the activities of the first farmers on these islands.

A HEATHLAND HISTORY

. . .

Farming people first made their way across the sea from Europe and settled in Britain about 5,000 years ago. They found a heavily wooded country, and a small indigenous population that survived principally by hunting and gathering wild plant foods in the great forest, although they may have had small herds of semi-domesticated cattle and pigs.

A SHARED NAME
The word "heath" is used for both the heathland habitat itself, and also for a group of plants that grows on it. The cross-leaved heath, shown here, is found in damp areas and is often mistaken for heather. Cross-leaved heath flowers from June until early autumn.

HARESFOOT CLOVER
The feathery flowers of haresfoot clover (below) can be seen in heaths and sandy places. The plant's name refers to the shape made by its narrow leaflets, three of which make up a leaf.

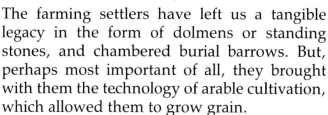

The farming settlers have left us a tangible legacy in the form of dolmens or standing stones, and chambered burial barrows. But, perhaps most important of all, they brought with them the technology of arable cultivation, which allowed them to grow grain.

With cultivation came settlement. As their technology evolved, so the farmers cleared more and more forest. On some of the lighter and thinner soils, the ones most easily won for cultivation, clearance produced irreversible changes in the structure and chemical processes of the soil. These led rapidly to a loss of soil fertility and crop yields declined. After a period, the soil became exhausted, and the farmers were forced to seek new ground.

Once cultivation had been abandoned, wild plants moved in. Among the plants growing

A SURREY HEATH
The National Trust holding at Frensham Common in Surrey (above) *covers almost 400ha (1,000 acres), much of it open heathland. Surrey is famous for its heaths, which have developed over deposits of sand and gravel that also extend into the adjoining counties of Sussex and Hampshire. Throughout southern England, much of the original heathland has either reverted to woodland or been built on, but a few large expanses still remain. Frensham Common is extensive enough to give a good impression of the heaths in their heyday.*

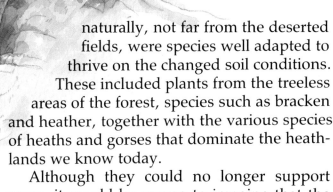

THE THREATENED SMOOTH SNAKE
The lowland heaths of southern Britain are the home of the smooth snake, a reptile that is becoming increasingly rare in this country. Smooth snakes reach about 60cm (2 feet) in length. They are not venomous, using their teeth simply to hold their prey before swallowing it.

naturally, not far from the deserted fields, were species well adapted to thrive on the changed soil conditions. These included plants from the treeless areas of the forest, species such as bracken and heather, together with the various species of heaths and gorses that dominate the heathlands we know today.

Although they could no longer support crops, it would be wrong to imagine that the newly created heathlands were seen by our remote ancestors as wasteland. In the place of crops, a heathland economy developed that was based on grazing and the use of a whole range of wild plants, including heather, bracken and gorse as well as trees. The heath-dwellers depended on the plants around them, and it was this that for centuries ensured the survival of the heath.

Grasses and heather were grazed. Bracken was of no use as an animal food but, like heather, it did make good thatching and bedding material. Gorse, cut and dried, burns well, and it helped to keep the household fires alight. Where a few trees grew they were managed by pollarding (*see pp. 58–9*), so that they provided a steady supply of new shoots which were used for fuel and animal feed.

A REFUGE FOR REPTILES
· · ·

Compared with woodland, for example, lowland heath is not an outstandingly rich habitat. But what makes it particularly interesting is that there are several animals and plants uniquely associated with it.

Reptiles, especially, find a hospitable

(see pp. 58–9)

HEAT-SENSITIVE HUNTER
Of Britain's three species of snake – the adder, grass snake and smooth snake – only the adder is capable of harming humans. However, the chances of being bitten by an adder are very small. At the first signs of an approaching walker, an adder's reaction is to seek cover, and only when taken by surprise or trodden on will it bite. A mature adder measures about 60cm (2 feet). Its pale zigzag patterning and relatively stout body readily distinguish it from the grass snake and smooth snake. Adders feed mostly during the day, detecting their prey with the help of heat-sensitive organs, one just in front of each eye.

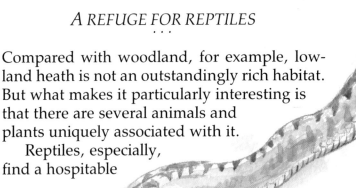

refuge in patches of sparse vegetation on the light soils, which warm quickly in the early spring sun. These creatures are cold-blooded and need this warmth, especially in northern latitudes, to quicken their still torpid bodies when they emerge from their winter hibernation in March or April. If disturbed, a basking snake or lizard can make a ready escape into the tangle of the heath.

Our rarest snake, the smooth snake, now restricted to central southern England, and our rarest lizard, the sand lizard, are exclusively heathland creatures. But other snakes, and the common lizard, also inhabit the heath.

Lizards feed on insects, spiders and worms, the last of which they suck dry and then swallow. They also feed on caterpillars, which they suck dry, discarding the body. The smooth snake hunts chiefly at dusk, feeding on voles, mice and shrews, killing them first by squeezing them in its coils. It will also eat slow-worms and small snakes. The adder, identified by its characteristic zigzag markings from head to tail, paralyses its prey by poisoning it before swallowing it whole.

In countries warmer than Britain, most reptiles lay their eggs in the ground where they hatch. Here, the only reptile to lay its eggs in this way is the sand lizard. In order to incubate its eggs, the grass snake often uses the heat of decomposition found in compost heaps. The young of other British reptiles

HEATHLAND LIZARD

Like the smooth snake, the sand lizard depends very much on lowland heaths for its survival. Female sand lizards dig holes in open patches of light, sandy soil and use them as nests to hold their eggs. Each nest contains up to a dozen eggs, and these may take as long as three months to hatch. Sand lizards spend much of their time searching for food in thick cover, and so are not easy to see.

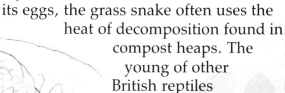

A SOUTHERN HEATH

FRENSHAM COMMON, SURREY · LATE SUMMER

. . .

*I*n late summer, when most of the wild flowers of the countryside have
bloomed and set seed, the heathland year reaches its climax. The heath and
heather flowers create a sea of red, pink and purple, while gorse – a plant
with a much longer flowering season – stands out as islands of yellow.
By this time of the year, the Scots pine has scattered most of its seeds,
adding to the perennial problem of tree encroachment. Neither heaths
nor heather can grow indefinitely in shade, and so, picturesque though
the pines may be, they have to be kept in check if the heathland, and
the animals that depend on it,
are to survive.

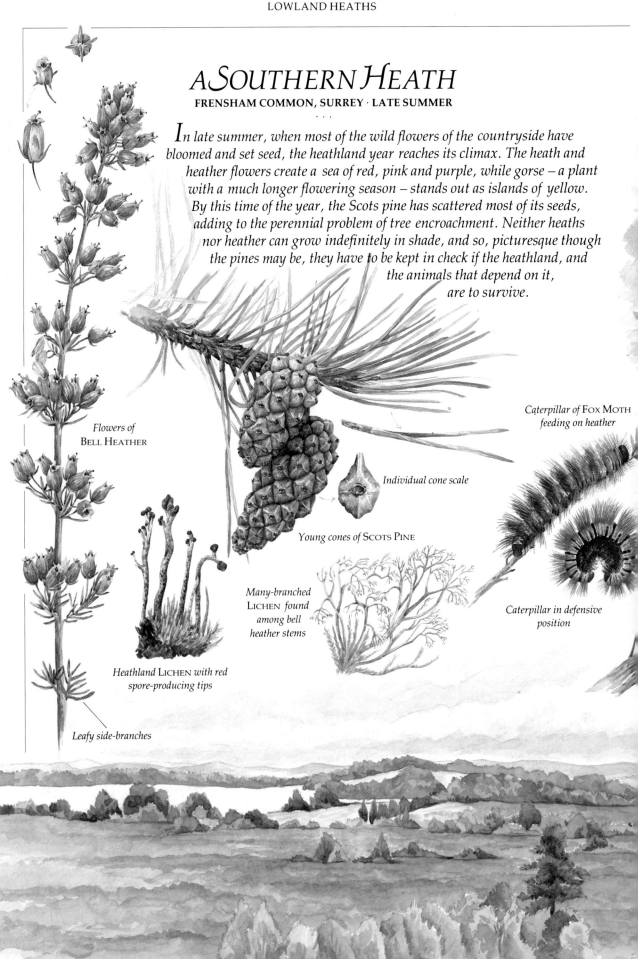

Flowers of
BELL HEATHER

Caterpillar of FOX MOTH
feeding on heather

Individual cone scale

Young cones of SCOTS PINE

Many-branched
LICHEN *found
among bell
heather stems*

*Caterpillar in defensive
position*

Heathland LICHEN *with red
spore-producing tips*

Leafy side-branches

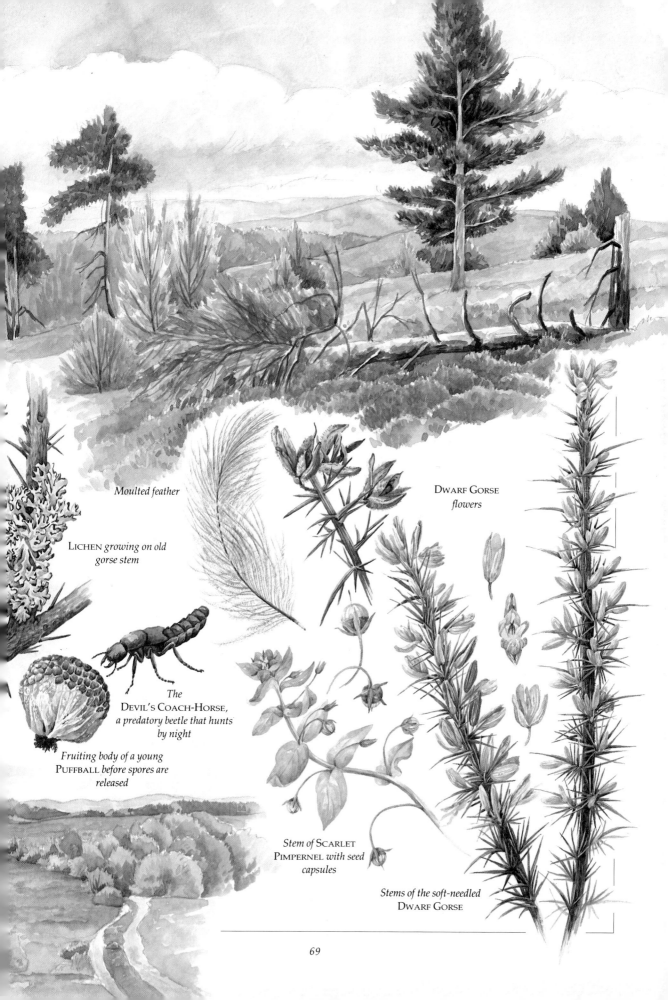

Moulted feather

Lichen growing on old
gorse stem

Dwarf Gorse
flowers

The
Devil's Coach-Horse,
a predatory beetle that hunts
by night

Fruiting body of a young
Puffball before spores are
released

Stem of Scarlet
Pimpernel with seed
capsules

Stems of the soft-needled
Dwarf Gorse

69

hatch at almost the same moment that the egg is released by the mother, some four months after fertilization. In these species, incubation takes place almost entirely within the mother's body.

PREDATORS AND SONGSTERS

For the visitor to the heath, sightings of reptiles are often dramatic. So, too, is the sudden appearance of birds of prey. The hen harrier spends much of the summer on upland moors, but in winter it hunts over the lowland heather and open farmland, with a slow, buoyant flight, taking birds and small mammals on the ground. Measuring about 46cm (18 inches) from head to tail, the hen harrier is one of the largest heathland birds. The female has the mottled brown colour that is typical of many birds of prey, but the male is grey and white with black wingtips, giving it an almost gull-like appearance.

When seen in pursuit of swallows or martins, the slate-grey hobby is one of the most breathtaking of all predators. A swift and agile

THE NODDING HAREBELL

The delicate flowers of the harebell appear from about July until the end of September. Harebell is always found on poor soils, those of heathland suiting it as much as those of grassland.

HIDDEN IN THE HEATHER

Nightjars are nocturnal, feeding by night and roosting on the ground by day. Their camouflaged plumage is so effective that it is possible to pass in full view of a roosting bird without noticing it. The best time to see nightjars is at dusk against a fading sky. They fly rapidly on pointed wings, darting after moths and other insects.

GORSE

Of all our wild flowers, gorse – or furze as it is also known – has one of the longest flowering periods. If the winter is mild, common or European gorse – one of three different species – will flower almost year-round, while dwarf gorse and western gorse usually flower from June until well into November. The gorses are members of the pea family, and they bear their seeds in pods. On warm dry days in spring and early summer, the pods explode with an audible crack.

hunter, it is a summer visitor to Britain, often choosing to nest among the branches of heathland trees. Hobbies are elusive even where they are known to breed.

Sometimes at dusk, between May and early August, the sustained churring song of the nightjar interrupts the silence of the heath. The monotony of the song is broken only as the tone changes when the bird moves its head. The nightjar is active only at dusk, when it takes to the air with an agile flight, catching insects on the wing. Large, owl-like eyes enable it to hunt in the twilight, and as it flies, bristle-like feathers on the sides of its beak funnel prey into its mouth. Locating a feeding nightjar is difficult but, if you are patient, not impossible. Finding one roosting in its daytime retreat on the ground is a different matter altogether. Nightjars have superbly camouflaged plumage, and when resting look just like broken pieces of wood, mottled with lichen.

Less dramatic, but rather more easy to see, are small birds such as the stonechat. Listen during the spring and summer for a sound like two stones being tapped together, and then look for a robin-sized, handsomely marked bird flicking its wings and flaunting its tail on top of a gorse bush.

In the early spring on the heaths of the southern counties, another bird may be seen singing from the gorse, characteristically flicking its long tail up over its back. This is a true heathland rarity, the Dartford warbler. This small bird is one of the few warblers that stay in Britain

ON AN ACID SOIL

Like many heathland plants, trailing St. John's wort is found mainly on acid soils. After flowering, it produces seeds in hollow capsules, which split open when ripe.

A SLOW DEVELOPMENT

It takes three years for a Scots pine cone to mature and release its seed. In the first year, the cone is small, green, and tightly closed. In the second year, the cone grows in size, but it is not until the third year that it turns hard and woody. Warm weather makes the cone scales open, releasing the winged seeds that fall gently to the ground. The needles of pines grow in clusters of twos, threes or fives. Those of the Scots pine are in pairs.

SCOTS PINE *cone*

SCOTS PINE *shoot*

Paired needles

throughout the year. It is at the northern edge of its European range here, and harsh winters prove devastating. Even in a good year, there are no more than a few hundred of these warblers in the entire country. Studland in Dorset, Frensham Common in Surrey and Ludshott Common in Hampshire are good places to search for the warbler when it is at its most active in early spring.

HEATHLAND MAMMALS

. . .

Few mammals of note haunt the heaths, other than the ponies, cattle and sheep that commoners still graze on some of them – most notably in the New Forest. Voles and shrews are not infrequent, foxes and rabbits also, no doubt finding easy burrowing in the light soils. That other great digger, the badger, prefers heavier soils where its cavernous sett will not so easily collapse.

Deer will often cross the heath, but they soon seek denser cover. Survival on the heath has always been for those that can hide below ground or take cover among the small shrubs and scrub – and it is this that makes them so vulnerable to the works of man.

COLOUR AND CAMOUFLAGE

. . .

There is one butterfly that is characteristic of the heath in summer. To the walker in July or August, the grayling materializes as if from nowhere, flies rapidly but in-directly to another patch of sunlight, and then, just as abruptly, disappears again. The grayling's vanishing trick works

FOX MOTH CATERPILLARS

The fox moth lays its eggs on heather, heath and bramble. As the caterpillars grow, they change in appearance. The bristly hairs of the mature caterpillars make them unattractive to birds.

Young FOX MOTH *caterpillars*

Mature FOX MOTH *caterpillars*

A FLAWED FORECASTER

Contrary to the claims of folklore, the scarlet pimpernel does not forecast the weather. Its flowers simply react to the weather as it is, opening when it is sunny and closing quickly when the sun is hidden by cloud. After flowering, it produces seeds in capsules with detachable lids.

in two ways. Not only is it beautifully camouflaged, but when it lands on the ground in strong sunlight, it also leans edge-on to the sun, so that it casts no shadow. The grayling is not restricted to heathland, but well adapted to it.

Rather less often seen, but typical of heathland, is the green hairstreak, a small butterfly with a wingspan of just under 3cm (1$^{1}/_{5}$ inches). Its caterpillars feed on gorse. The metallic green undersides of the wings, which it displays when sitting, are unlike those of any other British butterfly.

Undoubtedly the speciality butterfly of heathland is the silver-studded blue. It is now restricted almost entirely to the heathlands of southern Britain, with one or two surviving strongholds on limestone grassland in Wales. It dislikes dense mature heather, preferring the young growth that appears after cutting or burning, or sparse leggy heather where light can reach the ground.

Like the Adonis and chalkhill blues (*see p. 48*), the silver-studded blue enjoys a strong, mutually beneficial relationship with ants. The caterpillar is always attended by black ants and is commonly found within ant nests. The ants feed on a sugary fluid secreted by the caterpillar, and the caterpillar benefits from the protection of a "private army" of ferocious ants.

THE GRAYLING
The grayling is a rather local British butterfly, flying from July to early autumn, and laying its eggs on fine grasses and dead twigs. The caterpillars feed mainly in the following spring and early summer, when they pupate. Unusually for a British butterfly, the pupa or chrysalis is found underground.

WINTER EGGS
The silver-studded blue lays its eggs in June on heather and plants of the pea family, including gorse and birdsfoot trefoil. The eggs remain intact until the spring of the following year, when the bright green caterpillars hatch and begin to feed. With the arrival of midsummer, the caterpillars pupate and become adults, and the yearly cycle begins once again.

HEATHLAND SPIDERS AND HUNTING INSECTS
. . .

Dewfall or frost on the heather reveals an incredibly extensive and complex distribution of spiders' webs, but many heathland species do not make webs at all. The long-legged wolf

spider is an active hunter, stalking its prey with the help of its keen eyesight. It paralyses its victims by stabbing them with a pair of poisonous fangs. During spring, the female wolf spider carries her eggs in a silk ball slung beneath her body, making her conspicuous as she scuttles over bare ground and dead bracken.

The pink crab spider waits in flower-heads to seize suitable insects as they feed on the nectar. If you see a butterfly at a flower flapping its wings in an agitated way without taking off, a close look will often reveal the crab spider clutching its prey and beginning to feed.

Dragonflies, breeding in ponds and wetlands, regularly hunt over heaths. Other insect predators are found closer to the ground. The female sand wasp paralyses caterpillars and

FIGHT FOR SURVIVAL

At one time, heaths like that at Frensham Common (above) occupied large tracts of southern Britain, especially in Dorset, Hampshire, Surrey, Sussex and also East Anglia. The heath that remains today has to be protected not only from encroaching trees and shrub, but also from the threat of development.

HEATHLAND LICHENS

On heaths, lichens (right) flourish both on the ground and on the stems of woody plants such as heather and gorse. Lichens do not have flowers. In some heathland lichens, the reproductive bodies are brightly coloured.

drags them into burrows in the dry sandy soil. The wasp lays her eggs on the immobilized caterpillars, which then act as a source of food for the wasp grubs when they hatch.

A TIME OF CHANGE
· · ·

In the twentieth century, technology has given us the power to achieve rapid and dramatic change in the countryside. With fertilizers, even the hungry heath soils can now be put to productive use, and many of the heaths in the already overcrowded south of England have been planted with conifers, or bulldozed to make way for industry or housing.

The extent of the main areas of lowland heath in Britain fell from 140,000ha (350,000 acres) in 1830 to 40,000ha (97,000 acres) in 1980, and it is still falling today. The loss of 70 percent of heathland in that period is also typical of other countries of northwest Europe, which is the only part of the world where significant areas of lowland heath exist. The remnant is therefore precious.

HERALDS OF AUTUMN

Many kinds of fungi live closely associated with pine trees, and as autumn approaches, the ground around heathland pines often has a scattering of toadstools. Slugs find toadstools by smell, climbing over them to feed on the soft flesh.

Mountains & Moorlands

. . .

Britain's upland country provides some of our most dramatic and unspoiled scenery. Superficially at least, cloud-covered mountains and windswept moors appear to have little to offer wildlife but, in reality, this is far from true. The animals and plants that live here are well adapted to the wind and cold in an environment that offers little shelter. Indeed, some of them are so specialized for mountain life that they cannot successfully compete against other species at lower altitudes.

Geologically, Britain is divided into two almost equal halves. A line drawn between the River Tees and the River Exe marks the division between the relatively young, soft rocks of the south and east, and the old, hard rocks of the north and west. Most of the soft rocks have long ago eroded into low-lying, fertile land, but the hard rocks, being more resistant to weathering, remain to form Britain's mountain backbone.

About half of Britain is upland, so mountains and moorlands make up a significant part of our countryside. This great expanse of land includes a wide variety of wildlife habitats, and discovering their plants and animals is one of the pleasures of being in hill country.

ROCK AND RAIN

. . .

The type of upland found in any particular area of Britain depends on a number of factors, the most important being the nature of the underlying rock and the local climate.

LIVERWORT *growing on rock*

Stems of
LEAFY LIVERWORT
with overlapping leaves

CREEPING LIVERWORTS

Liverworts are small, simple plants. They are very common on mountains and moorlands, the best places to see them being on rocks splashed by flowing water or on sloping waterlogged ground. Some liverworts look like little branched ribbons, while others – known as leafy liverworts – have tiny leaves arranged on either side of a central stem.

THE POWER OF EROSION

This mountain torrent in North Wales flows through a rock-strewn landscape that is a testament to the effects of erosion. Nearly all this erosion is caused by water. Water not only scours the hillsides, but also splits open the rock by flowing into cracks and then freezing when temperatures fall in winter. As water turns to ice, it expands with an almost unstoppable force. This breaks up the rock, sending huge boulders tumbling down the hillsides.

Although upland rocks are hard, they do erode gradually. Solid rock is cracked open by frost, boulders shatter into smaller stones and eventually stones turn into grit loose enough for plants to root in. The complete process takes tens of thousands of years, but the different types of rock gradually break down, each producing a different type of soil.

Limestone, basalt and dolerite are alkaline rocks. They break down to form a soil that, even where it is thin, is relatively fertile. On a high limestone hillside, such as at Malham Tarn in Yorkshire, the slopes are clad in grass, and in spring this is rich in wild flowers, the speciality here being the delicate birdseye primrose. Limestone is a fairly widespread rock found over much of Britain. Basalt and dolerite, which are both volcanic in origin, occur in more localized outcrops.

By contrast, the dark millstone grit of the Pennines creates a less hospitable habitat. Here, the rock erodes to produce an acidic soil, one that far fewer plants find to their liking. Heather and coarse grass often dominate these hillsides, and this kind of upland landscape comes into its own in August, when the heather is in flower.

FRUIT OF THE FELLS

To the walker, the fruits of the bilberry offer a delicious treat after a toil up a long slope. Bilberries, whortleberries or blaeberries, as they are also known, have for long been collected for use in jam or fruit pies, although like cranberries and cowberries (see pp. 100–1), they are small and therefore time-consuming to pick. Bilberries are important to mountain wildlife, particularly birds.

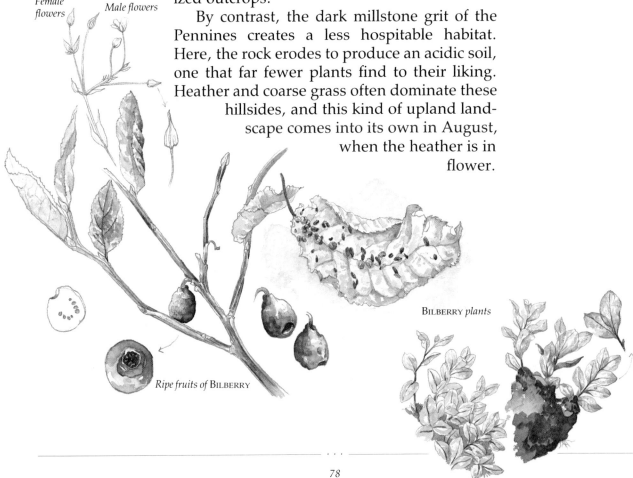

Female flowers

Male flowers

Ripe fruits of BILBERRY

BILBERRY *plants*

Male flowers

Female flowers

Britain's mountains bear the brunt of the prevailing westerly winds that bring in air laden with moisture from the Atlantic. As the air is forced upwards by high ground, it becomes cooler and is able to hold less water. The result is mist, drizzle and rain.

Rainfall can vary enormously over quite short distances. For example, at sea level in Cumbria the annual rainfall is about 90cm (35 inches). However, at an altitude of 900m (3,000 feet) in the mountains of the Lake District which lies nearby, as much as 300cm (120 inches) of rain can fall in a year.

In these very wet areas, the constant soaking, together with low temperatures, slows down the decomposition of plants. A thick blanket of waterlogged peat builds up, forming extensive bogs that can make hill walking a treacherous business.

UPLAND PLANTS
· · ·

The conditions on mountains and moorlands are too extreme for most trees and shrubs. A few stunted hawthorns, elders and oaks may survive where there is sufficient shelter, but the graceful rowan, or mountain ash, is the only tree that is naturally at home in this habitat.

The dominant upland vegetation consists of various combinations of grasses, such as clumps of mat grass, purple moor-grass, hair-grasses, bents and sheep's fescue,

SEPARATE FLOWERS
Yellow sedge (left) grows in damp ground on mountainsides. Each plant has male and female flowers, growing in separate spikelets. The male flowers are at the tip of the flowering shoot, and the female flowers further down.

LONG-DISTANCE TRAVELLER
The inconspicuous New Zealand willowherb has successfully taken to Britain's mountainsides after having arrived from the other side of the world. It is a small creeping plant that, like all willowherbs, has feathery seeds which are released from long narrow capsules.

A High Mountain Valley

CWM IDWAL, GWYNEDD · EARLY AUTUMN

At Cwm Idwal in Snowdonia, water not only shapes the scenery, it also creates perfect conditions for many simple, non-flowering plants. Mosses, liverworts, ferns and clubmosses all enjoy damp conditions, and their delicate and often beautiful shapes can be seen in abundance on stream banks, around boulders and on boggy, waterlogged slopes. All these plants reproduce by tiny spores that develop in special structures either on leaves, or on special slender stalks.

In early autumn, as the last hillside flowers bloom, countless spores are shed into the air to be blown far and wide by the mountain wind.

POLYTRICHUM moss with unripe spore capsules

Non-flowering stems of MOSSY SAXIFRAGE with leaves in rosettes

OMPHALINA toadstool

Feather-like stems of THUIDIUM moss

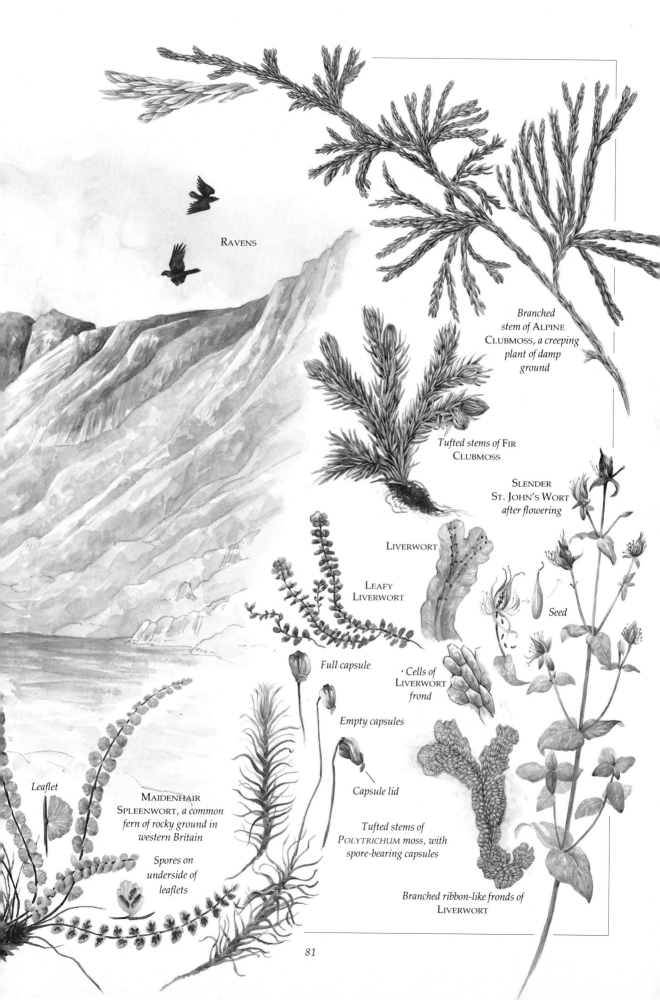

RAVENS

Branched
stem of ALPINE
CLUBMOSS, *a creeping
plant of damp
ground*

Tufted stems of FIR
CLUBMOSS

SLENDER
ST. JOHN'S WORT
after flowering

LIVERWORT

LEAFY
LIVERWORT

Seed

Full capsule

· Cells of
LIVERWORT
frond

Empty capsules

Capsule lid

Tufted stems of
*POLYTRICHUM moss, with
spore-bearing capsules*

Leaflet

MAIDENHAIR
SPLEENWORT, *a common
fern of rocky ground in
western Britain*

Spores on
underside of
leaflets

Branched ribbon-like fronds of
LIVERWORT

together with rushes and dwarf shrubs such as heather and bilberry. These plants are all low-growing, and have tough leaves that do not suffer in strong winds.

Grazing by sheep has a profound effect on mountain and moorland plants. Where sheep are plentiful, heather and bilberry often give way to grasses and rushes. A wide range of other plants can grow on mountains and moorlands, but if grazing is heavy, they are only encountered where the sheep cannot reach them. These inaccessible places include rocky ledges, crevices, the banks of streams and also islands set in streams or pools. Because it is not grazed, island vegetation is often much more lush than that around it.

SUMMER VISITORS
· · ·

Like plants, mountain birds also include those that have become adapted for life at high altitude. But, unlike plants, birds are able to choose their habitat according to the seasons. Many mountain birds migrate to lower ground, or in some cases much further afield, at the end of the breeding season. They only return just before the breeding season begins again.

The merlin, Britain's smallest bird of prey, and the golden plover, a short-billed wader, both nest on the ground among heather or grass.

HIGH-SPEED HUNTER

The peregrine lives at all altitudes, often using mountainside crags for nesting. It feeds on other birds, diving from high above and then striking with its talons. It has been estimated that in a dive a peregrine can momentarily reach a speed of 280 km/h (175 mph). At one time endangered by the effects of DDT, which weakened the shells of its eggs, the peregrine is now staging a steady comeback.

STONE-BREAKER

Saxifrages (below) are short, low-growing plants that often grow in rocky places. The name "saxifrage" means stone-breaker, describing their ability to grow out of the most unpromising rocky cracks and crevices. This is mossy saxifrage, a species that can be found in damp places on hillsides. Like many mountain plants, it has long been cultivated in gardens.

The agile merlin feeds on small birds that it pursues through the air, while the plover probes in soft ground for insects and worms. Once their young are independent, both leave the high ground until breeding begins again in the following spring. The dotterel and the ring ouzel also breed high up. The dotterel, a plump-bodied bird rather like a lapwing in shape but lacking a crest, can be seen in the Lake District and in Scotland. The ring ouzel, which looks like a blackbird with a white throat, is more wide-spread, living in the mountains of Wales, the Pennines, the Borders and the Scottish Highlands. It can sometimes be picked out by its powerful, short alarm call – much like a blackbird's – which echoes around hillsides between April and September.

A MOUNTAIN RETREAT

. . .

Many of the animals and plants that live in mountains or moorlands have no special liking for high altitudes. They live here either because hillsides form part of a much wider range that includes lowlands as well, or because this open habitat offers them safety or lack of disturbance.

Heather, for example, grows not only on high northern moors, but also on lowland heaths

A HAUNTING CALL
Hearing the call of the curlew (above) is one of the most memorable experiences in moorland country. Its name comes from its call – an echoing cur-lee – but more evocative still is its song, a series of haunting, bubbling notes that carries far over open ground. Curlews use their long, curved bills to extract small animals from mud and peat. Like those of most wading birds, their bills are very sensitive, and can detect food as well as collect it.

PREPARING FOR WINTER
Every year the leaves and stems of perennial plants such as the orpine wither away, leaving just the swollen base and roots to withstand the harsh mountain winter.

near the south coast. The russet-coloured small heath butterfly, which can be seen holding its own against the wind on moorland, is equally at home in lush meadows. The same is true of the lively meadow pipit, while a much rarer species, the peregrine falcon, which is one of the world's fastest birds on the wing, also lives on both high and low ground.

Some plants are widespread in lowland Britain, but also grow as rarities higher up. Thrift, for example, is a common sea-cliff and salt-marsh plant. It therefore comes as a surprise to see its pink flower-heads on mountain ledges in places such as the Lake District, but it does survive here, far above its more usual habitat.

The largest animal that lives on high ground, the red deer, is also more at home at lower altitudes. Red deer are originally animals of open woodland, but the reduction of Britain's forest cover has driven many of them to higher, more open ground. Approaching truly wild red deer calls for some expertise as the animals are wary and have keen senses. The slightest sign of danger will send them into a brisk but orderly retreat.

STREAMSIDE MOSSES

Mosses not only grow in low tufts – some species that grow near running water have long stems that straggle over the ground. Each stem is surrounded by tiny, tooth-shaped leaflets.

Branched Moss stems

LATE SUMMER SPECTACLE

Heather flowers from July to September, turning the dull dark green of heather moorland into a carpet of pale purple. Heather plants are very resilient, living for perhaps 30 years and becoming progressively more woody as they age. The woody base sprouts from near the ground after it is burned on managed grouse moors.

HEATHER MOOR

. . .

Heather moorland is a particularly important feature of upland country. The most extensive stretches of it can be seen on the slopes of the

Branched Moss stems

Curled Moss stems

Leaflet

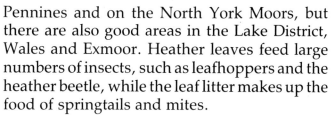

PLANTS FROM THE PAST

Clubmosses belong to an ancient family of plants that once included species taller than many of today's trees. The clubmosses that survive today are mostly just a few centimetres high, and they produce short stems that either grow upright or spread horizontally over the ground.

Pennines and on the North York Moors, but there are also good areas in the Lake District, Wales and Exmoor. Heather leaves feed large numbers of insects, such as leafhoppers and the heather beetle, while the leaf litter makes up the food of springtails and mites.

Heather, and the animals that feed directly on it, make up the first links in a food chain that includes the habitat's most famous predator – the golden eagle. Animals such as springtails and mites are eaten by birds such as meadow pipits and the chicks of the red grouse, golden plover and dunlin. Common and pygmy shrews also take their share. These animals in turn provide food for the carrion feeders, which include the raven, and birds of prey, ranging in size from the merlin and buzzard to the golden eagle itself, which has a wing span of between 180–210cm (6–7 feet).

Landowners manage heather moors by burning patches in rotation, which creates a mosaic of heather plants at different stages of growth. This makes better feeding for sheep and also for red grouse, which are reared for shooting, but it is not necessarily good for other animals, because it reduces the wildlife of the soil and kills lichen and moss. On heather moors owned by the National Trust, burning is closely monitored to prevent this kind of damage.

Remains of Clubmoss *stem showing surface scales*

ALPINE CLUBMOSS

NATURAL RECYCLING

On high moors, small toadstools show where fungi are living on the remains of decaying plants, or on old patches of droppings from grazing animals.

LAKES & RIVERS

· · ·

THERE IS ALMOST ALWAYS something to see in or near freshwater. In spring there are the large golden-yellow flowers of the marsh marigold; in summer, the dashing flight of the dragonfly in pursuit of flying insects; in autumn, the sudden swirl of fish taking food from the surface; in winter, the noisy flocks of ducks and stately swans parading for bread. Only a skin of ice stops this pageant, and even then, life goes on below the surface, hidden from view. The variety of that life is huge, with plants ranging in size from microscopic algae to tall grasses, and animals as different as minute, single-celled amoebae and mammals.

Freshwater habitats may be encountered almost anywhere in Britain. There are bubbling streams that flow over rocks on mountains and moorlands, deep lowland lakes lined with mud, shallow village ponds fringed with trees, and puddles that appear after storms, to vanish a few days later. These and many other types of ponds, pools, lakes and rivers all have their particular collections of plants and animals.

A WORLD OF WATER

· · ·

What is it that makes the life in a mountain stream different from that in a lake? The factors that influence life in water are many, and they include the speed with which the water moves, its depth, acidity and the supply of mineral nutrients dissolved in it. But, above all,

WATER SNAILS
Aquatic snails feed mainly on the tiny algae that flourish in freshwater. Most species, including these great pond snails, are found in ponds and rivers with hard or calcium-rich water. They need the dissolved calcium to make their shells, and also to make the rows of teeth that they use for rasping away at their food.

BANKSIDE PROFUSION
The deep, enticing lushness of a summer riverbank is created by the special conditions near the water's edge. Where the banks are steep, the shelter of the low-lying ground protects tall plants, and the fertile soil and abundant water supply enable them to grow vigorously.

GREAT WILLOWHERB

BULRUSH

YORKSHIRE
FOG

WINTER CRESS

life in freshwater is dominated by the need for oxygen and light. Nearly all organisms, including fish and submerged plants, depend on oxygen for survival. Oxygen dissolves in water, but water rarely contains more than five percent of the oxygen present in air. In some cases – stagnant pools in woodlands for example – it may contain none at all.

An important factor for plants is the limited ability of light to penetrate water. If the water is loaded with mud or thick with algae, the leaves of flowering plants can only work in a relatively thin surface layer.

Living in water does, however, have its benefits. Because of the buoyancy which water gives plants and animals, they do not need to develop strong supporting structures to keep them upright or in shape. Large water plants do not need trunks like trees but can manage with delicate stems. Fish do not need heavy bones like mammals but can survive with much more lightweight skeletons. Water is also slower to heat up and slower to cool down than soil.

Plants and animals living in water therefore benefit from relatively constant temperatures. Even if temperatures do fall very low, it is rare for a pond or lake to freeze solid, and under the ice there is normally enough water for organisms to survive.

STREAMS AND TORRENTS
. . .

Water movement has a profound effect on freshwater wildlife. In fast-flowing upland streams, few plants can survive the continual battering of the current and few animals can find shelter to prevent themselves being washed downstream.

**POLLEN
ON THE WIND**
On the damp ground along rivers and around lakes, grasses often escape cutting or grazing, allowing their flowers to develop fully. Grasses are pollinated by the wind, and so do not need brightly coloured petals to attract insects.

**PLANTS IN
FLOWING WATER**
*In a shallow lowland
river, such as the Stour at
Kingston Lacy in Dorset
(opposite), water plants
can take root in the
riverbed. Some plants,
such as the waterlilies,
have leaves that float on
the water's surface. In
others, the leaves are
submerged. A few plants
have two or even three
types of leaves. Common
water crowfoot, for
example, has finely
divided submerged leaves
and buttercup-like leaves
above the surface.*

Like many insects found in
streams, rivers and lakes, adult
stoneflies live in the air but lay their
eggs on the water or on vegetation
that grows in it. Their eggs develop into larvae which live, perhaps
for several years, underwater. When
fully developed, the larvae turn into
adults, which emerge in spring to mate
and lay another generation of eggs. The
dull-coloured adult stoneflies flutter
weakly over the water, and die after
two or three weeks.

Insect larvae are an important source
of food for fish. Fast-flowing streams
are generally well-supplied with oxygen,
and this suits fast-swimming fish such as
the trout, which can hold its own against the
strongest currents. The neat grey wagtail, with
its grey back and yellow underparts and rump,
may often be seen feeding at the stream side.
In winter months this handsome bird may
also be found alongside slower-flowing
lowland rivers.

Less widespread is the fat,
short-tailed dipper, which flies low
over the water from rock to rock before
plunging into it in search of a meal. The
dipper uses its wings to swim underwater,
turning stones with its beak to find
animals such as insects, snails and freshwater shrimps on which it feeds. Dippers
also eat small fish. The dipper's plumage is
much denser than that of most birds and has
an unusual downy under-layer, features that
keep it warm and dry. Unlike most waterbirds,
it does not have webbed feet, and so has difficulty swimming at speed on the surface.

*Flowers and flattened leaves
of* YELLOW WATERLILY, *also
known as* BRANDY BOTTLE

A FLEETING FLIGHT

Further downstream, as the land levels out and the water speed declines, so the number of plants and animals begins to increase. Plants with narrow, finely divided or strap-shaped leaves, such as the water crowfoot, can survive in the more sluggish water. It is in this part of the river that insects such as mayflies and caddisflies become common. Like stoneflies, these

A LOWLAND RIVER

RIVER STOUR, KINGSTON LACY, DORSET · MIDSUMMER

· · ·

*In summer, slow-flowing lowland rivers abound with
insects. Butterflies and bees visit the waterside flowers
for pollen and nectar, while delicate damselflies flutter low
over the water, courting and laying their eggs on stems and
lily-pads. A visit to a riverbank at this time of the year is often
rewarded with the sight of spectacular dragonflies, pursuing and
catching insects in mid-air. Some dragonflies, known as
hawkers, search for their food on long airborne patrols.
Others, the darters, make sudden swoops from
waterside perches.*

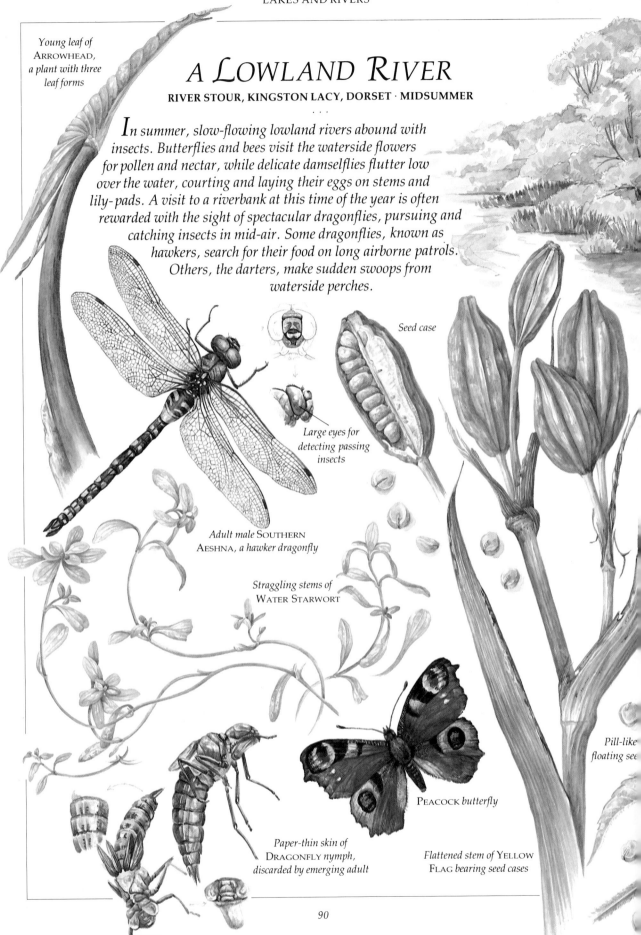

Young leaf of
ARROWHEAD,
*a plant with three
leaf forms*

Seed case

*Large eyes for
detecting passing
insects*

Adult male SOUTHERN
AESHNA, *a hawker dragonfly*

Straggling stems of
WATER STARWORT

*Pill-like
floating see*

PEACOCK *butterfly*

Paper-thin skin of
DRAGONFLY *nymph,
discarded by emerging adult*

Flattened stem of YELLOW
FLAG *bearing seed cases*

Tall flowering stem of
PURPLE LOOSESTRIFE

BANDED AGRION *damselfly
perched on plant*

Flowers of WATER
SPEEDWELL

Flowering stem of
WATER MINT

Floating DUCKWEED,
*Britain's smallest flowering
plant*

Leaf

Roots

BUMBLE BEE

Seed-head of YELLOW
WATERLILY

too spend most of their lives underwater as larvae. Emerging adult mayflies are a favoured food of the trout, a fact exploited by fly-fishermen. They are also relished by swooping swallows and house martins. Those adults that survive these attacks live for only a few days, being unable to feed.

Caddisfly larvae build protective cases of pebbles, sand grains or plant material, and live in these until they emerge as moth-like adults. The cases not only shield the soft larvae, but also camouflage them. The heavy case helps to keep its occupant in place against the tug of the current. Most species of caddisfly build their cases from a particular type and size of material, but some seem to use almost anything that is available, from shells to grass.

PLANTS OF THE RIVERBANK
. . .

In the middle reaches of rivers, bankside vegetation begins to develop, with trees such as the damp-loving alder and willows being typical. A particularly good example of riverbank alders can be seen in the Horner Valley at Holnicote on Exmoor. Although alders are broadleaved trees, they bear their seeds in woody "cones" that superficially look very much like those produced by conifers. When branches of trees hang over the water they form perches for hungry kingfishers, waiting to dive after fish. Kingfishers usually nest in high banks of soft earth, where they excavate an upward-sloping tunnel, but they can nest among the tree roots. As the water flow slows, the type of

SPREADING OUT
Brooklime is a species of speedwell – one of more than 20 found in Britain – that has adapted to life in shallow water. As it grows its stems sprawl horizontally, and they produce roots that become anchored in wet mud. Many other water plants, including watercress, grow in this way.

SAWFLIES

REED BEETLES *on leaf*

Long-snouted WEEVILS

INSECT CAVALCADE

The larger insects of a riverbank – dragonflies, butterflies and damselflies – are easy to see, especially as they are often in the air. But countless smaller insects, many of which are brightly coloured, can be found on riverside plants, feeding on sap, pollen, seeds or other insects. Among the most beautiful of these are the leaf-beetles, small shiny-bodied insects that glisten like raindrops caught in the sun.

PLANT BUG

Larva of LADYBIRD

Metallic-coloured LEAF BEETLES

rock or soil may begin to affect its flora and fauna. A stream on chalk or limestone fed by spring water, such as the River Dove in Derbyshire, will be clear and rich in plants such as the lesser water-parsnip and water crowfoot, which produces beautiful floating carpets of buttercup-like flowers. In contrast, streams on clay are often made turbid by silt in the water and may have many fewer species of plant. One of these is water-plantain, which in June bears delicate white, pink-tinged flowers on stout stems. It grows up to 1m (3 feet) high by slow-flowing water.

In small rivers arrowhead can be found along muddy banks. This plant produces leaves of three types, and is a living demonstration of how different forms of leaf are suited to different conditions. Underwater, arrowhead leaves are long and strap-shaped. This shape is an advantage because it presents little resistance to the flow of water and reduces the chance of the plant being uprooted and washed away. On the water's surface, arrowhead has floating leaves. These are roughly oval, a shape that may allow light to be used most efficiently. Their leaf-stems are flexible, enabling the leaves to move with the wind and current. Above the surface, the leaves are broad and arrow-shaped, and are borne on strong stems to prevent them falling into the water.

A number of water plants have two types of leaf, but the arrowhead is unusual in having more than this. This striking plant is common at Wicken Fen in Cambridgeshire.

As the river becomes deeper in its lower reaches, so most flowering plants become confined to the sides. Along the river edge, dense stands of tall plants such as common reed and

RAPID REPRODUCER

The small tortoiseshell is on the wing from March until October, feeding on nectar and laying its eggs on nettles, where the caterpillars grow and feed. There may be as many as three generations of small tortoiseshells in a year, so that the butterflies on the wing in the autumn are the "great-grandchildren" of the ones that laid their eggs in the preceding spring.

bur-reed may develop, providing nesting sites for swans and cover for water voles.

The water vole, sometimes incorrectly called the water rat, feeds on a wide range of water plants and can readily be seen by the quiet observer. If disturbed, it will rapidly dive underwater or retreat to its riverbank tunnel. The burrow contains a nest made of rushes, where several small litters of young may be born each year.

THE WILDLIFE OF LAKES
. . .

Lakes differ almost as much as rivers. At the two extremes are upland lakes, such as Wastwater in the Lake District, and lowland lakes, such as the Norfolk Broads. Upland lakes have clear, acidic water and rocky or gravelly shores with little vegetation, while lowland lakes often have water that is clouded by silt and algae, and are usually surrounded by muddy shores with tall plants.

The infertile waters of upland lakes do not provide many opportunities for wildlife. The numbers of birds – especially in winter – are low. One typical species is the red-breasted merganser, which feeds on fish. It has a bill with serrated edges, like the teeth of a saw, which helps it to hold its catch.

By contrast, lowland lakes are always of great interest to the birdwatcher. The noisy coot, which feeds mainly on plant material, including algae, is very evident at all seasons. Another bird likely to be seen throughout the year is the great crested grebe, a fish-eater, whose complex and elegant courtship display is

YEAR-ROUND RESIDENT

With its brilliant plumage, the kingfisher looks more like a bird of the tropics than one suited to Britain's cool climate. But the kingfisher is very much a British bird. It does not migrate in the winter, but may move downstream towards the coast at this time. Normally, it rarely travels far from its own stretch of a river.

DOMESTIC DUCKS

The common wild duck of rivers and ponds is the mallard, a bird that is found throughout the whole of the British Isles. Mallard drakes are grey with green heads, and the females brown. Large ducks of other colours – especially white, as here – are usually domesticated birds, or the offspring of mallard and domestic crosses.

so impressive in the spring. This display is well worth going out of your way to see as the pair of birds, the feathers around their necks spread out in a ruff, dance together in the water.

Lowland lakes are often rich in plants. In water up to about 2m (6 feet) deep, the large, almost circular leaves of the white waterlily or the less common yellow waterlily may cover extensive areas, as at Bosherston Lake at Stackpole in Wales. Thick belts of common reed or reedmace can be frequent around the shoreline, and the dead remains of these plants may accumulate in shallow water, gradually building up to form dry land. Over many years, this may fill a lake completely.

LIFE IN PONDS AND DITCHES
. . .

The water in ponds and ditches, and in some rivers, moves very little, creating the right conditions for plants that dislike a current. Small, freely floating plants, such as the bright green duckweeds – our smallest flowering plants – may form a continuous layer on the water, covering it so completely that it looks like dry land. In some ditches in the Norfolk Broads, the rare, strangely shaped and cactus-like water-soldier is found. This plant floats to the surface to flower, afterwards

PATIENT HUNTER

Although the heron is one of Britain's largest birds, measuring almost 1m (3 feet) from head to tail, its fishing technique is based on a very effective form of concealment. The heron wades into shallow water and then remains absolutely still. When a fish passes, the heron strikes with a sudden stab of its bill, pausing to grasp the fish head-first and then swallowing it whole.

WATERLOGGED NEST

The coot makes its nest by piling up vegetation in shallow water. A nest may contain up to eight eggs, and a pair of birds can raise up to three broods in a year. Coots are aggressive and pugnacious, and in the breeding season fights often break out between rivals with much noise and splashing.

sinking to the bottom. Ponds have very abundant animal life, much of it microscopic, and it is this that provides food for the bladderwort. This unusual plant of still water has yellow, pea-like flowers that are produced in July or August. It has no roots, and small bladders take the place of some of its leaves. If a passing animal touches one of these bladders, the bladder springs open, sucking the animal inside and trapping it. The animal is then slowly digested to supply the plant with the necessary minerals for growth.

Larger animals of ponds include the amphibians, of which the frog and toad are by far the most common. Frogs (*see p. 107*) and toads spend much of the year, including their winter

NEARING JOURNEY'S END
Where it is spanned by the old bridge at Kingston Lacy, the River Stour is only a few miles from the end of its journey from Wiltshire to the sea near Bournemouth. Long stems of water crowfoot trail in the shallow, slow-flowing water, while on the riverbanks, grasses and teasels make a deep mass of vegetation.

FLAVOURINGS AND REMEDIES
Riverbanks are the home of a number of aromatic and edible plants. Water mint has a traditional use as a cure for digestive ailments, while the sharp-tasting leaves of watercress are still used today in soups and salads. Yellowcress leaves are edible but much less flavoursome.

hibernation, on land, returning to water in the spring to breed. Shaded ponds where branches have fallen into the water seem to be a favoured spot for the rare great crested newt. The smooth newt is more common, living in garden ponds. The female is drab and elusive, but the brightly coloured male, which has an orange underside spotted with black, is more easy to see.

For all freshwater wildlife, but amphibians in particular, changes in the countryside are a constant hazard. Upland lakes and streams have been little affected by man, but in lowland areas, the story is very different. Drainage schemes, often designed for the benefit of agriculture, have damaged many streams and rivers, converting some into little more than canals. Lowland lakes and rivers have been affected by pollution from fertilizers applied to farmland, from industrial chemicals and from sewage effluent. Freshwater habitats are particularly sensitive to pollution, and careful conservation is needed to ensure that the plants and animals in our rivers, lakes and ponds continue to add richness to our countryside.

GREAT YELLOWCRESS

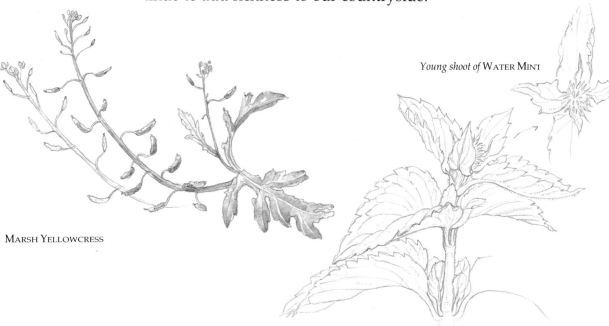

Young shoot of WATER MINT

MARSH YELLOWCRESS

BOGS & FENS

. . .

THE WATERLOGGED SOILS beneath bogs and fens are among the most revealing windows into the history of the British landscape. Entombed in them are the remains of massive trees, such as the 5,000-year-old bog oaks of the East Anglian fens, Iron Age villages with wooden walkways and palisades, and – most dramatic of all – mummified bodies, hundreds or thousands of years old.

But as well as having a great historical interest, fens in particular abound with wildlife. Few other habitats offer such diversity – the flash of the boldly coloured swallowtail butterfly in the Norfolk Broads, the imperious passage of the marsh harrier as it hunts for prey over reed-beds, the thrilling beat of the snipe's display flight at Wicken Fen in the spring, or the bright yellow flowers of the bog asphodel in the bogs of Brimham Rocks in Yorkshire. Of all parts of the countryside, bogs and fens are the hardest to explore. Most bogs are in inaccessible hill country while fens are clothed in dense vegetation, and at dawn and dusk often throng with mosquitoes. Both these habitats owe their unique wildlife and inaccessibility to two important characteristics they have in common – water and peat.

PEAT – THE NATURAL PRESERVATIVE

. . .

Peat is formed from the partially decomposed remains of plants. In most habitats bacteria, fungi and animals rapidly break down dead plants, converting leaves, stems and roots into

a crumbly material known as humus. Over a period of years, even something as large as a tree-trunk can be broken down in this way. However, this process can only take place where oxygen is available. In wet places such as bogs and fens, water prevents oxygen reaching the decomposing organisms, and so there is little or no decay. The remains of dead plants build up over decades and centuries without decomposing, and the result is a layer of peat, often several metres thick.

Although the plant remains in peat are compressed under the weight of those above them, much of their structure is preserved. Ancient stems can be made out with the naked eye, while under a microscope, the pollen grains of past generations of plants are also visible. From the record of this pollen we can trace the slow invasion of plants from continental Europe

A BOGGY BLANKET
As peat builds up, the centre of a bog tends to become higher than the edges, creating a slightly domed surface. The only plants that can grow are those that can tolerate waterlogged conditions and an acid soil. These include heather, mosses, a few flowers such as the bog asphodel and some grasses.

as the ice of the last glaciation retreated northwards 10,000 years ago. We can also detect the forest clearances of Neolithic man and the impact of nineteenth-century industrialization.

But peat is not only a historical record. It is also a valuable resource. Before coal became readily available, peat was an important fuel. The Broads in Norfolk's fenland are the flooded remains of open-cast peat mines of the thirteenth and fourteenth centuries, and in Ireland much peat is still dug today for fuel. Some peats, such as those of Cambridgeshire and Lancashire, are ideal for growing vegetables, and are extensively used for this. In some places, peat is dug on a huge scale for use in horticulture and market gardening.

These various forms of exploitation have led to many areas of peat being drained or lost, especially in the lowlands. This process is still continuing in places such as the Somerset Levels, making peat habitats among the most reduced and most threatened in the country.

PEAT BOGS AND THEIR PLANTS

. . .

Peat bogs occur mainly in hilly and mountainous areas, such as the Kinder Scout region of Derbyshire. Here the ground is wet because of high rainfall and low evaporation. Many uplands are composed of hard, acid rocks that release the minerals essential for plant growth only slowly. Temperatures in these areas are also low for much of the year.

This combination of coolness, dampness and a poor soil creates a habitat inhospitable to most flowering plants, and

MOSSES OF WET GROUND

Mosses are simple plants that do not have flowers and reproduce with tiny spores rather than seeds. Many mosses need damp conditions, and this makes peat bogs an ideal habitat for them. Compact mounds of Sphagnum *mosses, which are often found in peat bogs, are a sure sign that the ground beneath is waterlogged and often unsafe for walking.*

Ripe fruit of CRANBERRY

Flowers of CRANBERRY *with backswept petals*

FRUITS OF THE BOG

Every year Britain's bogs and hillsides yield an almost unnoticed harvest – crops of tiny berries (above) *produced by cranberry and cowberry plants. The berries taste delicious and are rich in vitamin C, but it takes a lot of patience to gather them in any quantity.*

Fruit of COWBERRY, *an evergreen shrub*

mosses are the main vegetation. In bogs, the commonest mosses are the dozen or so species of *Sphagnum*, and it is these mosses that contribute most to the formation of peat. *Sphagnum* mosses form springy mounds that range in colour from deep red to pale green, depending on the species. Each mound is made up of many tightly packed shoots, and these are tipped with rosettes of tiny leaves. *Sphagnum* mosses are extremely absorbent. The living moss holds water almost as well as a sponge, and until early this century, *Sphagnum* was collected, dried and used for lining bandages.

Of the flowering plants that do manage to grow on bogs, grasses and sedges are the most prominent. One of these, purple moor-grass, is unusual because it sheds its pale green leaves in the autumn. It is a common plant, and provides valuable grazing in spring.

The two species of cotton-grass produce drifts of white flower-heads in summer that look like small tufts of cotton. Cotton-grasses are actually sedges, and like all sedges they have solid stems, whereas the flowering stems of grasses are hollow. One species of cotton-grass produces three flowering heads on each shoot and the other species only one.

Another plant that resembles a grass but which is not is the bog asphodel (*see p. 98*). This small member of the lily family has broad, scimitar-shaped leaves about 15cm (6 inches) long and a spike of attractive yellow flowers. Common shrubs of this kind of wet ground include the bog myrtle, which is easily identified by the aromatic smell produced by its crushed leaves, and heather, which covers extensive areas in sites such

COTTON-GRASS

There are few sights more characteristic of high, boggy ground than the flower-heads of cotton-grass (below) fluttering in the blast of a strong wind. Common cotton-grass often grows alongside dark pools on bare, wet peat.

FLORETS IN A FLOWER

Sneezewort grows at the edges of peat bogs and anywhere where the ground is damp and the soil frequently acid. It is a member of the daisy family and, like the daisy, it has composite flowers. What look like single flowers are in fact clusters of tiny florets. Some form the outer petals, while others produce pollen and seeds.

AN UPLAND FEN
MALHAM, YORKSHIRE · LATE SUMMER
· · ·

*The Malham Estate in Yorkshire is made up of over
1,600ha (4,000 acres) of moorlands, hillsides and
spectacular limestone cliffs and pavements. The estate
includes Malham Tarn, England's highest large freshwater
lake, which has been studied by naturalists since the last
century. At high altitudes, damp ground is usually infertile
and acid, but at Malham the lime-rich water draining from
the surrounding hills has created a unique combination of
peat bog and flower-rich fen. The plants that grow in and
around the fen are a fascinating mixture of those found on
high ground, and those that are more often seen in
fertile fens much lower down.*

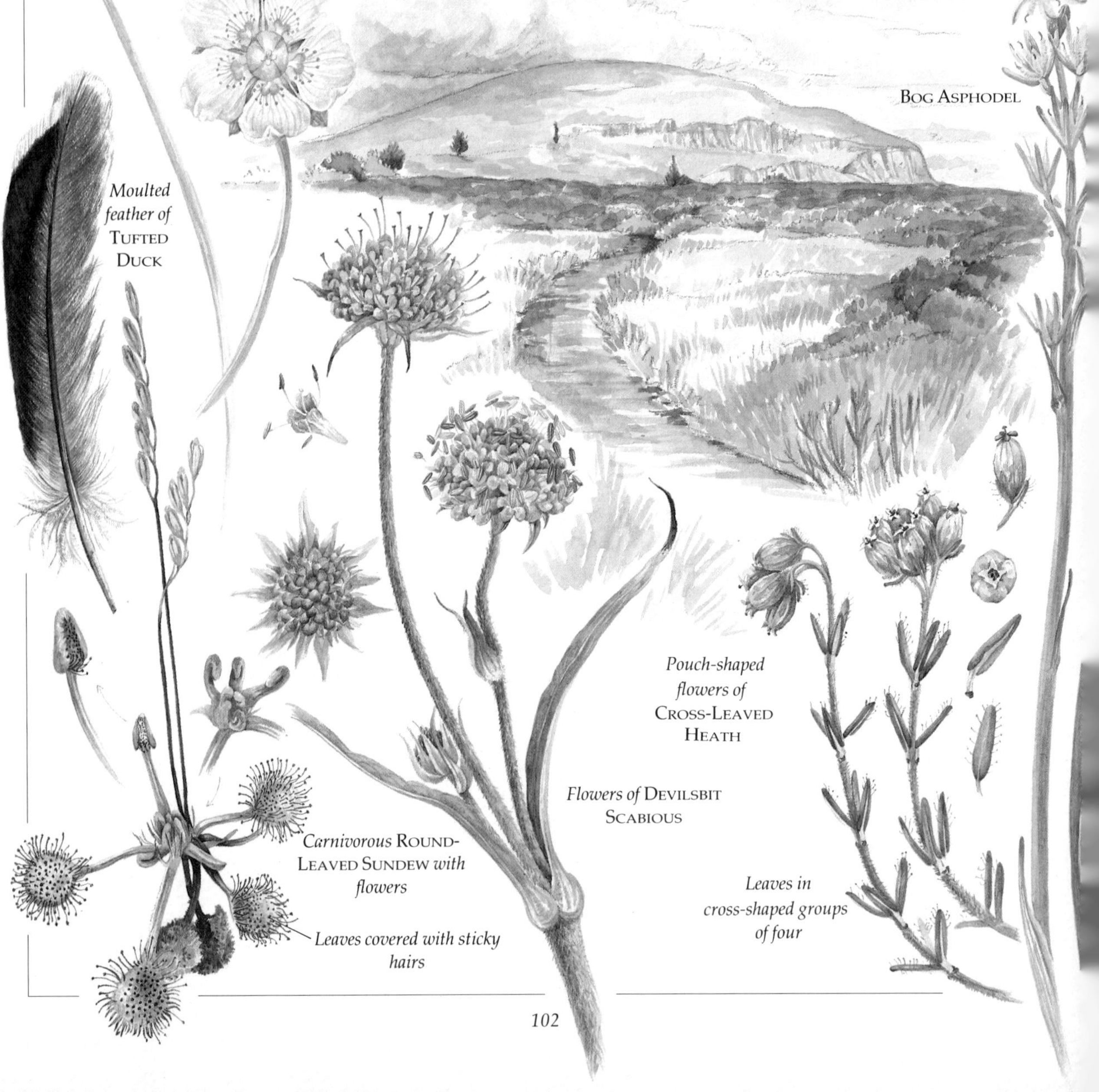

Five-petalled flowers of
GRASS OF PARNASSUS

BOG ASPHODEL

Moulted
feather of
TUFTED
DUCK

Pouch-shaped
flowers of
CROSS-LEAVED
HEATH

Flowers of DEVILSBIT
SCABIOUS

Carnivorous ROUND-
LEAVED SUNDEW *with*
flowers

Leaves covered with sticky
hairs

Leaves in
cross-shaped groups
of four

Flower-head of
MEADOWSWEET *with
developing seeds*

HARD RUSH

HEATHER

Dry seed-heads of
MARSH CINQUEFOIL

*Water-absorbent
leaflets*

Single shoot of
SPHAGNUM *moss*

as the Migneint in North Wales. Trees are notable by their absence, save where conifers have been planted. With a few exceptions, trees dislike waterlogged ground, and the drainage necessary for successful tree planting can soon destroy the entire character of a bog.

CARNIVOROUS PLANTS

Some bog plants make up for the shortage of minerals in the peaty soil by an unusual dietary supplement. The sundews and butterworts catch insects that settle on their sticky leaves, digesting them and absorbing the minerals produced. Their traps work in different ways. A sundew's round or oval leaf – the exact shape depends on the species – is covered in hairs, each of which is tipped with a glue-like substance. When an insect settles on the leaf, it becomes stuck fast. As it struggles, the hairs around the insect bend towards it, making escape even more difficult. Like all carnivorous plants, the sundew only digests the soft parts of its victims. Once the minerals they contain have been absorbed by the plant, the hard external skeletons and wings drop to the ground.

The butterwort's leaves are also covered in hairs, but these are much smaller than those of the sundews and do not move. Instead, the margins of the leaf roll inwards, trapping insects in a sticky, tube-like prison.

THE ANIMAL LIFE OF PEAT BOGS

The animal life of bogs is limited, in part because there is a restricted supply of food and in part because the environment is harsh. The characteristic butterfly of northern bogs is the

THE CALMING VALERIAN

Valerian grows on damp and often fertile ground. Traditionally, the juice extracted from its roots is supposed to have a calming effect, and it is still used to make herbal tea.

**FLOWERS
OF THE FENS**

*The nutrient-rich soil of
fens and their margins
suits far more wild flowers
than the acid peat of bogs.
Devilsbit scabious, marsh
lousewort and lesser
spearwort are all found in
fens. The devilsbit
scabious is so named
because its root ends
abruptly, as if bitten off.*

large heath, a gregarious, grey and russet species that lives as high as 600m (2,000 feet). Its
caterpillars feed on sedges and cotton-grass.
Apart from the large heath, butterflies are
uncommon, because most require warm,
sunny conditions. Although it is damp, snails
too are rare. This is because there is very little
calcium from which they can build their shells.

In bogs, birds are perhaps the most obvious
animals. Wading birds probe the damp soil for
food, and often the mournful cry of the golden
plover, the bubbling song of the curlew (*see p.
83*), or the sharp call of the dunlin are the only
animal sounds to be heard. These birds all feed
on worms and insects along the edges of the
peaty pools and among the tussocks.

MARSH ORCHID

*There are a number of
species of marsh orchid in
Britain. To make
identifying them more
complicated, they often
interbreed to produce
hybrids. All have pink or
red petals and long,
pointed leaves. This plant
has finished flowering and
seed formation is
underway.*

THE WILDLIFE OF FENS
. . .

In contrast to bogs, fens are highly fertile, and
they have an abundance of plants and animals.
Fens occur mainly in the lowlands. Here, drainage waters are generally rich
in nutrients,

DEVILSBIT SCABIOUS
*with visiting
hoverfly*

Flowers and seed capsules of
MARSH LOUSEWORT

LESSER SPEARWORT, *a
buttercup with spear-shaped
leaves*

FROM FEN TO WOODLAND

If a fen's plant cover is not regularly cut, trees gradually spread and the fen begins to change into damp woodland. At Malham, an extensive boardwalk allows this process to be seen at close hand. The sallow and birch scrub is periodically cleared away to preserve the character of the fen.

especially calcium, so that conditions for plant growth are good. Tall plants such as common reed and various species of sedge thrive, giving rise to peat that instead of being acid is alkaline. Wicken Fen – the first National Trust nature reserve – is a prime example of this.

Over 500 species of plant and 2,500 species of animal have been recorded in the 240ha (600 acres) of Cambridgeshire that make up Wicken Fen. One factor contributing to this diversity is the range of different conditions created by man's activities. The fen has been used not only for digging peat, but also for harvesting reed for thatching, sedge for thatching and for fuel, and grass for fodder. Where harvesting has ceased, many areas have developed into scrub or woodland, creating yet more habitats.

The greatest range of flowering plants is found in areas that are cut in the summer – either annually for fodder, or at intervals of three or four years for thatch. The longer the cutting interval, the more likely it is that the great fen sedge will become the dominant plant. The tough leaves of this sedge are up to 2m (6½ feet) long and have sharp edges that can cause serious cuts. Despite this, they are ideal for thatching, but when living they cast a dense shade that few other plants can tolerate for more than a few years.

THE YEARLY CUT

Annual cutting discourages the great fen sedge, and when this happens other species of sedge, grass and rush take over, with purple moor-grass being common. Other plants found in these conditions include the purple and yellow loosestrifes, forms of which are cultivated in gardens.

The tall flowering spikes of the marsh thistle are also a frequent sight in this habitat. Less often seen is milk parsley, sometimes known as fen carrot because of its finely divided leaves. This species is important because in England it is the only plant on which the caterpillars of the rare swallowtail butterfly will feed. The swallowtail – Britain's largest butterfly – still breeds on Horsey Mere in East Anglia, which is owned by the National Trust, and it seems to be holding its own in Norfolk.

Cutting in winter generally favours the common reed, which forms almost pure stands when harvested in this way. This reed thrives because the dead shoots that are removed by cutting are of no further use to the plant, all food being stored in extensive underground stems.

LIVING ON LEAVES

Willows are among the first trees to take root in the wet surface of a fen. In summer, their leaves (above) often bear raised red swellings. These are bean galls, caused by the larvae of a sawfly that feeds on the leaves.

MARSH CINQUEFOIL

The marsh cinquefoil (left) has flowers of a curious dull brownish-red colour, looking quite inconspicuous alongside many other flowers of damp ground. After the flower withers, the seeds form in an open cup. The plant's name is derived from the French for "five leaves".

FENLAND FROGS

At one time frogs were common throughout Britain, but as more and more land has been drained, their numbers have fallen. Fens are one habitat where they can still thrive. Frogs spend the winter in hibernation, emerging in early March onwards to mate and lay their eggs. In spring, shallow ditches in fen country often contain frog spawn, or masses of floating, jelly-like eggs.

REED-BED BIRDS
. . .

For the birdwatcher, reed-beds and the lagoons within them are a fascinating habitat to visit. Reed-beds are the home of two rare species in particular – the bittern, a large brown heron-like bird that has an extraordinary call, rather like a foghorn, and the bearded tit, a long-tailed bird that flutters among the reed stems. In spring, the reed-beds are full of bird song, and often this is the only clue to the birds' presence in the impenetrable vegetation. The sedge warbler, a migrant with distinctive white eye-stripes, produces a grating call as birds pair up and build their nests, slung between stems of reeds or sedges. The reed warbler produces a similar but harsher song, but the song of the grasshopper warbler, which also perches on reed stems, becomes alternately louder and softer as the bird turns its head from side to side. Unlike other warblers, grasshopper warblers continue their song long into the night.

The wet grassland that often borders reed-beds is an ideal habitat for snipe. This small wader is usually a secretive bird, but in spring it takes to the air and flies high up, diving towards the ground and producing a loud drumming noise. Unlike most sounds that birds make, the snipe's drumming is mechanical rather than vocal. As it falls in a dive, it spreads out two tail feathers, and it is their beating against the rushing air that produces the sound.

Throughout the year, the large and very rare marsh harrier flies low over the reeds in search

HIDDEN IN THE REEDS
Like many fenland birds, the reed bunting can be difficult to see because it is often concealed by reeds or thickets. When it does perch in the open, the male can easily be identified by its black head, marked with a white streak on each cheek. At a distance, female reed buntings look very much like sparrows.

MASSED FLOWERS
The individual flowers of plants such as valerian and amphibious bistort are small and inconspicuous, but because they grow together in a flower-head, the effect is much more striking. Cultivated varieties of bistort are often seen in gardens.

VALERIAN

AMPHIBIOUS BISTORT

of mammals and birds. Its flapping and gliding flight is characteristic of harriers, making it easy to recognize. In winter, the smaller hen harrier (*see p. 70*) uses fens as overnight roosting sites. It often appears in small groups, possibly moving in from continental Europe.

Mammals are rarely seen in this kind of habitat, but regularly cut fens are the home of very large numbers of woodmice. The grass snake is also common here, and if surprised, is just as likely to slip into water and swim away as to slither through the vegetation. Snakes, unlike humans, have no difficulty moving about in this waterlogged world.

COLOURED FOR PROTECTION

Caterpillars feature in the diet of many fenland birds. To escape attack, some caterpillars are brightly coloured, warning birds that they have an unpleasant taste. Once a bird has sampled a few of these caterpillars, it is reluctant to repeat the experience.

SAFEGUARDING THE FUTURE
· · ·

The main threats to the wildlife of both bogs and fens are undoubtedly drainage and changing use. Preserving wet fenland, with all its plants and animals, often calls for expensive work to isolate it from the drainage systems around it. It also has to be protected from peat extraction. The vegetation of bogs can be affected by overgrazing by sheep, while fens can quickly change into scrub and then woodland if the yearly cutting of reed or sedge is abandoned. Bogs and fens take thousands of years to develop, and it is part of the National Trust's work to ensure that they have a continuing place in our landscape.

FISHING FOR FOOD

The webs of orb-web spiders are particularly noticeable in autumn, when the spiders mature and their webs catch the morning dew. Some spiders use a hunting technique rather like rod-fishing: they pull in their catch as soon as it blunders into the web and feed on its soft parts and juices. Others use their webs like drift-nets. They make a nightly catch of small insects, pulling the haul in at dawn. The web and insects are then swallowed together.

MOTH CATERPILLAR *on grass of Parnassus*

DUNES, SALTMARSHES & MUDFLATS

· · ·

BRITAIN'S COASTLINE is constantly changing, and few parts of it are as impermanent as sand dunes, saltmarshes and mudflats, with their grains of sand and particles of silt and clay that are easily moved by wind and wave. The sand in a dune shifts in the sharp sea-breeze, while in saltmarshes and mudflats, the sediment stirs and settles in the tide's twice daily ebb and flow.

TIME AND TIDE
In the Newtown Estuary on the Isle of Wight (below), decaying wooden posts are all that remain of attempts to drain the ground and use it for fields. As fast as the banks are built up, the tide carries them away again.

Despite this ceaseless movement, these habitats are of considerable importance to wildlife. Dunes provide breeding sites for some of our rarest seabirds, and mudflats offer winter refuge to waders in their hundreds of thousands. Even the

seemingly inhospitable expanse of a saltmarsh abounds with plants.

For plants especially, life in sand dunes, saltmarshes and mudflats is not easy. Those that succeed and thrive here do so not only because they have overcome the instability of the sand and sediment but also because they have solved another and even more taxing problem – a shortage of water.

SURVIVAL IN A HARSH ENVIRONMENT
. . .

In dunes, the freely draining sand holds little moisture. In order to survive, many of the plants of sand dunes have features to maximize water uptake and minimize its loss. Marram

ROOTED IN THE SAND

On the dunes facing Studland Bay in Dorset (above), clumps of spiky marram grass anchor the sand with their roots. Stable dunes like these are used as nesting sites by skylarks and meadow pipits. Some seabirds, including the ringed plover and the delicate and rare little tern, prefer open dunes and the less stable shoreline nearer the high-water mark.

grass, for example, has roots that grow down many metres to reach water and thick, tightly curled leaves to conserve it.

Another successful way of conserving water is shown by "winter annuals", plants such as the rue-leaved saxifrage, which has white flowers, and the low, pale purple field madder. These germinate in late summer and flower the following spring, surviving the dry summer as drought-resisting seeds.

On saltmarshes water is abundant, but because it is very saline, plants have difficulty using it. Some plants overcome this problem through cutting down their need for water by having fleshy stems and leaves that act as water-tanks. These "succulents" – species such as glasswort, with its plump, cylindrical leaves – are very similar to many plants of hot, dry places. Other plants, such as sea-lavender, have glands on their leaves which secrete salt that has entered the plant.

Because the soil of a saltmarsh is full of water, it contains very little air. This poses a problem for plants whose roots require oxygen in order to grow. One species that does grow well in these conditions is cord grass. Its roots have large empty cells which can carry air to their tips. The ancestry of this vigorous plant can be traced back to a natural hybrid between a European species and an introduced American species which occurred in Southampton Water about 100 years ago.

Although sand dunes and saltmarshes are both poor sources of water for plants, they differ markedly in their supplies of the mineral nutrients that plants need to grow. The sand in dunes is made up of materials low in useful

FROM COAST TO GARDEN

Common catsear is a widespread plant of dunes and waste ground. It is also a very successful weed of lawns. Like the dandelion, it spreads by seeds that float on feathery parachutes.

SEASIDE HEATHER

The seaside may seem an unusual place to find bell heather (above), but this plant is just as much at home on the sandy ground of old dunes as it is on high moors. Bell heather thrives in poor soil and its narrow, evergreen leaves are well able to withstand the drying effect of the coastal wind.

minerals, and what minerals are present are easily washed through by rain.

Fresh supplies of sand are one of the few sources of additional minerals, and plants such as marram grass rely on this. If sand no longer accumulates, then marram grass loses its vigour and ceases to flower. This change is very often evident as you walk away from the sea across dunes, moving from the bluey-greenness of younger dunes to the greyness of older ones.

By contrast, the soil of a saltmarsh may have abundant supplies of minerals. This richness, coupled with easy cultivation, explains why so many saltmarshes have been embanked, drained and used for intensive agriculture.

THE LIFE HISTORY OF A DUNE
. . .

Sand dunes are generally found on exposed shores, where winds are strong and there is a supply of sand offshore. A wind speed of more than about 16km/h (10mph) is enough to carry dry sand inland from beaches and begin the process of dune formation. If the wind speed drops below this critical level, as it may do when it encounters the strand line with

MERMAID'S PURSE
Empty dogfish egg-cases, or "mermaid's purses", (below) are often washed up on beaches. The leathery tendrils wrap themselves around seaweed fronds, anchoring the case while the fish inside develops and eventually hatches.

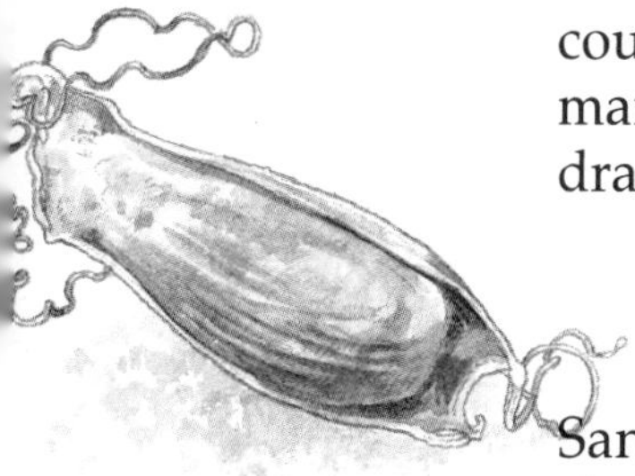

CLOSE COUSINS
From a distance, the pretty sea bindweed (below) looks very much like common bindweed, a rampant weed that is detested by gardeners. However, sea bindweed has rounded rather than arrow-shaped leaves, and instead of twining around or "binding" other plants, it sprawls across the ground.

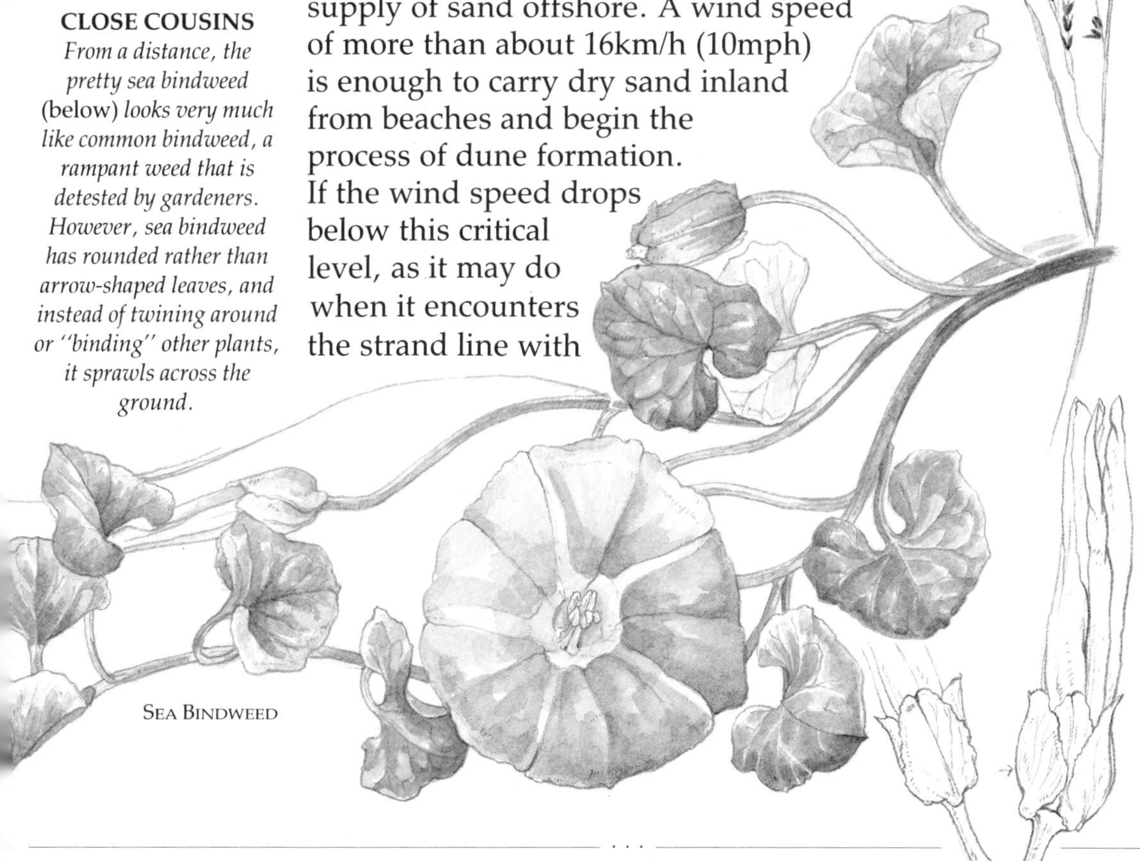

SEA BINDWEED

COMMON BENT

LESSER COCKROACH

Slender-waisted
SAND WASP

A LIVING LARDER
*Few animals live on the
open, shifting sand of
dunes. But where plants
hold the sand together,
plant-eating and
predatory insects are
common. It is here that
sand wasps nest,
excavating shallow
burrows to house their
eggs. Each parent wasp
stocks its nest with
paralysed caterpillars and,
after hatching, the larvae
grow rapidly on their
living food.*

its fish boxes, rope and seaweed, then the moving sand is deposited. Over time a small heap of sand may accumulate out of reach of all but the highest tides.

If plants colonize this mound, there is a chance that a new dune may form. Vegetation reduces wind speed dramatically, and therefore considerably increases the rate at which sand collects. Among the plants found on these "embryo" dunes are the low-growing sea rocket, which produces small, lilac-coloured flowers in late summer, and the tall sand couch-grass, which has stiff upright leaves. Sand couch-grass has an extensive root system which is particularly effective in binding the sand and holding it in place.

Many embryo dunes last only a year or two, being washed away by winter storms, but some persist and grow higher over the years. As a dune ages other plants, notably marram grass, begin to colonize it. Marram is probably the most common plant in sand dunes. It is certainly the most important species in trapping and holding sand in older dunes because it has extensive roots and underground stems and can grow up through fresh layers of sand.

From such small beginnings, a growing dune ultimately reaches a height, which may be as much as 30m (100 feet), at which no further sand accumulates. From this time the vegetation begins to change. Starved of a fresh supply of sand, marram grass begins to decline and low-growing plants begin to move in. These include the bloody cranesbill, whose purple-crimson flowers form sheets of colour in some Northumbrian dunes, and the common centaury, with its clusters of light pink flowers.

**RESILIENT SHORE
PLANTS**
*Both marram grass and
sea holly (right) grow on
older dunes. The edges of
marram grass leaves roll
up in dry weather to
conserve water. Sea
holly's grey-blue leaves
not only have vicious
spines but also a hard
surface which protects
them from the drying
wind. Some kinds of sea
holly have become popular
as garden plants because
they can be dried and used
in flower arrangements.*

Low-growing grasses also appear, and on the older "grey dunes", the gaps between flowering plants are filled with lichens and mosses.

BETWEEN THE TIDES

MARRAM GRASS

SEA HOLLY

Sand dunes are features of exposed coasts. Saltmarshes and mudflats, on the other hand, are normally found in sheltered areas, especially where rivers bringing sediments eroded from the land meet the sea. If sand dune and saltmarsh do occur side by side, as at Scolt Head in north Norfolk, it is because the dunes provide the necessary shelter.
In contrast to the steep slopes of dunes, saltmarshes are virtually flat. The often turbid tidal water ebbs and flows through winding creeks and seeps into

STUDLAND'S SANDY SHORE
The shore of Studland Bay in Dorset (above) is flanked by a long sweep of old dunes covered in marram grass and heather. Between dunes of different ages there are often valleys known as dune slacks, sheltering plants and animals that cannot live on dry sand.
These may include orchids, yellow flag, snails, spiders and, in a small number of sites such as Formby in Merseyside, the rare and distinctively striped natterjack toad.

muddy pools and open pans. Sometimes it evaporates to leave a layer of salt on the surface that sparkles in the sun. Saltmarshes show a characteristic pattern of vegetation. Different plants are frequently confined to separate areas of the marsh, forming bands or zones, often composed entirely of a single species. This zonation is mostly due to the effect of the tide. The sea aster, for example, with its daisy-like flowers, is always found at the front edge of marshes. It can withstand being flooded by the high tide longer than thrift, which is found at the upper reaches.

Regular tidal flooding causes problems for some animals, especially land-based insects and spiders. These need a supply of oxygen at high tide when they are covered by water. One common saltmarsh spider has a hairy body that traps bubbles of air, acting as an aqualung while the spider is underwater.

Flooding is also a problem for breeding birds, as it can wash their nests away. Despite this, saltmarshes are vital breeding areas for some birds, particularly the noisy redshank, with its long red bill and legs.

THE OYSTERCATCHER

With its black and white plumage and bright orange beak, the oystercatcher (above) is among the most conspicuous birds of the seashore. Oystercatchers are easy to pinpoint because, apart from being brightly coloured, they are very noisy. They make a loud piping sound, and birds on the ground often call to those flying overhead. Oystercatchers use their beaks to open the shells of cockles and other molluscs of muddy shores.

EBB AND FLOW

Tide, not time, regulates life in an estuary (above). As the tide rises, feeding birds are forced to leave the mudflats to roost on banks and islands. When the water begins to recede they return, sifting through the mud or picking out small animals buried in it.

The tides that submerge the marsh also bring fresh supplies of the fine sediments that make up saltmarsh soils. These sediments are either deposited on the marsh surface at high tide, when the water is still, or trapped by the dense vegetation. Saltmarsh plants often have a dusty appearance which is due to freshly deposited particles from the most recent tides.

THE HIDDEN LIFE OF MUDFLATS
· · ·

Mudflats, such as those along the Newtown Estuary in the Isle of Wight, are flooded for longer each day than saltmarshes. As a result, they are less stable and have few flowering plants. However, eelgrasses and green algae may be present in large amounts, and these are a nourishing winter food for ducks and geese.

Despite their unpromising appearance, mudflats do harbour huge numbers of tiny animals. In a single square metre of mud, as many as 100,000

AWAITING THE TIDE'S TURN
For redshanks, curlews, shelduck and gulls (below), *high tide is a time for resting, preening, or probing along the water's edge. For brent geese, which also feed on land, the state of the tide is less important. Geese are unusual among birds in being able to digest grass, but as grass is not a particularly nourishing food, they, like grazing mammals, have to eat large quantities to survive.*

RED-LEGGED WADER
The many different kinds of wading birds that feed on our estuaries can baffle even skilled birdwatchers. But one of them – the redshank (above) *– is instantly recognizable. It is not only its "shanks" or legs that are red, but also its straight, sharp beak, which it uses for snatching crustaceans and worms out of the mud.*

SALTMARSH & MUDFLATS

NEWTOWN ESTUARY, ISLE OF WIGHT · WINTER

Nearly all of Britain's wildlife habitats have most to offer the visitor in spring and summer. But, for birdwatchers at least, the marshes and mudflats around our estuaries come into their own with the approach of winter. As the days shorten in the Arctic and Scandinavia and the temperature drops, huge numbers of waders and waterfowl fly south to spend the winter in the relative warmth of our coastline. Newtown Estuary, with its drowned fields and fertile mud, provides food to nourish its share of wintering birds. At a time of year when so much of the countryside seems devoid of life, flocks of geese create a dramatic spectacle against the winter sky.

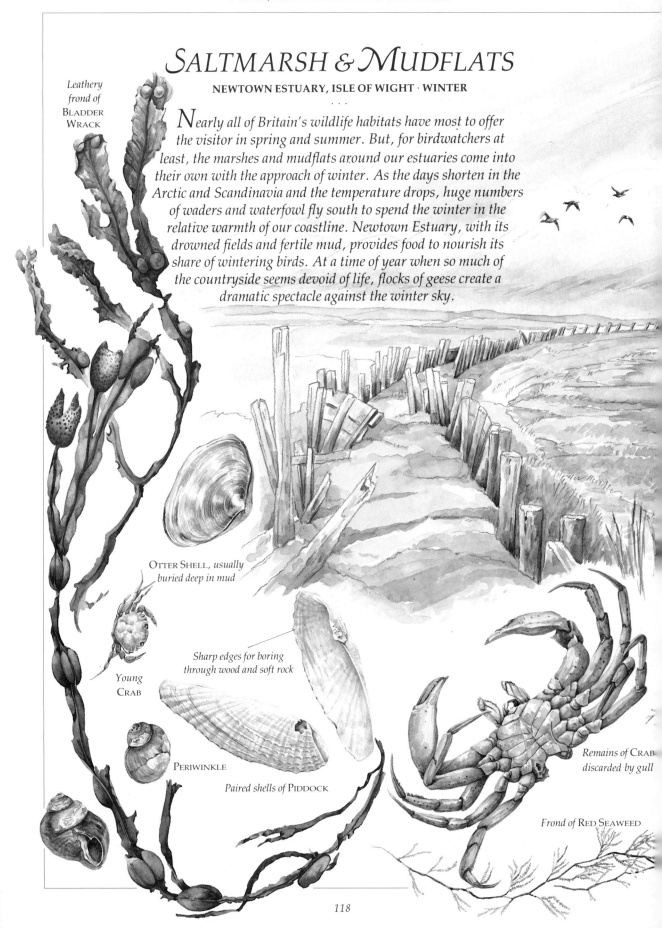

Leathery frond of BLADDER WRACK

OTTER SHELL, *usually buried deep in mud*

Young CRAB

Sharp edges for boring through wood and soft rock

PERIWINKLE

Paired shells of PIDDOCK

Remains of CRAB *discarded by gull*

Frond of RED SEAWEED

BLADDER WRACK

Air-filled bladders

Fleshy stems of GLASSWORT

COCKLE *shell*

Cockle shells

SEA ASTER *root with developing leaves*

Deeply ridged shell of OYSTER

worms, snails and crustaceans may live on or below the surface. These animals feed on still smaller organisms in the silt, or filter food particles out of the water.

One of the commonest of these hidden animals is *Corophium volutator*. This small, shrimp-like crustacean can sometimes be seen walking over the surface of the flooded mud, but it spends much more of its time in a vertical burrow, scraping food from the surface with a pair of specially modified antennae.

In numbers it is rivalled only by *Hydrobia ulvae*, a tiny snail that scours the mud for microscopic plants and animals. At low tide, *Hydrobia* crawls out across the mud, but as the tide turns, it makes a raft of bubbles and is carried upside-down towards the shore, feeding as it floats effortlessly inshore once more.

These animals are food for the large numbers of birds found in British estuaries. The most easily recognized of these is the shelduck, a large bird with a green head and brown, white and black body. At low tide, the shelduck walks over the mudflats, sifting animals out of the mud with sweeping movements of its beak.

DEEP DIVER
The cormorant (above) feeds on fish. It finds its quarry by paddling on the water's surface and dipping its head at intervals to peer into the depths. To help it dive, its feathers absorb water more easily than those of other waterbirds. Between periods of diving, the cormorant has to dry out to keep warm. It does this by holding its wings apart, often for an hour or more at a time. It will do this even in light rain, making a forlorn sight on a cold day.

SIFTING FOOD
The shelduck (below) and the handsome pintail (right) both use their broad bills to sift particles of food from water or mud. The pintail does this by "dabbling", keeping its bill outstretched in the water as it swims forward. The shelduck uses a similar technique, but instead of sifting its food from water, it sifts it from wet mud. The shelduck breeds in many places along the British coastline, but only a few hundred pintails live and breed in Britain.

This action leaves a characteristic pattern of zigzag markings on the mud's surface.

The shelduck is found on our mudflats throughout the year. Other birds use them as winter homes, travelling to them in the autumn from as far away as Canada, Greenland, Iceland and Siberia. The knot is one of these winter visitors. It forms huge flocks of thousands of birds, which turn, climb and dive in an extraordinary display of aerial coordination.

Other birds use the mudflats as staging posts on journeys that take them further afield. The black-tailed and bar-tailed godwits, two waders with slightly upturned bills, stop to feed in British estuaries in spring and autumn as they fly between southern Europe and Scandinavia. The tiny little stint, one of the smallest waders on British estuaries, pauses here on a flight that may take it from Siberia to Africa. For these long-distance migrants, the mudflats around our coast are a vital source of food.

BLACK-HEADED GULLS

The small and argumentative black-headed gull (left) has a wide-ranging appetite, and often prefers to steal food from other birds rather than find it for itself. It breeds in colonies, not only in coastal marshes but also inland. Black-headed gulls have black – or more accurately, dark brown – heads in the summer months only. In winter, they are white all over.

WINTER BREAK

In southern Britain, the wigeon (below) is mainly a winter visitor, flying in every autumn from as far away as Siberia. It feeds mainly on grass and water plants.

CLIFFS & ROCKY SHORES

THE COASTS of Britain are the scene of a primeval struggle between the surging force of the ocean and the solidity of the land. The ultimate winner is always the ocean, and over millions of years it has eaten into the shore, turning crevices into coves and promontories into islands, to create the coastline we know today.

On coasts with hard rocks, such as the granite of Cape Cornwall or the gabbro of St. David's Head in Dyfed, the sea wins only slowly, although fresh scars of fallen rock can be seen in most areas after the storms of winter. By contrast, the cliffs of soft chalk that make up the Seven Sisters in Sussex, or the even softer clays of parts of the Yorkshire coast, erode rapidly, sometimes losing a metre or more in their yearly battle against the sea.

The inevitability of this outcome is dramatically illustrated by the fate of man's habitations. For example, much of the Bronze Age hill-fort at Belle Tout near Eastbourne in Sussex has disappeared into the sea, with over 50m (160 feet) of earthwork being lost between 1910 and 1969. The whole of medieval Dunwich, once the second largest town in East Anglia, now lies underwater, 1.5km (1 mile) off the Suffolk coast.

The very different rock types around the coast produce different groups of plants and animals. Geographical location, too, is important because it determines both land and sea temperature and hence

CLIFF-FACE REFUGE
For nesting seabirds such as kittiwakes, the precipitous faces of cliffs are places not of danger but of safety. By nesting on ledges in otherwise sheer rock, the birds ensure that their eggs and young are beyond the reach of predatory mammals such as foxes.

BRAVING THE ELEMENTS
Despite the dainty appearance of its flowers, thrift (below) is an exceptionally tough plant. Its low, compact shape and thread-like leaves enable it to withstand scorching summer sun, salt spray and the battering of winter gales.

the frequency of frost, and also exposure.

Cliffs exposed to prevailing winds dry out quickly in the summer and become drenched with salt-laden spray during winter gales. Any plants that gain a foothold on them are pruned short by the wind and their animal life is sparse. In more sheltered spots, or in crevices which provide protection and a more humid atmosphere, plants can raise their heads and much more luxuriant vegetation can develop.

The small Glanville fritillary butterfly, black and orange above and orange and white below, shows just how important geology and climate

LAND IN RETREAT
Cliffs like those at Stackpole in Dyfed (above) are constantly undermined by the sea. Waves eat away at the rock between high and low tide marks, and once the foundations have been undermined, the cliff-face collapses to form a huge pile of boulders on the shore below.

DOG-WHELKS *feeding on barnacles*

LIVING BETWEEN THE TIDES

The animals and plants of the lower shore face difficult and demanding conditions. At low tide (above), they are exposed to strong, drying winds, while at high tide they have to withstand the

SHORE CRAB

onslaught of the waves. Crabs survive both by retreating into cracks in the rock.

can be. The Glanville fritillary is common in continental Europe, but in Britain is found only on the Isle of Wight. The reasons for this are that the butterfly needs high temperatures in summer and the caterpillars feed only on rib-wort plantain. Only the crumbling cliffs around the Isle of Wight provide both the warmth the butterfly needs and the bare ground that the plant requires to flourish.

LIFE ALONG THE SHORELINE
· · ·

Where the cliffs are of hard rock, the shoreline exposed at low tide is always fascinating. Most movement, and greatest colour, is in the rock pools.

KEEPING A GRIP

Dog-whelks (above), winkles and sea anemones (below) anchor themselves to the rock with the help of muscular feet which grip the rock like suckers. Dog-whelks feed on mussels and barnacles. They eat mussels by boring a tiny hole into the shell, while they reach the soft bodies of barnacles by prising apart the shell-plates.

SEA ANEMONE

WINKLE

MUSSELS *tightly packed in a "bed"*

TENACIOUS THREADS

Mussels (above) anchor themselves to the rock by tiny threads. These threads are so strong that not even the pounding of the waves can break them.

Feeding arms

GLUED TO THE ROCK

Many sedentary animals of the shore, such as barnacles (above), spread by means of tiny, floating larvae. When a barnacle larva eventually settles on a rock, it glues itself fast and develops a hard shell.

Here, the stinging tentacles of brightly coloured sea anemones wave over sheets of algae which form a thin coating on the rock. Stealthy shrimps stalk for food and tiny fish dart in the shadows. Sea anemones use their tentacles to trap and kill their prey. When they are left out of the water by a falling tide, they withdraw their tentacles into the centre of their bodies, turning into miniature, jelly-like volcanoes.

The predominant colour of many exposed shorelines is brown, due to the brown sea-weeds which clothe the rocks and the large numbers of weed-encrusted limpets. The conical shell of the limpet, and the similarly shaped shell of the barnacle, are able to resist the pressure of the largest waves. The shell of a limpet has an irregular edge, and this fits precisely into the depression in the rock that is the limpet's home. When covered by the tide, a limpet moves around over fairly large distances, scraping algae off the rock. As soon as the tide begins to fall, it returns to its home, locking itself against the rock if touched.

By contrast, barnacles are permanently cemented to the rock. They feed on minute animals which they catch by waving their long arms in the water.

PLANTS OF CRAGS AND CLIFF-TOPS

· · ·

Above the shoreline on cliffs made of hard rock there are two separate habitats for plants – the cliff-face and the cliff-top. Exposed cliff-faces have no protection from the wind, are often swept by salt spray and have little or no soil. Where conditions are most

SCAVENGERS OF THE SHORE

Land habitats abound with insects, but few have adapted to life in or near salt water. Wingless bristletails (below) are among the insects of the upper shore. They feed on tiny scraps of organic matter.

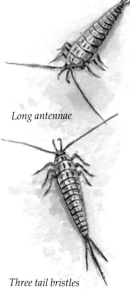

Long antennae

Three tail bristles

FIVE ARMS, MANY FEET

The five arms of a starfish (below) are equipped with large numbers of tubular feet. The starfish uses these to move about, and to pull apart the shells of mussels.

COASTAL CLIFFS

STACKPOLE HEAD, DYFED · MIDSUMMER

. . .

*F*ew sights equal the grandeur of cliffs plunging to the sea, with seabirds wheeling and gliding on the updraught of the onshore wind. But in summer, dramatic views are only part of the pleasure of walking a high coast path. Where the cliff- top has been left uncultivated, summer brings with it an exquisite display of flowers that revel in the sunshine. Sea campion and thrift bloom among the rocks, with vetches and birdsfoot trefoil in the short grass, while on dry cliff-tops, the bristly viper's bugloss can add patches of one of the most intense blues of any wild flower.

Tiny flowers of SEA SPURGE, *held in cup-like bracts*

KIDNEY VETCH

Seed-heads of QUAKING GRASS

Broken shell of GUILLEMOT *egg, with characteristic sharply pointed end*

Flowers of THRIFT or SEA PINK

Leathery, grass-like leaves

Shells of BANDED SNAILS

EYEBRIGHT, *a low plant of the cliff-top turf*

Seeds in long, slender pods

Stem of DISTANT SEDGE, with separate clusters of male and female flowers

SPRING SQUILL, *a flower of grassy cliff-tops that grows from a bulb*

BIRDSFOOT TREFOIL

FIELD FORGET-ME-NOT

VIPER'S BUGLOSS, *named after its traditional use as a remedy for snake bite*

Flowers in curved clusters

Seed capsule

Bristly leaves and stem

Flowers of SEA CAMPION

MILKWORT

severe, only lichens can survive. In these places, the bright orange circles of *Xanthoria parietina* or the green-grey fluffy tufts of *Ramalina siliquosa*, which is sometimes called sea ivory, decorate the rocks. Where there is some soil, plants with deep roots and thick glossy leaves can move in. The cushions of small grass-like leaves of thrift, whose rosy coloured flowers give it the alternative name of sea pink, are common on most coasts. The shiny dark green leaves of scurvy-grass, not actually a grass but a member of the cabbage family, are often found and the white-flowered stonecrop, again with fleshy leaves, is widespread. Less usual are sea-beet and sea-kale, wild ancestors of cultivated forms.

Where the cliff-top soil is deeper, grasses such as red fescue, with its bristle-like leaves, and Yorkshire fog, with its soft hairy leaves, become dominant. It is in such areas that the small bluebell-like flowers of spring squill may be found in April and May.

In a very few places, such as the north coast of Cornwall, oak woodlands have developed on exposed cliffs. These woods are rarely more than 2m (6 ½ feet) high.

A COASTAL CURE

Scurvy-grass (above) gets its name from its former use as a cure for scurvy, the disease caused by a deficiency of vitamin C. At one time, scurvy particularly affected sailors on long voyages. Eating scurvy-grass, a seaside plant rich in vitamin C, would have helped to produce a rapid recovery.

CLIFF-TOP TABLES

Gulls and other birds often carry small shore animals to the cliff-top where they feed on them. Moulted feathers, broken shells and the remains of crabs can often be found alongside cliff-paths far above the shore.

Young flower-head

AMONG TURF AND ROCK

Compactness is a characteristic shared by plants of cliff-faces and the turf above (left). One of these plants, rock samphire, is able to live on ledges facing the sea. In Elizabethan times, its fleshy leaves were very popular as a vegetable, and the plants were gathered by men lowered down cliff-faces on ropes.

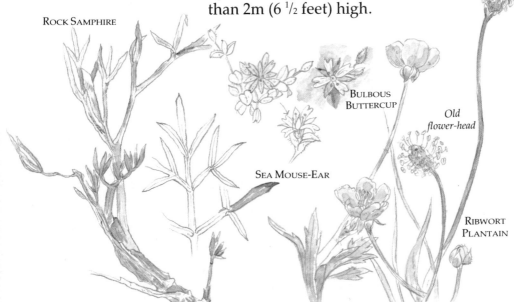

ROCK SAMPHIRE

BULBOUS BUTTERCUP

SEA MOUSE-EAR

Old flower-head

RIBWORT PLANTAIN

(see p.69)

STARS IN THE GRASS

The sky-blue flowers of the spring squill (below) look like small, six-pointed stars in the short cliff-top grass. The spring squill is a relative of the bluebell, and like the bluebell it grows from a small bulb.

On cliff-tops, short, soft-stemmed plants frequently give way to low-growing shrubs such as heather or gorse. There are three species of gorse: the common, tall-growing European gorse, formerly planted as a fuel crop, the autumn-flowering dwarf gorse (see p.69), and the western gorse, intermediate in size between the other two and confined to the west of the country. In more sheltered valleys, thickets of blackthorn may develop and bracken is frequent.

The plants that grow on soft cliffs are very different from those on rocky coasts. Water is not generally in short supply and the major problem that they face is the shifting ground beneath them. These conditions favour species such as coltsfoot and plantains, which either have runners or abundant seed, enabling them to colonize bare ground rapidly.

SOUTHERN SPECIALITIES

· · ·

SEA SPURREY

Sea spurrey (below) is a plant of salty, damp ground. It can sometimes be seen in sheltered places on low cliff-tops where drainage is poor.

With its mild climate and closeness to continental Europe, England's south coast has a number of unique plants and animals. One place particularly notable for plants is the Lizard in Cornwall.

The Lizard is England's most southerly point. Its warm climate and unusual soil, which is produced by an underlying rock found nowhere else in England or Wales, contribute to a remarkable flora. Probably no other area in the country has so many species of plant that are found in that place and nowhere else. These include the twin-headed and

SEA SPURREY

LEAST SOFT BROME

Long awn or bristle

DOWNY OAT *grass*

SMALL COPPER

ON THE ALERT

The small copper is a common butterfly of flower-filled grass, whether on the tops of cliffs or far inland. A highly territorial insect, it challenges other butterflies that may wander into the piece of grassland that it has occupied.

A LIFE UNDERGROUND

Crane-flies, or daddy-long-legs, (below) spend most of their lives as "leatherjackets", brown burrowing larvae that feed on the roots of grasses and other plants. The adults emerge in spring and summer.

upright clovers, the annual dwarf rush, and the strange dwarf land quillwort, a small tuft-like plant that reproduces by spores instead of seeds.

Many of these plants are normally found on the southwest coasts of Europe, and the Lizard is their northern limit. The mild climate also favours introduced species from much further afield, especially the Hottentot fig from South Africa. This plant's trailing stems, with their fleshy, rather banana-like leaves, form extensive sheets on some cliffs, shading out the native vegetation. The only factor controlling their spread seems to be the infrequent frosts that from time to time kill the parts of the plant above ground.

Young LICHEN

CLICK BEETLE

BANDED SNAIL

130

CRICKETS AND BUTTERFLIES
· · ·

The warmth of the cliffs along the English Channel is appreciated by insects, particularly grasshoppers and crickets. About half Britain's species occur here, and their rasping song is an almost constant feature of warm summer days.

A few species, such as the grey bush-cricket, are confined to cliffs. Unlike grasshoppers, bush-crickets eat insects as well as plants, and can be easily identified by their very long antennae, which can be up to twice the length of the body. The female grey bush-cricket has a scimitar-like organ at the end of its abdomen which, despite its fearsome appearance, is used for nothing more sinister than laying eggs.

The cliffs along the south coast can also be good spots to see butterflies. Some, such as the Glanville fritillary or the Lulworth skipper, found mainly in southeast Dorset, live only on or near the coast.

BIRDS OF ROCKY COASTS
· · ·

It is difficult to imagine cliffs without seabirds, and a seabird nesting-cliff in the height of the breeding season is one of the most exciting wildlife spectacles that Britain has to offer. Relatively few stretches of coast in England, Wales and Northern Ireland support large numbers of breeding seabirds, but where cliffs offer the right combination of protection from predators, rocky ledges and access to a good food supply, then the crush can be extraordinary.

Guillemots and razorbills lay their eggs on bare rock, always choosing ledges on the most

A GLIMPSE INTO THE PAST
The cliffs of southwest Wales have been formed where high ground meets the sea. As the sea cuts into the rock, it reveals separate layers, or strata, in the rock. The lower the layer, generally the further back in time it was laid down.

LICHENS

LONG-LIVED LICHENS
Lichens are abundant where the rock is hard, but rarely grow on cliffs of chalk or other soft rocks. One reason for this is that they are slow-growing, and need a durable surface on which to develop.

MARATHON FLIERS
Birds are not the only migrants to make a landfall on our coasts. Every year, many butterflies and moths also cross the Channel. Fast-flying hawkmoths can reach Britain from as far away as North Africa. The privet hawkmoth (above) is mainly a year-round resident, but its numbers are swollen in summer by arrivals from further south.

precipitous cliffs. From late winter onwards, the black-and-white adult birds arrive to pair and breed, and as the available space is gradually used up, the colony becomes busier and noisier by the day. The male and female of each pair share the task of incubating the single carefully protected egg. While the incubating bird perches on the cliff with the egg held between its feet, the other flies out to sea to collect fish. By May, the air around favoured cliffs is filled with guillemots and razorbills arriving and departing on stubby, whirring wings, while their partners growl and croak excitedly from the rocky ledges.

Cliff-ledges are also used by the kittiwake, one of seven species of gull that breed around our coast. The kittiwake breeds in colonies, laying between one and three eggs in a shallow, cup-like nest made of seaweed. It gets its name from its piercing *kitti-week* call, which in volume is more than a match for its noisy neighbours.

The short turf of cliff-tops provides a nesting site for the colourful puffin, which, like the guillemot, spends much of the year far out to sea, coming ashore for a short period to breed. Puffins nest in burrows, loosening the earth with their beaks and then shovelling it away with their feet. Because they nest on slopes near cliff-tops, and not on inaccessible ledges, their eggs and young are more at risk to predators such as foxes.

Cliffs are also important for birds other than seabirds. They are a favoured breeding area of peregrines (*see p. 82*), now fairly common after a serious decline between 1955 and 1965 due to poisoning by

ON THE ROCKS

High cliffs and clear water create ideal conditions for seal-watching. Two species of seal live along Britain's coastline – the common seal, which is brown in colour, and the grey seal, which is much more spotted. Both spend much of their time out of the water on flat rocks and sand banks.

GREY SEALS *basking*

THE SEARCH FOR A SPACE

On a cliff where seabirds breed, competition for space is often intense. Each species has its own particular requirements that have to be met before egg-laying can begin. The kittiwake, for example, needs enough space to construct its small nest, while the razorbill prefers narrower crevices or ledges. Guillemots use the most exposed ledges. Both the razorbill and guillemot lay their eggs directly on the rock, without making a nest.

agricultural pesticides. The scarce chough – a black-bird with a curved red bill and red feet – is virtually confined to the coast, where it nests, often in caves, and feeds on cliff-tops or nearby fields. Choughs can be seen on the Lleyn Peninsula in North Wales or at Fair Head in Northern Ireland.

A WESTERN RARITY
The chough is a natural aerobatic performer, diving and swerving around cliffs with great sureness and control. Unfortunately, few choughs now remain in Britain, so watching them in the air is a rare treat.

The grey-brown rock pipit is a sparrow-sized bird that, although also confined to the coast, lives on almost all rocky shores. In winter it may be joined by the dumpy purple sandpiper, a wader that breeds in Scandinavia and the Arctic.

CONSERVING THE WILDLIFE OF ROCKS AND CLIFFS

Most cliffs, and many cliff-tops, have escaped disturbance by man, although in places urban development or agriculture has reached right to the cliff edge. The National Trust's *Enterprise Neptune*, launched in 1965, has resulted in over 800km (500 miles) of coast now being protected from such developments. Many other stretches of coast are still in need of protection.

One important change on Britain's coasts over recent years has been a marked decline in the number of cattle and sheep grazing on cliff-tops, with the consequent spread of tall grass and scrub and the disappearance of many wild flowers. In several parts of the country, notably on the Lizard, the National Trust is reintroducing grazing to cliff-tops, to the considerable benefit of their special plant life.

GAZETTEER
· · ·

The following pages form a visitor's guide to over 150 National Trust sites of special wildlife interest, arranged alphabetically by county within eight regions. The sites have been chosen to give the widest possible variety of habitat and location. Some are within a short distance of towns and cities, while others are in the far reaches of the countryside.

REGIONAL INDEX
SOUTH AND SOUTHEAST **135–148** · SOUTHWEST **149–157**
EAST ANGLIA **158–161** · CENTRAL ENGLAND **162–169** · NORTHEAST **170–175**
NORTHWEST **176–178** · WALES **179–185** · NORTHERN IRELAND **185–187**

MAP REFERENCES
The map references that appear in the gazetteer enable sites to be located on Ordnance Survey 1:50,000 maps. They pinpoint either the centre of a site or a main point of entry to it. A map reference has three separate parts. In the map reference 175:SU611782, for example, the figures 175 identify the Ordnance Survey sheet. The letters SU identify the relevant 100,000 metre square. Finally, the figures that follow are the grid reference – in this case, 611 east and 782 north. In some large sites, a four-figure grid reference is used. Full details of map references appear on all 1:50,000 Ordnance Survey maps.

NORTHERN IRELAND

NORTH-WEST

NORTHEAST

CENTRAL ENGLAND

EAST ANGLIA

WALES

SOUTHWEST

SOUTH AND SOUTHEAST

SOUTH & SOUTHEAST

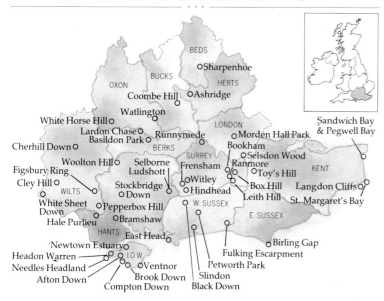

*D*espite *its large human population, southern England is remarkably rich in wildlife. Over the centuries, its land has been used in many different ways, creating a patchwork of habitats that range from heaths and downland turf to coppice woodland. The National Trust protects some of the most endangered and scenic of these habitats, as well as lengths of the region's often dramatic coastline.*

SHARPENHOE

– BEDFORDSHIRE –

Location
On the northern edge of the Chilterns, between the A6 (Barton-le-Clay) and the M1 (Harlington), 6 miles north of Luton.
Map reference 166:TL067300.

Habitats
Chalk grassland, scrub, woodland.

Nature conservation features
Intensive management has restored Sharpenhoe's grassland after many years during which spreading scrub gained the upper hand. Today the grassland has a scattering of typical lime-loving plants, including wild thyme, horseshoe vetch, several species of orchid, clustered bell-flower and autumn gentian. The insect life of the site is limited, but the nests of the yellow meadow ant are common in some areas. Mining bees, mining wasps and wolf spiders can all be seen here. The scrub, which is used by hedgerow birds, is made up mostly of hawthorn and elder. The areas of beech woodland have been planted; one is on the site of an Iron Age hill-fort.

· · ·

BASILDON PARK

– BERKSHIRE –

Location
Northwest of Reading on the A329 to Wantage; overlooking the River Thames 2½ miles above Pangbourne.
Map reference 175:SU611782.

Habitats
Parkland, woodland, chalk grassland.

Nature conservation features
The park surrounding the imposing Basildon House has a rich natural history. It covers an area of 164ha (406 acres), and is made up of open grassland with scattered trees and woods. Much of the woodland is of recent origin, but some areas are semi-natural, and are dominated by ash and yew. Some of the old yews are particularly fine specimens. Box grows well here. The park boasts four species of helleborine – the violet, white, green and narrow-lipped – and a small area of chalk grassland contains stemless thistle, cowslip, purging flax and bee orchid. The park's birds include the sparrowhawk, kestrel, little owl and tawny owl, and among its butterflies is the white admiral.

WILD THYME

LARDON CHASE & LOUGH DOWN

– BERKSHIRE –

Location
Overlooking the River Thames just north of Streatley and to the west of the A417.
Map reference 174:SU588809 and 588813.

Habitats
Chalk grassland.

Nature conservation features
This is one of the largest remaining areas of chalk grassland in Berkshire. Its steep east- and south-facing chalk slopes give good views of the Chilterns and the valley of the Thames. This is a good place for the butterfly enthusiast, with a variety of species, including blues, on the wing in summer. Chalk milkwort, autumn gentian and clustered bellflower are among the site's many chalkland plants.

LARDON CHASE A view of the chalk hillside at the height of summer, with plantains, hawkbit and many different grasses in flower.

BRAMSHAW COMMONS Mixed woodland encourages many different birds.

COOMBE HILL & LOW SCRUBS

– BUCKINGHAMSHIRE –

Location
On the northern edge of the Chilterns between Wendover and Princes Risborough; just to the south of the B4010.
Map reference 165:SP849066 and 165:SP854061.

Habitats
Chalk grassland, scrub, woodland.

Nature conservation features
At 260m (852 feet), Coombe Hill is one of the highest viewpoints in the Chilterns. The nearby Low Scrubs is a fantasy world of strangely shaped trees. The steep slopes of Coombe Hill are rich in chalk grassland plants, including horseshoe vetch, kidney vetch and dropwort, which in turn attract many butterflies. Juniper grows here, bringing with it a range of special insects and other small animals that live only in association with this shrub. In the wooded areas, oak predominates and beech is common. The woodland is mainly of recent origin, but much of it was formerly coppiced and some ancient pollards can still be picked out.

· · ·

BRAMSHAW COMMONS

– HAMPSHIRE –

Location
Between Bramshaw, Cadnam and Plaitford, on the edge of the New Forest. South of the A36, 10 miles west of Southampton.
Map reference 184 and 185: SU2717.

HALE PURLIEU Scots pines are scattered over the open heath.

Habitats
Lowland heath, scrub, woodland, marsh, streams.

Nature conservation features
The 565 ha (1,400 acres) of Bramshaw Commons make up a typical New Forest landscape. The commons' expanses of open heath are fringed by scattered belts of woodland, containing a mixture of broadleaved trees and conifers. The wild flowers are especially diverse in wet and boggy places, and they include bog pimpernel, sundew, bog asphodel, marsh St. John's wort, bogbean and bog myrtle. The bird life, too, is varied, with nightjars, linnets, stonechats, yellowhammers, lapwings, redshanks and curlews. Woodland birds are also here in numbers, including all three British woodpeckers, the nuthatch, treecreeper, marsh tit and sparrowhawk.

HALE PURLIEU

– HAMPSHIRE –

Location
On the northwestern edge of the New Forest, about 3 miles northeast of Fordingbridge, adjacent to the B3080.
Map reference 184:SU200180.

Habitats
Lowland heath, scrub, woodland, pools.

Nature conservation features
With its open ground and dense thickets, Hale Purlieu is a good example of a mix of habitats that is common throughout the New Forest area. Heather, bell heather, cross-leaved heath, dwarf gorse and purple moorgrass grow in the well-drained, higher areas. Heather and purple moor-grass also grow on the wetter low-lying ground, alongside oblong-leaved sundew, cottongrass and meadow thistle. The New Forest is famous for its bird life, and Hale Purlieu is no exception to this. Nightjars nest on the heath, and can be seen on the wing at dusk in summer.

· · ·

LUDSHOTT COMMON & WAGGONER'S WELLS

– HAMPSHIRE –

Location
About 1½ miles west of Hindhead, on the south side of the B3002.
Map reference 186:SU855350 (Ludshott Common) and 869338 (Waggoner's Wells).

Habitats
Lowland heath, scrub, woodland, ponds.

Nature conservation features
Much of Ludshott Common is covered by lowland heath. Heather, which is now regenerating after a severe fire in 1980, is common throughout the heath, as are gorse and bracken. The common's butterflies include the silver-studded blue, grayling and green hairstreak. Many different species of spider live in and near the heather. The woods near the old hammer ponds at Waggoner's Wells contain fine old beech trees and also sessile oaks, which are uncommon in Hampshire. These woods are believed to be a surviving fragment of ancient woodland. Redstarts and wood warblers nest in the trees, while nightjars, stonechats, linnets, redpolls and nightingales breed on the margins of the heath.

SELBORNE

– HAMPSHIRE –

Location
Adjoining the village of Selborne, about 4 miles south of Alton on the B3006.
Map reference 186:SU735333.

Habitats
Woodland, scrub, grassland.

Nature conservation features
Selborne is inseparably linked with the writings of the Rev. Gilbert White. The beech hangers adjoining the village – hallowed ground to the naturalist – still live up to the descriptions so faithfully recorded in *The Natural History of Selborne*. The main hanger, along the chalk slope to the west of the village, has a rich array of wild flowers, including woodruff, yellow archangel, wood spurge and wood anemone as well as the birdsnest orchid. This is also one of the best places in Britain to see land snails, with dozens of species – some just a few millimetres long – living in the woods. Above the hanger, on the plateau of Selborne Common, is an area of oak and ash with clearings bordered by shrubs. Over 30 species of butterfly have been found here, including the silver-washed fritillary, the brown, purple and green hairstreaks and the majestic white admiral.

· · ·

STOCKBRIDGE DOWN

– HAMPSHIRE –

Location
1 mile east of Stockbridge, on the north side of the A272.
Map reference 185:SU379349.

SELBORNE The famous beech hangers cling to a low chalk hillside.

Habitats
Chalk grassland, scrub.

Nature conservation features
This area of Hampshire chalkland is common land, and unusually for a common it has a long history of being cut for hay. It has a distinctive mix of grasses and plants such as horseshoe vetch, knapweed broomrape and bee orchid. The wide range of butterflies includes the holly blue and brimstone, and the insect life of the area also features a native species of cockroach. The dry chalk suits some interesting shrubs, including juniper as well as the more common yew, dogwood and blackthorn, and these provide cover for birds such as the blackcap and linnet.

WOOLTON HILL: THE CHASE

– HAMPSHIRE –

Location
About 3 miles southwest of Newbury, close to the west side of the A343.
Map reference 174:SU442627.

Habitats
Woodland, grassland, stream, lake.

Nature conservation features
The Chase is made up principally by woodland through which a chalk stream winds, eventually flowing into a picturesque lake. The woodland contains oaks, beeches and conifers, while

alders grow on the stream banks. The flowers of the wet ground are one of the attractions of this nature reserve, with marsh marigold in early spring followed by gypsywort, meadowsweet, hairy willowherb, golden saxifrage, hemlock and water dropwort. Goldcrests and crossbills are attracted by the conifers, and several species of warbler, including the blackcap, garden warbler, willow warbler, chiff-chaff and wood warbler, are known to breed here.

. . .

ASHRIDGE

– HERTFORDSHIRE –

Location
3 miles north of Berkhamsted, at Northchurch, between the A41 and B489 and astride the B4506. Map reference 165:SP9812.

Habitats
Woodland, chalk grassland, heath.

Nature conservation features
At the northeastern end of the Chilterns overlooking the Vale of Aylesbury, this extensive stretch of downland has several nature walks and paths. Oak, ash, beech, cherry, birch and sycamore all thrive on the hill slopes. Yellow archangel, wood anemone and wood sorrel grow on the woodland floor, while the chalk downland has many species of orchid, as well as vetches, squinancywort, rock-rose, hairy violet, gentian, twayblades and restharrow. The woodland is the home of fallow deer and two species of deer from the Far East – the muntjac and Chinese water deer. The dormouse is also found here, as are the pipistrelle and long-eared bats.

AFTON, COMPTON & BROOK DOWNS

– ISLE OF WIGHT –

Location
On the southwest coast, from 3 miles south of Yarmouth eastwards. Access by the A3055. Map reference 196:SZ350858 (Afton Down), 376850 (Compton Down), 395851 (Brook Down).

Habitats
Farmland, chalk grassland, scrub, cliffs.

Nature conservation features
From the top of this bold chalk ridge there are marvellous views over land and sea in every direction. The major biological interest is in the chalk grassland on the south-facing slope, which is very rich in plants. This slope is hot and dry in the summer and exposed to gales in the winter, factors that combine to keep the

COMPTON BAY *Eroded cliffs showing the thin topsoil.*

vegetation short even in the absence of grazing animals. Most of the characteristic plants of chalk grassland, such as the horseshoe vetch, dwarf thistle, rock-rose and kidney vetch, are common. Orchids grow here in abundance. Where the vegetation is sparse, the exposed chalk rubble is clad with lichens. Snails are plentiful and butterflies, notably the chalkhill and small blues, can be readily found in favoured sheltered spots. The flamboyant yellow-horned poppy grows on the exposed cliff-edge to the south of the road.

. . .

COMPTON TO SHIPPARDS CHINE CLIFF

– ISLE OF WIGHT –

Location
On the southwest coast between Brook and Totland. Access by the A3055. Map reference 196:SZ376850 (Compton Down), 378841 (Shippards Chine).

Habitats
Cliffs, grassland.

Nature conservation features
These unstable sandy cliffs are always changing as the sea eats away at their feet. The consequent slumping creates ideal conditions for a wide range of plants and animals, notably the Glanville fritillary butterfly whose caterpillars feed on ribwort plantain. Other plants that do well here are the sea fern grass and burrowing clover. The loose, warm sand encourages mining bees and wasps, which can be seen in late spring excavating and stocking their burrows.

HEADON WARREN

– ISLE OF WIGHT –

Location
Near the Isle's western extremity, facing the Solent.
Map reference 196:SZ310851.

Habitats
Cliffs, heathland, woodland.

Nature conservation features
The cliffs of Headon Warren are made up of sandy deposits similar to those at nearby Alum Bay and very different from the chalk of the Needles to the West. They support one of the few remaining heathlands on the Isle of Wight. The main dwarf shrubs are heather, which is very closely grazed by rabbits, and bell heather, with smaller amounts of gorse. The mottled grasshopper, grayling butterfly and common lizard are among the heath's inhabitants. In some years Dartford warblers may be seen.

THE NEEDLES TO TENNYSON DOWN

– ISLE OF WIGHT –

Location
Southwest of Freshwater. Access to the Needles via the B3322. Map reference 196:SZ300848 (the Needles Headland), 330855 (Tennyson Down).

Habitats
Cliffs, chalk grassland.

Nature conservation features
This impressive chalk ridge, with vertical chalk cliffs on its southern edge, is topped with grassland, and the nature of this grassland varies with the level and type of grazing. Tennyson Down's wild flowers include clustered bellflower, autumn gentian, tufted centaury and frog orchid. West High Down is grazed by sheep and has fewer plants, while the ungrazed section near the Needles is covered with rough grass. Even in this exposed location, chalkland butterflies are common. Cormorants, kittiwakes, guillemots and shags regularly nest on the cliffs, while peregrines have also been known to breed.

. . .

NEWTOWN ESTUARY

– ISLE OF WIGHT –

Location
Midway between Newport and Yarmouth, north of the A3054. Map reference 196:SZ424906 (Newtown village).

Habitats
Farmland, woodland, river, saltmarsh, mudflats.

Nature conservation features
The National Trust owns much of this unspoiled estuary, three-quarters of which is covered by the high tide. In winter, up to 10,000 waders and waterfowl feed out on the mud, either on the algae or on the abundant animal life concealed in the mud. Birds that are seen regularly here include the golden plover, curlew, black-tailed godwit, Brent goose, wigeon and pintail. Shelduck also breed here, along with the oystercatcher, redshank, ringed plover and two species of gull. The edges of the estuary are bordered by typical saltmarsh plants. The woodland is made up of oak, ash, hazel and field maple. It is particularly important to wildlife because it harbours both red squirrels and dormice. The silver-washed fritillary, white admiral and purple hairstreak butterflies also live within it.

THE NEEDLES *Chalk pinnacles at the Isle of Wight's western tip.*

NEWTOWN ESTUARY *The estuary at high tide, with saltmarsh plants in flower. Few species can tolerate these saline conditions.*

VENTNOR

– ISLE OF WIGHT –

Location
On the southeast coast, approached by the A3055 coast road or the B3327.
Map reference 196:SZ570782 (St. Boniface Down), 563784 (Littleton and Luccombe Downs).

Habitats
Chalk grassland, scrub, farmland.

Nature conservation features
The National Trust's holdings at Ventnor include St. Boniface Down, which at 233m (764 feet) is the highest point of the Isle of Wight. In early summer, horseshoe vetch produces beautiful sheets of yellow flowers in the grassland areas. Rock-rose,

autumn gentian and woolly thistle are common, and slender centaury, common broomrape and bee orchid also grow here. This is also the only place on the Isle of Wight where the stripe-winged grasshopper is found, and in summer, the chalkhill blue and brown argus butterflies are a common sight.

· · ·

LANGDON CLIFFS

– KENT –

Location
1 mile northeast of Dover, above Dover Eastern Docks.
Map reference 179:TR335422.

Habitats
Cliffs, chalk grassland, scrub, woodland.

Nature conservation features
Langdon Cliffs form part of the majestic wall of chalk for which the coast around Dover is so famous. Its rich grassland is full of chalk-loving plants. These include the pyramidal, bee and fragrant orchids, and also meadow clary and a rare species of parasitic broomrape. The small blue is among the many butterflies that can be seen here in warm, sunny weather. The shrubby thickets near the cliffs are important staging posts for migrating birds, especially warblers, and a number of small birds also breed in them.

· · ·

SANDWICH BAY & PEGWELL BAY

– KENT –

Location
3 miles north and 2 miles northeast of Sandwich.
Map reference 179:TR347620 (Sandwich Bay), 343627 (Pegwell Bay).

Habitats
Sand dunes, saltmarsh, shingle, beach, foreshore.

Nature conservation features
Separated by the estuary of the River Great Stour, these two bays are both managed as nature reserves. The reserves lie on a migration route for birds and butterflies. Over 150 species of bird have been recorded, and wildfowl and waders overwinter in large numbers on the estuary. The dunes and shingle provide a habitat for plants such as marram grass, sea bindweed, sea holly and sea sandwort. Marsh and pyramidal orchids can sometimes be seen.

St. Margaret's Bay

– Kent –

Location
4 miles northeast of Dover, approached via the A258 Dover-Deal road.
Map reference 179:TR370455 (Bockhill Farm).

Habitats
Cliffs, farmland.

Nature conservation features
The largest of the National Trust's holdings on the chalk cliffs northeast of Dover is Bockhill Farm. It lies in a part of southeast England that is believed to have remained as grassland when the rest of Britain was covered in forest. It is a refuge for grassland plants, some of which are only found in this locality. The cliffs shelter fulmars and kittiwakes. The peregrine, which

ST. MARGARET'S BAY *The chalk cliffs, looking westwards.*

once bred here regularly, now appears to be returning.

· · ·

Toy's Hill

– Kent –

Location
2½ miles south of Brasted, 1 mile west of Ide Hill.
Map reference 188:TQ465517.

Habitats
Woodland, heathland.

Nature conservation features
Standing on the greensand ridge of the North Downs, Toy's Hill has superb views over the northern part of Kent. From early times, this area was part of the Brasted Chart Commons, and was used for firewood and for feeding pigs and cattle. The beech woods were cut for charcoal to fuel the Wealden iron trade, and also by local oasts to dry hops. In places, old beeches and oaks still remain, but the great storm of 1987 blew down nearly all the trees on the woodland plateau. The slopes lower down the hill are covered with bluebells in the spring and with many other woodland flowers throughout the summer.

· · ·

Morden Hall Park

– London –

Location
On the east side of the Morden Road (A24) and Mordenhall Road (A297).
Map reference 176:TQ259687.

Habitats
Parkland, fen, river.

Nature conservation features
Morden Hall Park is a rich oasis for wildlife in south London, with its riverbanks, fen and parkland trees. The River Wandle has many aquatic plants, including duckweed and curled pondweed, and dragonflies patrol over it in search of insects. Grey wagtails and kingfishers both nest along the river. The trees and shrubs harbour a range of woodland birds, including the nuthatch and great spotted woodpecker. Like many birds in towns and cities, those in the park are used to humans and therefore easy to watch.

· · ·

Selsdon Wood

– London –

Location
3 miles southeast of Croydon, ½ mile southeast of Selsdon, along the Farleigh Road.
Map reference 177:TQ357615.

Habitats
Woodland, grassland, pond.

Nature conservation features
At one time, Selsdon Wood was in deepest countryside. Today, it lies on the very fringes of London, offering a welcome respite from the busy city. About three-quarters of its area is made up by broadleaved woodland divided by wide rides, the rest being rough meadows. In May, large tracts of ground are carpeted with bluebells, and herb Paris is one of the more unusual woodland plants. Selsdon's bird life contains no great rarities but it is abundant. The woodland butterflies include the comma and the more scarce white-letter and purple hairstreaks, with browns and skippers in the meadows.

WATLINGTON HILL

– OXFORDSHIRE –

Location
1 mile southeast of Watlington, east of the B480.
Map reference 175:SU702935.

Habitats
Chalk grassland, scrub, woodland.

Nature conservation features
With its marvellous chalk grassland full of wild flowers, Watlington Hill is one of the biological highlights of the Chilterns. Horseshoe vetch, kidney vetch, rock-rose and squinancywort are all common, and the frog orchid, bee orchid, pyramidal orchid, autumn gentian and Chiltern gentian can all be found here. The grassland is the home of about 30 species of butterfly. Other habitats of interest include areas of yew woodland and two kinds of scrub, one over the chalk with lime-loving shrubs such as wayfaring tree, dogwood, whitebeam, privet and juniper, and another quite different kind on areas of acid soil, with gorse, hawthorn and blackthorn.

. . .

WHITE HORSE HILL

– OXFORDSHIRE –

Location
6 miles west of Wantage, 2 miles south of Uffington, on the south side of the B4507. Map reference 174:SU301866.

Habitats
Chalk grassland.

Nature conservation features
This chalk hill, with its earthworks and famous white horse, lies on the ridge of the Lambourn Downs. Much of the land around the ridge is now intensively farmed, but the hill still retains many tropical chalkland flowers, such as birdsfoot trefoil, and a variety of butterflies.

. . .

BOOKHAM COMMONS

– SURREY –

Location
2½ miles west of Leatherhead and north of Great Bookham. Map reference 187:TQ1256.

Habitats
Grassland, woodland, scrub, ponds, streams, marsh.

Nature conservation features
The large expanse of wooded and open common land at Bookham is rich in animal life and has over 500 species of flowering plant. The commons' grassland, grazed for centuries, fell into disuse after 1947 and now contains plants such as hogweed, rosebay willowherb and bracken. The woodlands are largely of oak with many fine old trees and an understorey of holly and hawthorn. Woodpigeons, blackbirds, woodpeckers, tawny owls and woodcock all breed in the woods, while the streams are visited by kingfishers, herons and grey wagtails. In summer, warblers and nightingales are common in the scrub. All three species of newt live in the ponds, and grass snakes are numerous.

WATLINGTON HILL The wooded hill rises above open farmland.

BOX HILL

– SURREY –

Location
1 mile north of Dorking, 1¹/₂ miles south of Leatherhead, to the east of the A24.
Map reference 187:TQ1751.

Habitats
Woodland, chalk grassland, scrub.

Nature conservation features
This well-known beauty spot is probably one of the most visited parts of the Surrey countryside. Yet in places it retains a sense of solitude and tranquillity, and the hill abounds with wildlife. The box and yew trees, which are a feature of the hill, have such thick foliage that little can grow beneath them, but many plants grow in the areas of old mixed woodland. The downland grass is rich in wild flowers, including seven species of orchid and lime-loving plants such as sainfoin, salad burnet and marjoram. Box Hill is considered to be one of the best butterfly sites in Britain.

CLUSTERED
BELLFLOWER

FRENSHAM COMMON

– SURREY –

Location
Astride the A287 Hindhead to Farnham road.
Map reference 186:SU8540.

Habitats
Heathland, woodland, scrub, bogs, reedbeds, lakes.

Nature conservation features
This property, part of which is a country park, is a fine example of Surrey heathland. The dry areas of the heath contain bell heather, ling, gorse, bracken, birch and Scots pine, while mosses, sedges and sundews grow where the ground is wet. The ponds provide a habitat for the yellow iris, sweet flag, common reed and bulrush, and in summer the reedbeds are the home of reed buntings and reed and sedge warblers. The heathland birds include the elusive nightjar, as well as the stonechat, whinchat, snipe and redshank.

. . .

HINDHEAD COMMON

– SURREY –

Location
Northwest of Haslemere and east of the A3/A287 junction.
Map reference 186:SU8936.

Habitats
Heathland, woodland, farmland, stream.

Nature conservation features
The National Trust's land at Hindhead Common includes Gibbet Hill and the great amphitheatre of the Devil's Punchbowl. Woodland of many types

can be found here, some made up of Scots pine, others of mixed species including oak, beech, whitebeam and rowan. In some areas of open ground, repeated fires have inhibited the heather and allowed bracken to take over. Great spotted and green woodpeckers live in the woods, and where scrub has become established, it provides cover and a supply of insects for blue tits, long-tailed tits, coal tits and goldcrests. Roe deer also live on the common, but are rarely seen.

. . .

LEITH HILL

– SURREY –

Location
About 4 miles southwest of Dorking, approached via the A29 and then the B2126, or by following signs south from the A25 between Dorking and Abinger Hammer.
Map reference 187:TQ139432.

Habitats
Woodland, heathland, grassland.

Nature conservation features
At 294m (965 feet), Leith Hill is the highest point in southeast England, giving extensive views across the Surrey-Sussex borderlands. Its well-wooded slopes are covered with a mix of broadleaved trees such as oak and birch, and conifers such as Scots pine. The fine show of bluebells and the spring colours of the rhododendrons in Mosses Wood are a local highlight, as is the white admiral butterfly, which lives on the hill in some numbers. Woodland birds, including woodpeckers, nuthatches, treecreepers and wood warblers, find the dense tree cover to their liking.

LEITH HILL Seed-heads of traveller's joy decorate a thicket.

RANMORE COMMON

– SURREY –

Location
2 miles northwest of Dorking.
Map reference 187:TQ1451.

Habitats
Woodland, common, fields.

Nature conservation features
This wooded common lies on the slopes of the North Downs. The woodland here is predominantly composed of beech, oak and ash with some yews interspersed among the taller trees. Columbines, white helleborines, bluebells, foxgloves and wood anemones can be seen on the woodland floor in spring. The common is the haunt of roe deer, and also of numerous foxes and rabbits. Its woodland butterflies include the purple hairstreak, white admiral, dark green fritillary and silver-washed fritillary. Sparrowhawks, wood warblers, woodcock and all three of our native woodpeckers live and breed in the woods.

. . .

RUNNYMEDE

– SURREY –

Location
On the Thames, $^1/_2$ mile above Runnymede Bridge, on the south side of the A308.
Map reference 176:TQ007720.

Habitats
Meadows, marsh, woods, hedges, ponds, riverbank.

Nature conservation features
These historic meadows, where King John set his seal on the Magna Carta, are today a haven for wetland plants and animals. The ponds contain the fringed waterlily, duckweed, frogbit, water dropwort and the flowering rush. On nearby Cooper's Hill, the rich turf contains many species of flowering plants.

. . .

WITLEY & MILFORD COMMONS

– SURREY –

Location
1 mile southwest of Milford.
Map reference 186:SU9240.

Habitats
Heathland, chalk downland, woodland.

Nature conservation features
Until early this century, cattle and horses were grazed at Witley and bracken was cut for pig litter. Today, after being occupied by the army in two world wars, the character of the commons has changed. This is particularly noticeable where "foreign" soil has been brought in to restore the habitat. Bell heather and ling – two typical heathland plants – have been joined by chalk downland species such as stemless thistle and marjoram. The mixture of broadleaved trees encourages a variety of birds. Siskins and redpolls feed on birch seeds, and woodpigeons and jays eat the plentiful acorns. A vast variety of insects feed on the trees and scrub. Common lizards and adders both live on the commons, as do roe deer and a small number of red deer.

BIRLING GAP

– East Sussex –

Location
5 miles west of Eastbourne, south of Friston which lies on the A259.
Map reference 199:TV554961.

Habitats
Chalk grassland, cliffs, rocky shore.

Nature conservation features
Birling Gap nestles in some of the most spectacular coastal scenery on the Sussex coast, where high chalk cliffs form a vertical rampart which is constantly being eroded by the sea. A ladder allows access to the shingle beach. At high tide, only a narrow strip of shingle remains above the water, but low tide exposes chalk flats capped with flints that have been sculpted and hollowed by the sea. The chalk provides a foothold for seaweed, and also for small animals such as limpets, mussels and sea anemones. Gulls, fulmars and jackdaws patrol the cliffs, making use of the strong updraught created by the onshore wind.

· · ·

BLACK DOWN

– West Sussex and Surrey –

Location
1 mile southeast of Haslemere.
Map reference 186:SU9230.

Habitats
Woodland, heath, old pasture.

Nature conservation features
The sandstone plateau of Black Down is the highest point in Sussex, standing 280m (918 feet) above the well-wooded countryside of the Weald. Majestic

beeches grow on the eastern slopes, and the top of the hill is clad with birch, scrub oak, Scots pine, gorse and heather. Oak and rhododendron also grow on the slopes, with rowan and alder buckthorn. The damper areas are home to many moisture-loving plants such as whortleberry, *Sphagnum* moss and sundew. Green and great spotted woodpeckers are common near tree cover, as are warblers, tree pipits, wrens and the occasional crossbill. Meadow pipits, linnets and yellowhammers can be seen over open ground.

· · ·

EAST HEAD

– West Sussex –

Location
On the east side of the entrance to Chichester Harbour. Access by the A286 and B2179.

***EAST HEAD** Extensive sand and shingle flats exposed at low tide.*

Map reference 197:SU766990.

Habitats
Sand and shingle beach, sand dunes, saltmarsh, mudflats.

Nature conservation features
East Head is a narrow spit of sand and shingle beach that juts out into Chichester Harbour. At the mercy of storms and high tides, its shape and position are constantly changing. Almost one hundred species of flowering plant have been found on East Head, from glasswort, thrift and sea-lavender to the rare sea heath, sea bindweed, golden samphire and evening primrose. Chichester Harbour is, as might be expected, a haven for many seabirds, wildfowl and waders. Shelduck live here in their thousands. Brent geese, wigeon, pochard, teal, mallard, golden-eye and merganser share the rich mudflats and inshore waters with redshank, curlew, grey plover, sanderling and bar-headed and black-tailed godwits. Terns nest on the shingle.

· · ·

FULKING ESCARPMENT & NEWTIMBER HILL

– West Sussex –

Location
5 miles northwest of Brighton, and immediately south of Poynings, Fulking and Edburton.
Map reference 198:TQ2411.

Habitats
Chalk grassland, woodland.

Nature conservation features
Following its South Downs Appeal, the National Trust has recently begun to acquire large areas of this steep chalkland

escarpment. Orchids are common in the short turf. Chalkland butterflies abound here, and they include several different species of blue. Carder bees and cardinal beetles live on the slopes, and a number of rare species of grasshopper can be found in the grass. The downland birds include the nightingale, as well as the occasional hoopoe, flying in from across the Channel.

. . .

PETWORTH PARK

– WEST SUSSEX –

Location
In the centre of Petworth, 5½ miles east of Midhurst, at the junction of the A272 and A283. Map reference 197:SU976218.

Habitats
Parkland.

Nature conservation features
Petworth Park, which was landscaped by "Capability" Brown, contains one of the finest deer parks in Britain. Its many ancient trees include gnarled oaks and sweet chestnuts. The abundant insects living on the trees provide food for treecreepers, woodpeckers and nuthatches, while the acorns and chestnuts are eaten by grey squirrels and jays. The park's fallow deer are particularly impressive in early autumn, when the antlers of the bucks are fully grown and the rutting season begins.

SLINDON WOODS

– WEST SUSSEX –

Location
6 miles north of Bognor Regis on the A29.
Map reference 197:SU9608 (Park Wood).

Habitats
Woodland.

Nature conservation features
The remains of the woods at Slindon are a testament to the power of the great storm that swept across southeast England in 1987. Although the disaster destroyed a large proportion of the woods on this estate, some plants have benefited from the increased light, as have the birds that feed among them. As the years progress, Slindon's woods will be a fascinating case-history of woodland reasserting itself.

. . .

CHERHILL DOWN & OLDBURY CASTLE

– WILTSHIRE –

Location
On the A4, between Calne and Beckhampton.
Map reference 173:SU046694.

Habitats
Chalk grassland, plantations.

Nature conservation features
The prominent chalk ridge of Cherhill Down, with its monument and White Horse cut into the turf, is flanked by steep slopes and dry coombes. The southern slope and adjacent land at the western end is the best place for wild flowers, which include the lesser butterfly orchid. Cherhill Down has large numbers of chalkhill blue

FULKING The chalk escarpment rises abruptly from the Sussex Weald.

butterflies, as well as the brown argus, marbled white and dingy skipper. Skylarks, meadow pipits and partridges can usually be seen.

· · ·

CLEY HILL

– WILTSHIRE –

Location
3 miles west of Warminster near the Somerset border, on the north side of the A362.
Map reference 183:ST838450.

Habitats
Chalk grassland, chalk, quarry.

Nature conservation features
This broad chalk hill, the site of an Iron Age hill-fort capped by Bronze Age burial mounds, is a landmark for miles around. At one time it was well known for its Adonis and chalkhill blue butterflies, but both disappeared in the 1970s. Happily, the Adonis blue is now back in some numbers, and the chalkhill blue has also returned. The hill's butterflies also include the marbled white and brown argus. Cley Hill's "unimproved" grassland has a profusion of chalk-loving flowers, including gentians.

· · ·

FIGSBURY RING

– WILTSHIRE –

Location
About 4 miles northeast of Salisbury, to the north of the A30 London road.
Map reference 184:SU188338.

Habitats
Chalk grassland.

Nature conservation features
Figsbury Ring's Iron Age earth-

CLEY HILL *A flat-topped chalk hill, covered in turf that is rich in wild flowers.*

works provide warm, south-facing slopes that suit many chalkland plants. Orchids are common here, with pyramidal, fragrant, bee, common spotted and frog orchids growing in the turf, which is regularly grazed by sheep. This is a particularly good site for butterflies, especially the chalkhill and small blues.

· · ·

PEPPERBOX HILL

– WILTSHIRE –

Location
5 miles southeast of Salisbury, on the north side of the A36.
Map reference 184:SU215248.

Habitats
Scrub, chalk grassland.

Nature conservation features
Pepperbox Hill, which gets its name from its seventeenth-century folly, is one of the few

sites in southern England where juniper thrives. The hill also has some good specimens of white-beam, dogwood, hawthorn, wayfaring tree, guelder rose and wild privet. Seven species of orchid bloom on the hill and its other plants include the greater knapweed, dropwort and chalk milkwort. A total of 80 species of butterfly and moth have been recorded on the hillside.

· · ·

WHITE SHEET DOWN

– WILTSHIRE –

Location
Off the B3092, 3 miles northwest of Mere, which lies on the A303.
Map reference 183:ST800348.

Habitats
Chalk scree, grassland, woodland.

Nature conservation features
White Sheet Down adjoins the National Trust's Stourhead Estate, and contains one of the richest prehistoric sites in Wiltshire. Like any area of "unimproved" chalk grassland, it is a haven for butterflies. It has the chalkhill and small blues, marsh fritillary, marbled white, and, in early summer, good numbers of grizzled and dingy skippers. Coltsfoot, cowslips and primroses grow on the chalk scree, and birdsfoot trefoil, harebell, salad burnet, yellow rattle, wild thyme and lady's bedstraw flower here in summer. Several species of orchid grow on the hill, and rock-rose flowers in profusion in summer, creating a carpet of yellow that contrasts with the late summer "blue period" when the devilsbit scabious comes into flower.

SOUTHWEST

· · ·

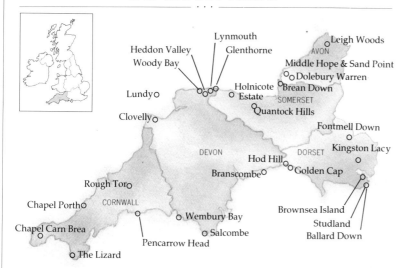

Heddon Valley
Woody Bay
Lynmouth
Glenthorne
Leigh Woods
AVON
Middle Hope & Sand Point
Dolebury Warren
Brean Down
Holnicote Estate
SOMERSET
Quantock Hills
Lundy
Clovelly
Fontmell Down
Kingston Lacy
DEVON
Hod Hill
DORSET
Branscombe
Golden Cap
Rough Tor
Chapel Porth
CORNWALL
Brownsea Island
Chapel Carn Brea
Studland
Ballard Down
Wembury Bay
Salcombe
Pencarrow Head
The Lizard

*J*utting out into the Atlantic like a crumbling finger, the Southwest peninsula contains some of the most spectacular coastal scenery to be found anywhere in Britain. Extensive sections of coastline are owned and protected by the National Trust. So, too, are many inland sites, which vary from high windswept moorland to lush, fern-filled woodlands deep in sheltered valleys.

DOLEBURY WARREN

– AVON –

Location
Near Churchill, about 12 miles south of Bristol, to the south of the A368 and east of the A38. Access via the A38, ¹/₂ mile south of its junction with the A368. Map reference 182:ST450590.

Habitats
Limestone grassland, heath, scrub, woodland.

Nature conservation features
Dolebury Warren's steep limestone ridge is crowned with a large and impressive Iron Age hill-fort with massive banks and ditches. The ridge rises to 180m (600 feet), and is an outstanding site for butterflies. Over 30 species have been recorded here, among them the small skipper, grizzled skipper, small blue, small heath and speckled wood. The flanks of the ridge are covered by grass, hawthorn scrub and also woodland, which is dominated by ash trees. In spring and summer, the grassland is studded with the flowers of common rock-rose, salad burnet, kidney vetch, wild thyme and yellow rattle. Heath has developed on the hilltop .

LEIGH WOODS

– AVON –

Location
On the western bank of the River Avon, just north of the Clifton Suspension Bridge. Map reference 172:ST560734.

Habitats
Woodland, scrub, grassland, cliffs.

Nature conservation features
These verdant woods cling to the limestone of the Avon Gorge, just a short distance from the centre of Bristol. They are in part ancient and in part woodland that once contained areas of pasture. A wide range of trees grows here, including oak, ash, small-leaved lime, wild cherry, and also a type of whitebeam that is unique to the Avon Gorge. The plant life of Leigh Woods is exceptionally rich, with some rare species. Ivy and bluebells grow on the woodland floor, together with more unusual plants, such as lily-of-the-valley and ivy broomrape. Ferns, which appreciate the damp conditions, are also abundant.

· · ·

MIDDLE HOPE & SAND POINT

– AVON –

Location
2 miles north of Weston-super-Mare on the coast road from Kewstoke. Map reference 182:ST335665 and 325660.

Habitats
Limestone grassland, scrub, rock, saltmarsh.

Nature conservation features

This very varied site is dominated by a limestone ridge 30m (100 feet) high that juts out into the Bristol Channel, giving views across to Wales and inland to the Mendips. The ridge becomes progressively more craggy towards its western tip, while at its eastern end, it grades into salt-marsh. Rock samphire and thrift grow on the rocks, while the rabbit-nibbled turf is rich in lime-loving flowers such as yellow-wort, common centaury, salad burnet, common rock-rose, wild thyme, dwarf thistle, bee orchid and green-winged orchid.

· · ·

CHAPEL CARN BREA

– CORNWALL –

Location

On the north side of the A30, about 3 miles northeast of Land's End. Access via a side-road between the A30 and the B3306. Map reference 203:SW385281.

Habitats

Heath, grassland, granite outcrops, scattered boulders.

Nature conservation features

Sometimes referred to as "the first and last hill in England", Chapel Carn Brea's exposed position, granite outcrops and steep slopes have marked effect on its plant life. The main vegetation here is heath, which is dominated by four plants – ling, bell heather, western gorse and bristle-leaved bent grass. Purple moor-grass and cross-leaved heath also grow in damper places, while heath milkwort, heath bedstraw and bluebells can also be seen. Many insects and

other invertebrate animals thrive in the shelter of crevices and hollows under the boulders.

· · ·

CHAPEL PORTH

– CORNWALL –

Location

About 1 mile north of Porth-towan and 1¹/₂ miles southwest of St. Agnes, from where it can be approached by road. Access also via the B3277 and from it by a track down the Chapel Combe Valley. Map reference 203:SW697496.

Habitats

Heath, grassland, marsh, old mining spoil.

Nature conservation features

Chapel Porth is a flat coastal plateau about 85m (280 feet) above sea level. Wind has had a profound influence on the natural history of this site. Ling and bell heather grow in wave-like clumps where they are most exposed, and in places the soil's fertility is increased by blown

CHAPEL PORTH *The rock-strewn beach seen from the cliff-top.*

sand. This has created a very rich plant life, with 16 nationally rare plants and a further six that are only found in a few localities. They include the hairy green-weed, black bog-rush, pale heath violet, bloody cranesbill, burnet rose, Dorset heath and salad burnet. The majestic royal fern thrives in damp places near the cliff-tops. Chapel Porth is a good place to see both reptiles and sea-birds. The common lizard, slow-worm, adder and grass snake have all been recorded here. Among the seabirds, razorbills breed on the cliffs nearer the northern end, and guillemots, kittiwakes and shags feed in the water offshore.

· · ·

THE LIZARD

– CORNWALL –

Location

South of Helston. Access via the A3083. Map reference 203 and 204:SW7015.

Habitats

Heathland, grassland, scrub, woodland, streams, marsh.

Nature conservation features

The Lizard's unusual geology, coupled with the mild coastal climate, have brought about a plant life unlike that of any other part of Britain. Some of its plants, such as several clovers and the dwarf rush, are generally found only in warmer parts of Europe. Cornish heath grows on the heathland, while spring and autumn squills, dyer's green-weed and chives can be found in the coastal grass. Hottentot fig, a fleshy-leaved plant from southern Africa, forms sheets that cover some of the cliffs.

PENCARROW HEAD, LANSALLOS, LANTIC BAY & LANTIVET BAY

– CORNWALL –

Location
East of Fowey, with access via footpaths from the Polruan-Lansallos road. The coast path runs along the entire frontage.
Map reference 200 and 201: SX1451.

Habitats
Scrub, grassland with bracken, cliffs, pools, shingle beaches.

Nature conservation features
The cliff-slopes on this site were once used for farming, but now are largely covered with bracken and scrub. Scrub woodland at the western end shows a later stage as nature takes over farmland. Here, ash and sycamore grow among blackthorn, hawthorn and elder. Although small and scattered, the numerous different habitats, including cliff-slopes, pools, rocky platforms, and a shingle beach at Lantic Bay, create great natural diversity. The parasitic ivy broomrape and the maidenhair fern, a rarity in the wild, both grow here, while the mown verges to the footpaths create a habitat for plants that cannot compete with the bracken. These less vigorous plants include the rare slender birdsfoot trefoil and also the hairy birdsfoot trefoil, a very local plant of low turf.

ROUGH TOR

– CORNWALL –

Location
Off the A39 at Camelford and about 3 miles southeast of the village.
Map reference 200 and 201: SX145806.

Habitats
Moorland, grassland, rocky outcrops.

Nature conservation features
Reaching over 365m (1,200 feet), this isolated and rugged granite tor is Cornwall's second highest point. Rough Tor rises out of an extensive sweep of moorland. Its grassland and peaty soils are clothed by plants typical of high, acid conditions. They include heath, common bent, sheep's fescue, and in damper places, purple moor-grass and bog asphodel. Bilberry, ling and bell heather are scattered thinly among them. Despite the apparently harsh conditions, insects can be abundant. Rough Tor's birds, although relatively few in terms of species, are easy to watch. Wheatears, ring ouzels, meadow pipits, kestrels and buzzards all live here in the summer.

· · ·

BRANSCOMBE & SALCOMBE REGIS

– DEVON –

Location
South of the A3052 and about 3 miles east of Sidmouth, approached by side-roads from the villages of Branscombe and Weston. The coastal footpath runs along the cliff.
Map reference 192:SY2188 and 1588.

ROUGH TOR High granite outcrops, scoured and sculpted by the wind.

Habitats
Chalk grassland, woodland, scrub, streams, shingle beach.

Nature conservation features
This coastal property is divided into two main sections, both lying at the most westerly point at which chalk is found in southern England. The chalk gives rise to a small but rich area of grassland along the cliffs. As well as many common plants and animals, a number of local species are found, such as Nottingham catchfly, blue gromwell, yellowwort, horseshoe vetch and wood vetch. The slopes and upper cliff near Weston Mouth are especially good places for these plants. The mixed undercliff scrub attracts many migrating warblers, including the willow warbler, blackcap and chiffchaff. Among the larger birds, buzzards and ravens are usually in the vicinity of the bare rocky outcrops, along with a scattering of herring gulls.

. . .

CLOVELLY: BECKLAND & FATACOTT CLIFFS

– DEVON –

Location
West of Clovelly, with access via small side-roads running north of the Hartland road, which turns off the A39 near Clovelly Cross. The coastal footpath runs along the cliffs.
Map reference 190:SS284265 and 190:SS265273.

Habitats
Woodland, grassland, heath, scrub.

Nature conservation features
Several detached sections make

HEDDON VALLEY A stream tumbles towards the sea through a steep valley, which is carpeted with heather and bracken.

up this coastal property, including land in the vicinity of Brownshams, where one of the easier points of access is situated. In the area from Beckland to Fatacott, low, wind-trimmed shrubs cover much of the undercliff. Here blackthorn, hawthorn and brambles are abundant. Where there is more shelter, rowans, sycamores and oaks also grow. Mixed woodland occurs in the relatively undisturbed Beckland Wood and at Brownshams. Old "unimproved" damp grassland still survives in a few scattered locations, for example in the Brownshams nature reserve.

. . .

GLENTHORNE

– DEVON –

Location
North of the A39, and about 3 miles east of Lynmouth. Access via three footpaths from the main road, or by the coastal footpath.
Map reference 180:SS7750.

Habitats
Woodland, heath, grassland, ravines, streams.

Nature conservation features
Glenthorne has a long, wild and beautiful coastal frontage, with steep slopes, landslips and ravines running to the sea. Much of the woodland is old coppiced oak, but there are also areas of ash, beech and sycamore. The open slopes are covered with bracken, grass, ling and bell heather, and at least two rare varieties of whitebeam grow among the rocks. Insects and snails thrive in the undisturbed dead wood, while abundant mosses and lichens show that this stretch of coast has largely escaped man's influence.

. . .

HEDDON VALLEY

– DEVON –

Location
North of the A399 and A39, about 5 miles west of Lynton. Side-roads to Trentishoe, Martinhoe and Hunter's Inn.
Map reference 180:SS6549.

Habitats
Woodland, heath, grassland, scree, cliffs, streams, meadows.

Nature conservation features
This extensive and varied area of countryside is deeply cut by wooded valleys that converge and run to the sea. Included within the boundary is an area of heathland, Trentishoe Down, and a long stretch of coastline with rugged cliffs and a small shingle beach. The woodland, mainly of oak and ash, is the haunt of the redstart, pied flycatcher, wood warbler, lesser spotted woodpecker, buzzard and sparrowhawk. Red deer also

LUNDY Jagged rocks create a habitat for many different cliff-plants.

pass through it. Butterflies, too, are abundant. The dipper, grey wagtail and heron can be seen along the streams, and the yellowhammer, linnet, stonechat, whinchat, tree pipit and wheatear live in the heathland. A variety of cliff-nesting birds, including fulmars and razorbills, help to make this a prime site for birdwatchers.

. . .

LUNDY

– DEVON –

Location
11 miles north of Hartland Point, 25 miles from Ilfracombe and 30 miles south of Tenby. Public access by boat from Bideford and Ilfracombe, and by helicopter from Hartland Point.
Map reference 180:SS1345.

Habitats
Cliffs, rocky shore, grassland, heath, scrub, woods.

Nature conservation features
Lundy lies in the Bristol Channel off the coast of north Devon, and is sufficiently far from the mainland to have a character all of its own. It is composed mostly of granite, which erodes only slowly to create cliffs with many ledges on which birds can nest. About 40 different species of bird breed on the island, the seabirds being the most obvious to the visitor. Among these are guillemots, razorbills, fulmars, kittiwakes, shags and a few puffins. As well as these breeding species, many more birds use Lundy as a stop-over point on their migrations. In all, over 400 species have been recorded, some extremely rare. One plant, the Lundy cabbage, is unique to the island.

LYNMOUTH

– DEVON –

Location
East of Lynmouth on both sides of the A39, including the deep valley of the East Lyn River. Extensive, well-maintained footpaths.
Map reference 180:SS7449.

Habitats
Woodland, streams, grassland, heath, scree, cliffs.

Nature conservation features
An extensive and varied area of the North Devon coast, the Trust's land around Lynmouth contains a mixture of both exposed and sheltered ground. The wooded areas provide breeding cover for buzzards, redstarts, pied flycatchers and wood warblers, while dippers feed in the fast-flowing streams. The woods are mostly of oak, but they also contain ash, birch, rowan and three rare local species of whitebeam. Woodland butterflies are also prominent. The dark-green fritillary flies over bracken-covered slopes in June, and a little later in July, the larger silver-washed fritillary feeds on bramble flowers along valley pathways. Heathland and cliffs complete the mix of habitats, and there are spectacular views over the Bristol Channel and its bordering coastline.

Acorn of
SESSILE OAK
eaten by insect larva

SALCOMBE

– DEVON –

Location
Flanking the Salcombe Estuary, and reached by side-roads from the A381 and A379. The coastal footpath runs along the shore. Map reference 202:SX7236 to 6639; 202:SX773350, 765355 and 740375.

Habitats
Cliffs, woodland, heath, grassland.

Nature conservation features
This extensive section of the south Devon coast, including Bolt Head, Portlemouth Down, Prawle Point and Gammon Head, is a magnificent destination for the birdwatcher. The scrub and rough ground attracts stonechats, whinchats, yellowhammers, linnets and many species of warbler. Along the steeper rocks and cliffs there are ravens, kestrels, rock-pipits and wheatears, with a scattering of herring gulls, fulmars and kittiwakes

WOODY BAY A view of the cliffs with rowan in the foreground.

nesting in more inaccessible sites. The seaward slopes and rocky outcrops are clothed in bloody cranesbill, spring and autumn squills, rock samphire and thrift. Sheltered spots are good places to see butterflies. Ants, grasshoppers and bush-crickets are also well represented in the heathland and grass.

· · ·

WEMBURY BAY & YEALM ESTUARY

– DEVON –

Location
5 miles southeast of Plymouth, approached via the A379. Map reference 201:SX530480.

Habitats
Cliffs, woodland, beach, mudflats.

Nature conservation features
The National Trust owns 2.5 km (1½ miles) of coastline from Wembury to Warren Point, and land on either side of the scenic Yealm estuary. Wembury Bay is notable for its marine conservation area, which was established in 1981. It has many rock-pools, and is an ideal place for exploring the plant and animal life of the lower shore. Wembury Point is an important staging point for waders and migratory birds. The Great Mew Stone, owned by the Ministry of Defence, is a breeding site for black-backed and herring gulls, cormorants, shags and buzzards. After storms, wagtails and turnstones can be seen hunting along the shore of Wembury Bay for insects, which they find among the mounds of seaweed flung up on the beach. Stonechats, whinchats, wheatears and nightingales breed inland.

WOODY BAY

– DEVON –

Location
About 3 miles west of Lynton and north of the A39, reached by side-roads from the A39 or from Lynton. Map reference 180:SS675487.

Habitats
Woodland, scrub, heath, cliffs.

Nature conservation features
In places, the oaks at Woody Bay extend to the very edge of the precipitous cliffs. Yew trees are also common here. Yew is believed to be a native tree at Woody Bay, one of the few places in Devon and Cornwall where this is so. Rare species of whitebeam, including the Devon whitebeam, perch precariously at the edge of rocky cliff overhangs. The seabirds that breed on the secluded rock stack and in the general region of Wringapeak are mainly herring gulls, kittiwakes, razorbills and guillemots. Fulmars, ravens and peregrines are all among the resident birds along the cliffs.

· · ·

BALLARD DOWN

– DORSET –

Location
On the coast immediately north of Swanage. Access by coastal and other footpaths. Map reference 195:SZ030810.

Habitats
Chalk grassland.

Nature conservation features
This dramatic chalk ridge rises to over 150m (500 feet) behind the coastal resort of Swanage. The steep, south-facing slope is a fine

example of "unimproved" chalk grassland, once so common in this area. Although no great rarities grow on Ballard Down, horseshoe vetch, kidney vetch, bee orchid and autumn lady's tresses make exploring its slopes in spring and summer an enjoyable experience. Many insects thrive in the warm climate of the Dorset coast. A total of 21 species of butterfly breed here, including the small blue and Lulworth skipper. The gorse provides cover and perches for whitethroats and stonechats.

· · ·

BROWNSEA ISLAND

– DORSET –

Location
In Poole Harbour, about 1½ miles southeast of Poole. Access by boat from Poole Quay and Sandbanks. Private boats may land at Pottery Pier at the west end of the island.
Map reference 195:SZ0288.

Habitats
Woodland, heathland, rhododendron scrub, lakes, lagoon, reedbeds, shore.

Nature conservation features
This fascinating island in Poole Harbour receives more than 100,000 visitors a year, but still retains sufficient peace and tranquillity to be the home of a wide range of birds and other animals. Almost half the island is a nature reserve, leased to the Dorset Trust for Nature Conservation. There are regular guided walks and a public hide gives views over the lagoon and its small gravel islets, which have been specially created as nesting sites for terns. Seabirds breeding on Brownsea include the great and

lesser black-backed gulls, herring gull and shelduck. Many waders can be seen on and around the island, including the curlew, oystercatcher, dunlin, greenshank, bar-tailed and blacktailed godwit, common and spotted redshank, and avocet. The island's woods are a stronghold for the red squirrel.

· · ·

FONTMELL DOWN

– DORSET –

Location
Between Shaftesbury and Blandford. Path from car park at Spread Eagle Hill, on the B3081. Map reference 183:ST884184.

Habitats
Chalk grassland.

Nature conservation features
Fontmell Down's rolling grassy slopes have never felt the effect

of the plough, and they have never been treated with fertilizers or herbicides. As a result, the plant and animal life remains much as it has been for hundreds of years. The turf abounds with squinancywort, quaking grass and other chalk-loving plants. Over 55 bird species have been recorded, including nightingales, grasshopper warblers, sparrowhawks, kestrels, buzzards and hen harriers. The sheltered coombes and the south-facing slopes are good places to find chalkland butterflies, including the elusive silver-spotted skipper.

· · ·

GOLDEN CAP

– DORSET –

Location
1 mile south of Morecombelake, halfway between Charmouth

GOLDEN CAP *Gorse and grass cling to the steep sandy cliff-face.*

and Bridport on the A35. Approached by side-road or footpath. Map reference 193:SY4092.

Habitats
Cliff, grassland, scrub, farmland, heath.

Nature conservation features
This steeply rolling countryside, with its cliffs, deeply incised valleys, small fields, ponds and heaths, is perhaps the epitome of the English landscape. The cliffs are of great geological interest, because they are made of soft sandy and clayey material that is rich in fossils. Erosion is rapid, and cliff falls are frequent. The terraces formed by these falls have a very diverse plant and animal life. Some areas are covered in willow scrub, while others have grass, heather or reeds that grow around small pools. The tangled scrub of the undercliff is a haven for migratory birds. A number of rare insects can be seen here, including the wood white and green hairstreak butterflies and the grey bush-cricket.

. . .

HOD HILL

– DORSET –

Location
About 4 miles northwest of Blandford, approached by footpath from the A350, or from the Child Okeford road. Map reference 194:ST857107.

Habitats
Chalk grassland, scrub.

Nature conservation features
Rising steeply above the River Stour and crowned by the ramparts and ditches of a hill-fort, Hod Hill is one of the richest sites for chalkland wildlife in

England. Thirty-five species of butterfly have been recorded here, although some of them – for example, the silver-spotted skipper and white-letter hairstreak – may have become extinct in recent times. In summer, the chalkhill blue, common blue, small blue and brown argus can all be seen on the hill, and another scarce species, the marsh fritillary, also lives here. Over 200 species of flowering plant have been recorded.

. . .

KINGSTON LACY ESTATE

– DORSET –

Location
About 2 miles northwest of Wimborne Minster on both sides of the B3082 Blandford road. Map reference 195:SY978014.

Habitats
Woodland, scrub, parkland, chalk grassland, meadows, marsh, river.

Nature conservation features
This largely agricultural estate has several areas that are interesting for their wildlife, the most notable being Bradbury Rings and the banks of the River Stour. The plant life of Bradbury Rings includes the greater butterfly orchid, frog orchid and bee orchid. Bastard toadflax, adder's tongue fern and knapweed broomrape can also be found on this part of the estate. The River Stour attracts many birds, including sedge and reed warblers, kingfishers, mute swans and little grebes. A large black poplar – rare in Britain – grows near White Mill Bridge, and young trees are being propagated from it.

STUDLAND HEATH & GODLINGSTON HEATH

– DORSET –

Location
On the edge of Poole Harbour and about 5 miles southwest of Bournemouth. Map reference 195:SZ010820 to 040860.

Habitats
Woodland, scrub, heathland, bogs, sand dunes, saltmarsh, mudflats.

Nature conservation features
This extensive nature reserve is one of the National Trust's finest wildlife properties. Its complex mix of habitats can best be appreciated from the high ground near the golf clubhouse on the Corfe Castle–Studland road. From here, the great sweep of open heathland, with its wetter drainage lines and bogs, falls away dramatically to the distant dunes. Many interesting plants can be seen in the wetter areas – species such as oblong-leaved sundew, bog myrtle, marsh clubmoss, meadow thistle, marsh gentian and royal fern. The area's birdlife is very varied, with gulls and waterfowl, as well as the stonechat, nightjar and Dartford warbler. Common lizards, sand lizards, adders and slow-worms all thrive in the sunny climate and sandy soil.

. . .

BREAN DOWN

– SOMERSET –

Location
2 miles southwest of Weston-super-Mare, to the south of

Weston Bay. Access via Brean village.
Map reference 182:ST2959.

Habitats
Cliff, coastal moorland, scrub, grassland.

Nature conservation features
This wild, narrow promontory is of great botanical and archaeological interest. The steep south-facing slopes have a mixture of plants that is found nowhere else in Britain, including the white rock-rose, Somerset hair-grass and the dwarf sedge. The slopes also abound with insect life, including the chalkhill blue and dark green fritillary butterflies. In the spring and autumn, the scrub provides cover for migrating birds such as the wheatear, ring ouzel, whinchat, warblers and finches.

· · ·

HOLNICOTE ESTATE

– SOMERSET –

Location
Astride the A39, between Minehead and Porlock.
Map reference 181:SS8844.

Habitats
Moorland, bogs, grassland, woodland, rivers, cliffs, saltmarsh, shingle beach.

Nature conservation features
This wonderfully varied estate covers about 50 square km· (20 square miles) of north Somerset. The high windswept moorland – home of the estate's red deer – is dominated by heather, with patches of bilberry, bell heather and gorse. Lower down, Horner Wood has ancient oaks and ashes that are covered with lichens, mosses, liverworts and ferns. These steep wooded valleys are

HOLNICOTE ESTATE Horner Water, haunt of the dipper, seen here flowing through a lush glade in the broadleaved woodland.

inhabited by buzzards, sparrowhawks, green and lesser spotted woodpeckers as well as by pied flycatchers, wood warblers and redstarts. Fast-flowing Horner Water is home for the dipper and grey wagtail, while the coastal heath and cliffs provide a habitat for whinchats, stonechats, wheatears and nightjars. Throughout the estate, insects are abundant.

· · ·

THE QUANTOCK HILLS

– SOMERSET –

Location
Between Minehead and Bridgwater, touching the Bristol Channel near West Quantoxhead. Map reference 181:ST124397 (Bicknoller Hill), 181:ST158361 (Great and Marrow Hills),

181:ST1640 (Shervage Wood), 182:ST222320 (Fyne Court).

Habitats
Woodland, heathland, grassland, streams.

Nature conservation features
The National Trust owns several properties on this small but fascinating range of hills. Of these, Fyne Court is leased to the Somerset Trust for Nature Conservation, which has created several nature trails, providing a useful introduction to the region's natural history. The open hills have large areas of heather, but in places this has reverted to grassland and bracken. A good variety of birds can be found on the heathland, including the meadow pipit, stonechat, whinchat and nightjar. Red deer, introduced in the 1860s, can be seen on the high ground, together with ponies and sheep.

EAST ANGLIA

· · ·

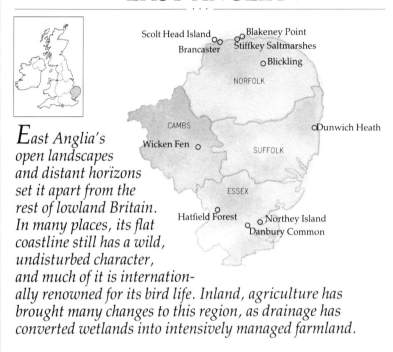

*E*ast Anglia's open landscapes and distant horizons set it apart from the rest of lowland Britain. In many places, its flat coastline still has a wild, undisturbed character, and much of it is internationally renowned for its bird life. Inland, agriculture has brought many changes to this region, as drainage has converted wetlands into intensively managed farmland.

WICKEN FEN *The massed flowers of reeds form a brown band on the horizon.*

WICKEN FEN

– CAMBRIDGESHIRE –

Location
South of the A1123. 3 miles west of Soham via the A142.
Map reference 154:TL5570.

Habitats
Fen, pools, woodland, scrub, grassland.

Nature conservation features
The flat, mysterious landscape of Wicken Fen is a reminder of what much of Cambridgeshire would have looked like before drainage became widespread. Wicken Fen is the National Trust's oldest nature reserve, and it contains a great variety of habitats for wildlife. Many kinds of plant line the water's edge, while the water itself teems with life, from microscopic plants to water voles and fish. A large artificial mere, created to attract waterbirds, is the winter home of large numbers of mallard and wigeon. Teal, pochard and tufted duck can all be seen here, and in spring great crested grebes use it as an arena for their elaborate courtship displays. The mere is fringed with reeds, providing nesting sites for reed warblers and an autumn roost for large numbers of swallows and sand martins. Bearded tits can sometimes be seen here, especially in winter. In parts of the reserve, the vegetation is cut down every four years, keeping trees and shrubs at bay. Where the fen has been left unmown, woody plants have taken over. Buckthorn, alder buckthorn and guelder rose thrive in the damp ground, but eventually these shrubs are ousted by trees – mainly birch, oak and alder. The scrub and woodland is the haunt of owls, woodcock and sparrowhawks.

DANBURY COMMON

– ESSEX –

Location
5 miles east of Chelmsford on the A414, to the south side of the road.
Map reference 167:TL7805.

Habitats
Grassland, heath, scrub, marsh, ponds.

Nature conservation features
It is easy to get lost in this complex mixture of habitats that has developed on hill-top gravel. In the past hundred years, much of the original heath has been invaded by scrub, birch and oak, and some areas have become covered with dense stands of gorse, broom and wild roses. However, heather does survive in a few areas, together with common milkwort and tormentil, and is spreading as the scrub is gradually cleared to recreate the heathland of days gone by. The common is rich in moths and birds. A small area of hornbeam is still regularly coppiced.

· · ·

HATFIELD FOREST

– ESSEX –

Location
3 miles east of Bishop's Stortford. Access from a side-road leading south from the A120 at Takeley Street.

Seed case of
SWEET CHESTNUT

DANBURY COMMON Mature silver birches among grass and bracken.

Map reference 166:TL540200.

Habitats
Woodland, parkland, grassland, scrub, marsh.

Nature conservation features
This large area of woodland and grassland is one of the most important relics of medieval forest in Britain. Its long history of exploitation, for timber, for coppice and pollard wood and for grazing, has created a wide variety of habitats. In the coppiced areas, the main trees are oak, hornbeam, ash, field maple and hazel. Altogether there are 36 native species of tree and shrub and 17 that have been introduced. Dyer's mercury is the most common plant of the woodland floor. The grassy rides have a wide range of plants that need damp conditions, including water figwort and common flea-bane. The impressive pollard trees in the open grassy areas are home to many insects and other animals. Nightingales, hawfinches, tree pipits and woodcock are among the birds of the coppiced areas. Great-crested and little grebes can be seen on the lake.

· · ·

NORTHEY ISLAND

– ESSEX –

Location
In the Blackwater Estuary, 1 mile east of Maldon, and reached by a causeway at low tide. Permits to visit the island must be obtained at least 24 hours in advance from the Warden, Northey Cottage, Northey Island, Maldon, Essex. Map reference 168:TL872058.

Habitats
Grassland, saltmarsh, mudflats.

Nature conservation features
Northey Island's main attraction is its bird life. Between October and March, up to 2,000 dark-bellied Brent geese can be seen feeding in the fields or on the saltmarshes. Other birds that regularly visit the island in winter include the short-eared owl and also many ducks and waders. In addition to its birds, Northey Island is renowned for its saltmarsh plants. Sea plantain, sea purslane, sea-lavender and common scurvy-grass all grow here. The dykes and sea walls are also rich in plants, while insects and other invertebrates live in the banks.

· · ·

BLAKENEY POINT

– NORFOLK –

Location
On the north Norfolk coast between Wells and Sheringham. Access by boat from Blakeney or Morston, both on the A149. Map reference 133:TG0046.

BLAKENEY POINT *A haven for birds on the Norfolk coast.*

Habitats
Shingle, sand dunes, saltmarsh, mudflats.

Nature conservation features
Blakeney Point is one of Britain's most important breeding sites for terns. In May and June, thousands of Sandwich, common and little terns throng the shingle spit, laying their camouflaged eggs directly on the pebbles. Large numbers of oystercatchers, ringed plovers and redshank also breed here. In winter, the mudflats provide food for Brent geese, which fly in from Russia and Greenland, arriving from October onwards. The point is often a landfall for migrating birds, and one of the attractions of visiting Blakeney is that so many species can be seen on passage. The sea itself is also worth watching, especially in autumn when seabirds move south, hugging the coast.

· · ·

BLICKLING ESTATE

– NORFOLK –

Location
1½ miles northwest of Aylsham on the A140. 15 miles north of Norwich, 10 miles south of Cromer astride the B1354. Map reference 133:TG1728.

Habitats
Meadows, heaths, hedgerows, woodlands, park, lakes, riverbank.

Nature conservation features
Having escaped many of the "improvements" of modern farming, Blickling's riverside meadows are a delight for all who appreciate wild flowers. In areas of open shallow water, the water whorl grass can be found –

a common plant in Norfolk, but rarely seen elsewhere. Tway-blade, climbing corydalis and lily-of-the-valley are among the less usual plants growing in the woodlands. The presence of the woods attracts breeding birds such as the hawfinch, redstart and lesser spotted woodpecker. Barn owls, wood warblers and nightjars also live on the estate. The lake is the home of the tufted duck, the great crested grebe and Egyptian and Canada geese, while the River Bure provides a habitat for kingfishers and water voles. Blickling is also a good place to see rabbits and hares.

· · ·

BRANCASTER

– NORFOLK –

Location
On the north coast of Norfolk between Wells and Hunstanton, close to the A149. Map reference 132:TF800450.

Habitats
Foreshore, sand dunes, saltmarsh, mudflats, reed-beds.

Nature conservation features
This sweep of coastline, over 7km (4½ miles) long, is made up of a rich variety of habitats that is particularly attractive to birds. Large numbers of reed warblers and sedge warblers nest in the reed-beds in summer, while the sand and mudflats are covered with algae, which provide winter food for flocks of Brent geese. The dunes are held in place by marram grass. Cord-grass grows in the lower saltmarsh, and above this are sea arrow-grass, sea-lavender and sea aster, the last two of which create a carpet of colour in late summer.

BRANCASTER The beach at low tide, backed by dunes with marram grass.

SCOLT HEAD ISLAND

– NORFOLK –

Location
Just off the north Norfolk coast, opposite Brancaster Staithe, on the A149, from where boats leave for the island.
Map reference 132:TF8146.

Habitats
Shingle ridge, sand dunes, saltmarsh.

Nature conservation features
This internationally important site for breeding seabirds is managed by the Nature Conservancy Council as a National Nature Reserve. Common, Sandwich and little terns breed on the shingle and dunes, and the rare natterjack toad also lives here. In winter, large numbers of wildfowl and waders feed on the saltmarsh and mudflats. Scolt Head Island is also an exceptionally good place to see the plant life of dunes and saltmarshes.

· · ·

STIFFKEY SALTMARSHES

– NORFOLK –

Location
On the north coast of Norfolk between Wells and Blakeney. Access from the A149 at Stiffkey village.
Map reference 133:TG956439 to 991444.

Habitats
Shingle, saltmarsh.

Nature conservation features
Stiffkey saltmarshes abound with plants typical of this demanding habitat, especially sea-lavender and sea aster, and a visit in late summer sees these in bloom. In spring and early summer, the shingle bank at the outer edge of the saltmarsh is an important breeding area for terns and shelduck. The saltmarsh is also worth visiting in winter, because at this time it is a feeding ground for large numbers of Brent geese, wigeon, teal and other wildfowl.

· · ·

DUNWICH HEATH

– SUFFOLK –

Location
On the coast between Aldeburgh and Southwold, east of Yoxford. Access via the B1126, leaving it at Westleton.
Map reference 156:TM475683.

Habitats
Heathland, cliffs, shingle beach.

Nature conservation features
Dunwich Heath is a superb example of the heathland that was formerly so extensive on the sandy soil of this part of Suffolk. Near the sea, the heath is covered by wind-pruned bell heather, and clumps of gorse provide perches for stonechats, whinchats and warblers. Further inland, the heath has been overtaken by bracken, birch and pine, giving enough shelter to conceal roe deer. Nightjars nest in the clearings, and can be seen on the wing at dusk in summer. The slumping cliffs are a good demonstration of the erosive power of the sea. The cliff-face is pockmarked with the nesting burrows of sand martins, which swoop through the air in pursuit of insects. Beneath them, the small pebbly beach harbours the yellow horned poppy, grayling butterflies, lesser marsh grasshoppers and glow-worms.

CENTRAL ENGLAND

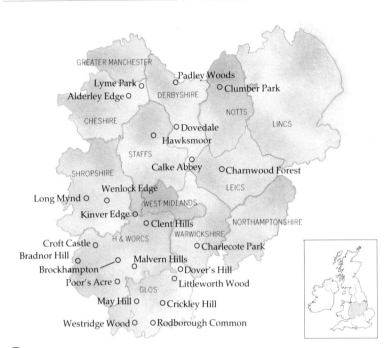

Central England is a region of fascinating natural contrasts. In the north, the high tops of the Peak District bring an upland flavour to the area, while to the south and east, the countryside is made up of open farmland, broad river plains or water-worn limestone hills. Moorland, deep gorges, ancient woodlands, fields and hedgerows all contribute to a mosaic of habitats for the region's plants and animals.

ALDERLEY EDGE

– CHESHIRE –

Location
Astride the B5087 Alderley Edge to Macclesfield road.
Map reference 118:SJ860776.

Habitats
Woodland.

Nature conservation features
This wooded escarpment is of both geological and biological interest. The area is rich in minerals, and copper was mined here for hundreds of years. This has left behind many old shafts and quarries. Much of the woodland was planted, but some sections are on ancient woodland sites. Oak, birch, beech and Scots pine make up a varied patchwork of trees that provides homes for many kinds of birds, including the redstart.

LYME PARK

– CHESHIRE –

Location
On the western edge of the Pennines and just within the Peak District National Park. Off the A6 at Disley, 6½ miles southeast of Stockport.
Map reference 109:SJ965825.

Habitats
Parkland, grassland.

Nature conservation features
Once a medieval deer park, the magnificent Lyme Park surrounds a large historic house. Deer are still very much in evidence today, with both red deer and fallow deer living within the park's perimeter. A visit in September will coincide with the red deer rut, a spectacular and noisy period when rival stags battle for supremacy. Much of the park, which rises to 300m (1,000 feet), is covered by grass growing over an acid soil. Fine-leaved grasses – mainly consisting of fescues and bents – dominate the lower levels, but on the upper slopes, purple moor-grass takes over. The meadow pipit and skylark are common birds, while snipe search for food in the damp ground and wheatears may be seen on the higher ground.

LYME PARK *A herd of red deer grazing in tree-studded grass.*

CALKE ABBEY

– DERBYSHIRE –

Location
9 miles south of Derby, on the A514 at Ticknall.
Map reference 120:SK368227.

Habitats
Woodland, parkland, fields, hedges, grassland.

Nature conservation features
Calke Abbey is hidden in rolling parkland of great interest for its natural history. Especially important for the park's wildlife are the many large, ancient oaks growing amid bracken and grassland. The dead wood of these trees provides a home for woodboring beetles found at very few locations in Britain. These stately trees are also an ideal habitat for green and great spotted woodpeckers, the spotted flycatcher, nuthatch and treecreeper. The acid grassland contains plants such as the heath bedstraw, sheep's sorrel, harebell and tormentil, as well as grasshoppers and the meadow brown, common blue and small heath butterflies. In winter, large numbers of waterfowl congregate on the park's ponds.

. . .

DOVEDALE

– DERBYSHIRE and STAFFORDSHIRE –

Location
4–7 miles northwest of Ashbourne, west of the A515.
Map reference 119:SK1453.

Habitats
Crags, woodland, limestone grassland, river.

Nature conservation features
Over millions of years, the waters of the River Dove have carved their way through a massive limestone plateau to create the deep and beautiful valley of Dovedale. The imposing crags that line the valley have the thinnest of soils and a special plant life, while the gentler slopes rising from the river are mostly covered in flower-rich grassland or woods. Dovedale's south-facing grassland slopes are a fascinating habitat, because they contain plants that are characteristic of northern or southern England, here growing side by side. These include the stemless thistle, Nottingham catchfly, dropwort, greater burnet saxifrage and northern bedstraw. Glow-worms and the northern brown argus butterfly also live on these slopes. The river teems with small animals, and these provide food for the grey wagtail and the dipper, both of which can be seen from the river's edge.

PADLEY WOODS

– DERBYSHIRE –

Location
8 miles west of Sheffield, just off the A625.
Map reference 110 and 119: SK2480.

Habitats
Woodland.

Nature conservation features
Padley Woods are an important relic of a type of woodland that was once much more widespread in this area. They are made up principally of sessile oaks, many of which have been coppiced, together with birch, rowan, alder, ash and introduced trees such as beech. Wavy hair-grass, wood sorrel, bilberry, mosses and ferns can be seen here, as can the rare climbing corydalis. Lichens thrive on the scattered rocks and boulders.

DOVEDALE Mixed woodland clings to the steep sides of a valley.

Nearly 50 species of bird breed in the wood. They include the pied flycatcher, three species of woodpecker, the hawfinch, redstart and tawny owl.

. . .

CRICKLEY HILL

– GLOUCESTERSHIRE –

Location
On the northern edge of the Cotswolds, overlooking Gloucester which lies 6 miles to the west. Entrances from the A417 and B4070.
Map reference 163:SO930165.

Habitats
Limestone grassland, woodland.

Nature conservation features
This impressive site, with its abundant flowers and insects, gives sweeping views over the Severn Valley. Its northwest-slopes are covered in limestone grassland, which contains a range of different grasses and also plants such as devilsbit scabious, salad burnet, birdsfoot trefoil and squinancywort. The damper areas are clothed by mosses and liverworts. A hill-fort stands on the western end of the limestone promontory, and wild thyme, clustered bellflower and autumn gentian can be seen in the drier grasslands around it.

. . .

DOVER'S HILL

– GLOUCESTERSHIRE –

Location
On the right of the B4035, between Chipping Campden and Weston-sub-Edge.
Map reference 151:SP137397.

Habitats
Woodland, grassland, ponds.

Nature conservation features
Dover's Hill lies on the edge of the Cotswold escarpment where the limestone hills drop steeply towards the Vale of Evesham. The grassland contains a local speciality – meadow saxifrage – and large numbers of snails live in some areas. The scrub is made up mostly of hawthorn, ash and sallow, and its tangled cover provides an excellent habitat for nesting birds, such as the whitethroat, garden warbler and turtle dove. The tawny owl, great spotted woodpecker and blackcap nest in the woodland. The large old pollards of ash, oak and field maple are home to many insects.

. . .

LITTLEWORTH WOOD

– GLOUCESTERSHIRE –

Location
3 miles southwest of Broadway, 4 miles west of the junction of the A44 and A424 and $^3/_4$ mile west of Snowshill village. Access by narrow lane.
Map reference 150:SP086338.

Habitats
Woodland, scrub.

Nature conservation features
With its stands of field maple, oak and hazel, the ancient semi-natural Littleworth Wood is partly managed as a coppice. Beneath the trees a dense shrub layer consists of hazel, spindle, wayfaring tree, whitebeam and hawthorn. These diverse trees and shrubs harbour a great range of insects, attracting birds such as the blackcap, goldcrest and green woodpecker. Deer and badgers also live in the wood. Littleworth contains a number of unusual plants, such as herb Paris, meadow saffron, four species of orchid and the adder's tongue and hard shield ferns.

. . .

MAY HILL

– GLOUCESTERSHIRE –

Location
About halfway between Gloucester and Ross-on-Wye, to the north of the A40.
Map reference 162:SO695215.

Habitats
Grassland, heath, ponds.

Nature conservation features
The steep climb to the top of this isolated hill, 275m (900 feet) high, is rewarded with spectacular views. The hill's vegetation consists mainly of acid grassland. Spreading gorse and bracken is now being controlled by cutting. The hill's butterflies include the small copper and green-veined white, and the ponds and marshy ground are the haunt of pondskaters, damselflies and newts. The plant life of these wet areas includes marsh pennywort, bog stitchwort, round-leaved crowfoot and bog pimpernel. The whinchat is a regular summer visitor, nesting among tussocks of grass. The adjacent and recently acquired May Hill Common is still largely covered by bracken.

GORSE *flowers*

RODBOROUGH COMMON Flower-studded grassland on the limestone plateau of the Cotswolds.

RODBOROUGH & MINCHINHAMPTON COMMONS

– GLOUCESTERSHIRE –

Location
In the Cotswolds between Stroud and Nailsworth, east of the A46 and southwest of the A419.
Map reference 162:SO850038 and 850010.

Habitats
Limestone grassland, scrub.

Nature conservation features
This very extensive area of limestone grassland lies on the plateau of the Cotswolds and the steep escarpment which forms the hills' abrupt western flank.

The commons, which are edged with scrub and furrowed by ancient earthworks, are still grazed by cattle owned by local people exercising their rights as "commoners". Abundant wild flowers, including 11 species of orchid, help to create a carpet of colour in spring and summer. The butterflies include the chalk-hill and small blues, marsh and dark green fritillaries.

. . .

WESTRIDGE WOOD

– GLOUCESTERSHIRE –

Location
On the western edge of the Cotswolds, 1 mile northwest of Wotton-under-Edge.
Map reference 162:ST753945.

Habitats
Woodland.

Nature conservation features
This small wood is characteristic of the many beautiful woods and copses that cling to the steep Cotswold escarpment. Beech is the most abundant tree, but ash, oak, whitebeam and field maple also grow well on the limestone slopes. Holly, spindle and wayfaring tree form a broken shrub layer. Springtime sees the woods carpeted in bluebells and dog's mercury, while patches of wood anemone, sweet woodruff and yellow archangel add further colour. The rare angular Solomon's seal also grows on the woodland floor. The animal life of the wood includes the striking scarlet tiger moth, many birds and the diminutive dormouse.

. . .

BRADNOR HILL

– HEREFORD & WORCESTER –

Location
To the north of and overlooking Kington. Access by side-road, leading to the golf club from the B4355.
Map reference 148:SO282584.

Habitats
Grassland, heath, scrub.

Nature conservation features
This broad, rounded hill, part of which is managed as a golf course, has extensive views over the Welsh mountains to the west and the Wye valley to the east. Its grasslands and grassy heaths contain birdsfoot trefoil, the uncommon upright chickweed as well as many mosses and lichens. Hares live on these stretches of open ground, and meadow pipits, whinchats and wheatears can also be seen here.

Yellowhammers, green wood-peckers, tree pipits and the tawny owl need more cover, and the hill's wooded northern slopes provide these birds with a suitable habitat.

BROCKHAMPTON

– HEREFORD & WORCESTER –

Location
About 1¹/₂ miles east of Brom-yard, north of the A44.
Map reference 149:SO682546.

Habitats
Woodland, ponds, streams.

Nature conservation features
Several nature walks have been laid out through this scenic coun-try estate. The original woods are mainly of old oaks, but in the past redwoods and cedar of Lebanon were planted for orna-ment. More recently, beech has been planted to provide hard-wood in the future. The wood-land plants include dog's mercury, yellow archangel and enchanter's nightshade. The younger plantations of larch and beech attract willow warblers and chiffchaffs, while tits, wood-peckers and redstarts prefer the older woodland.

. . .

CLENT HILLS

– HEREFORD & WORCESTER –

Location
About 2 miles east of West Hagley and just south of the A456, reached by side-roads with a main entrance near the village of Clent.
Map reference 139:SO9397.

BROCKHAMPTON *A mass of grasses, sedges and purple loosestrife lines the water's edge in front of the old manor house.*

Habitats
Woodland, grassland, heath, pond, streams.

Nature conservation features
The Clent Hills, which are man-aged as a country park, form a popular and heavily visited open space just a few miles from the centre of Birmingham. Most people visit the hill-slopes above the village of Clent, but Walton Hill to the southeast also falls within the park's boundary. The area's varied habitats, including patches of oakwood, hawthorn scrub and grassland, guarantee a wide variety of plants and animals. The scarce bird cherry grows in the broadleaved woodland, where many of the park's birds are also to be found. These include redstarts, wood

warblers, little and tawny owls as well as sparrowhawks. In more open areas, bilberry and western gorse grow in the remnants of shrubby heath. Over 20 species of butterfly have been recorded within the area.

. . .

CROFT CASTLE

– HEREFORD & WORCESTER –

Location
6 miles northwest of Leominster, via the B4361 from Leominster or the B4362 from the main A49 Ludlow to Leominster road.
Map reference 137:SO455655.

Habitats
Woodland, parkland, grassland, ponds, streams.

Nature conservation features
The extensive and many-faceted Croft Castle estate lies on the gently rising slopes of a limestone ridge. Its parkland is notable for massive and ancient oaks, many of which have been pollarded, and for the abundant insect life that they harbour. The scarce Natterer's bat lives in old buildings, while the woodland is the home of fallow deer and muntjac. Buzzards can often be seen soaring over the trees, and the pied flycatcher and lesser spotted woodpecker live among the woods. So, too, does the now scarce hawfinch, which feeds on the seeds of the hornbeam. Butterflies, which include the silver-washed fritillary, are an important part of the estate's wildlife.

· · ·

MALVERN HILLS: MIDSUMMER HILL & TACK COPPICE

– HEREFORD & WORCESTER –

Location
Mainly north of the A438 about 4 miles east of Ledbury.
Map reference 150:SO759375 and 762368.

Habitats
Woodland, scrub, grassland, marsh.

Nature conservation features
These two adjacent hill-tops near the southern end of the Malverns lie almost wholly within the ramparts of an Iron Age hill-fort, which crowns the steep slopes of the main ridge. In Tack Coppice, to the south of the main road, an open ash wood, its floor covered by the moss-clad remains of dead trees, covers the eastern part of

the slope. Higher up, scrub gives way to grass which is studded with hills made by yellow meadow ants. The grassland is one of the dwindling number of localities where glow-worms can still be seen. The boldly marked pied flycatcher, another rarity, lives in the woodlands.

· · ·

POOR'S ACRE

– HEREFORD & WORCESTER –

Location
Bordering the roadside between Mordiford and Woolhope, about 6 miles southeast of Hereford.
Map reference 162:SO590365

Habitats
Woodland.

Nature conservation features
Although of small size, Poor's Acre lies next to a much larger area of ancient woodland, giving its plants and animals a special quality. The wild service tree occurs in unusual abundance, and spurge laurel, a plant usually confined to old woodlands, also grows here. The wood's wildlife is notable for its wealth of moths and butterflies, with over 650 species having been recorded in the locality. The pearl-bordered fritillary, wood white, white admiral and white-letter hairstreak all occur in the area.

SMALL SKIPPER
on tufted vetch

CHARNWOOD FOREST: ULVERSCROFT

– LEICESTERSHIRE –

Location
6 miles southwest of Loughborough, between the B5350, B591 and B587.
Map reference 129:SK490126.

Habitats
Woodland, heath, grassland.

Nature conservation features
Ulverscroft lies on a ridge of high ground, rising to 240m (800 feet), with outcrops of syenite, an ancient volcanic rock. The oak woodland with its scattered beech trees is part of the ancient Charnwood Forest, and the old trees attract many woodland birds, including all three British woodpeckers, the nuthatch, redstart, treecreeper, tits and warblers. Small areas of heathland, now almost entirely covered by bracken, still contain some remnant patches of bilberry, a legacy of earlier days when the ground was more open.

· · ·

CLUMBER PARK

– NOTTINGHAMSHIRE –

Location
4$^1/_2$ miles southeast of Worksop, 1 mile east of the A1. Entrances from the A57, A614 and B6005. Map reference 120:SK645774 to 626746.

Habitats
Parkland, woodland, grassland, lakes, river.

Nature conservation features
This great park on the edge of Sherwood Forest is large enough, at 1,500ha (3,800 acres),

to absorb over a million visitors a year and yet still be a fascinating place for the naturalist. The extensive woodlands, together with the heathland and grassland, are remnants from a time when vegetation like this covered much of the area. Like many parks, Clumber is a haven for those insects that live in the wood of ancient oak and beech trees. The park's breeding birds include the nightingale, hawfinch, woodcock, lesser spotted woodpecker, redstart and long-eared owl. The large sweeps of acid grassland are dominated by wavy hair grass, and on them small-flowered cranesbill can be found, as well as spring vetch and buckshorn plantain, which is normally a coastal species. The butterflies here include the gatekeeper, small heath and small copper. The heathland, which is covered with heather, bell heather and gorse, provides a breeding area for nightjars, tree pipits, woodlarks and grasshopper warblers. The large lake is a magnet for wildfowl, the most notable being the gadwall, which breeds here.

. . .

LONG MYND

– SHROPSHIRE –

Location
15 miles south of Shrewsbury, west of the Church Stretton valley and the A49. Approached from Church Stretton, Ratlinghope or Asterton.
Map reference 137:SO430940.

Habitats
Moorland, grassland, heath, woodland, streams.

Nature conservation features
The Long Mynd's name comes

from the Welsh for "long mountain". It reaches a height of 530m (1,700 feet) and, on a clear day, gives breathtaking views as far as the Black Mountains to the southwest and Cheshire to the north. The animal and plant life around its sharp ridge is noticeably different to that of the gentle farmland below. Ravens, buzzards and curlews haunt the heather-clad upland plateau, while moorland birds such as the wheatear, stonechat, ring ouzel and red grouse are plentiful. Woodland birds include the tree pipit and pied flycatcher, while the dipper and grey wagtail patrol the streams for insects. On the high slopes, springs encour-

age moisture-loving plants such as butterwort and round-leaved sundew, bog pimpernel and *Sphagnum* moss. The common spotted orchid grows on the moorland, and heath bedstraw on the grassy slopes.

. . .

WENLOCK EDGE

– SHROPSHIRE –

Location
Between Ironbridge Gorge and Craven Arms, running northeast from the A49. Access via the B4371, which traverses the ridge. Map reference 138:SO595988

LONG MYND *Broken rock, grass and heather on the summit ridge.*

(Blakeway Coppice), 138: SO570965 (Easthope Wood), 127:SJ605002 (Harley Bank).

Habitats
Woodland, limestone crags and grassland, scrub, marsh.

Nature conservation features
This famous limestone escarpment provides superb views over the Shropshire plain. The National Trust's holdings on Wenlock Edge are mostly wooded areas. The trees include a mixture of conifers and broadleaved species, with beech, oak, ash, hazel coppice, wild cherry and birch. Holly, rowan, spindle and guelder rose grow beneath them, and in spring bluebells and violets bloom in the clearings. Woodcock, woodpeckers, tits and warblers feed in the woods and copses, while sparrow hawks, kestrels, tawny and little owls hunt in the woods or over open ground.

· · ·

HAWKSMOOR

– STAFFORDSHIRE –

Location
1½ miles northeast of Cheadle, on the north side of the B5417. Map reference SK035445.

Habitats
Woodland, pasture, farmland, river.

Nature conservation features
Hawksmoor is a haven for wildlife just a short distance from the busy Potteries. Over 60 species of bird are known to breed in its woods and open ground, and its mammals include the fox, stoat, weasel, hare and badger. The broadleaved woods are made up of sessile oaks, American red oaks,

field maple, beech, sycamore and glades of birch. The woodland birds include large numbers of warblers, and the older trees are ideal for woodpeckers and the treecreeper, nuthatch and redstart. Conifers have been planted in some places, and here the tiny goldcrest and coal tit hunt for insects. Skylarks, curlews and lapwings all feed on the open pasture, and the river birds include the kingfisher, dipper, common sandpiper and yellow wagtail. Four trails lead through Hawksmoor, making delightful walking especially in spring, when the woodland floor is covered in bluebells, moschatel, wild garlic and wood anemones.

· · ·

KINVER EDGE

– STAFFORDSHIRE –

Location
4 miles west of Stourbridge, 4 miles north of Kidderminster, 1½ miles west of the A449. Map reference: 138:SO835830.

Habitats
Woodland, heathland, sand, scrub.

Nature conservation features
This wooded escarpment and heath near Stourbridge is a surviving remnant of the vast forest that once clothed this area. The woodlands that remain today are of oak, which was at one time coppiced for charcoal, and birch. The oak trees provide food for a great many different insect species, which in turn make up the food of treecreepers, tits and warblers. Adders, slow-worms and lizards like the sandy soil of the escarpment, and can often be seen on hot, dry days basking in the sun.

CHARLECOTE PARK

– WARWICKSHIRE –

Location
5 miles east of Stratford-upon-Avon, 1 mile west of Wellesbourne on the west side of the B4088.
Map reference 151:SP263564.

Habitats
Parkland, pasture, riverbanks.

Nature conservation features
A walk through Charlecote's historic deer park gives access to a lake and the banks of the River Avon, and leads past ancient trees that provide homes for birds, insects and bats. Black poplars, uncommon in Britain, grow beside the church, and pollarded willows are scattered in the meadows. Treecreepers, woodpeckers and nuthatches nest in holes in the older trees, and in summer, the purple hairstreak butterfly can be seen on the wing. During the winter, regular flooding of the adjoining pastures attracts wildfowl.

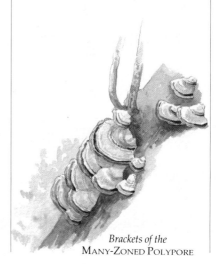

Brackets of the MANY-ZONED POLYPORE

NORTHEAST

T he northeast contains some of the most beautiful coastline to be seen in England, and its dunes, estuaries, saltmarshes and rocky islands attract seabirds by the thousand. Further inland, the high ground of the Pennines and the North York Moors dominates the landscape, providing a habitat for upland plants and animals, and spectacular walking throughout the year.

Map labels:
Farne Islands
Newton Links
Dunstanburgh Castle
Alnmouth
Cragside
NORTHUMBERLAND
Allen Banks
The Leas
TYNE AND WEAR
Moor House Woods
DURHAM
CLEVELAND
Roseberry Topping
Ravenscar
Bridestones Moor
Hayburn Wyke
N. YORKS
Malham Tarn
Fountains Abbey
Brimham Moor
HUMBERSIDE
Hardcastle Crags
W. YORKS
S. YORKS
Derwent Estate

ROSEBERRY TOPPING

– CLEVELAND –

Location
8 miles southeast of Middlesbrough, 2 miles east of Great Ayton, which lies on the A173. Map reference 93:NZ575126.

Habitats
Moorland, woodland.

Nature conservation features
The steep climb to the low but dramatic summit of Roseberry Topping, at an altitude of 322 m (1,057 feet), leads through three contrasting kinds of landscape – woodland, heather moor and bracken-covered ground. Newton Wood is dominated by oaks, but also contains ash trees, wych elms, alders and large-leaved limes. The wood is especially important to wildlife as a haven for breeding birds such as the pied flycatcher, wood warbler, tree pipit, redstart and green woodpecker. The heather on Newton Moor is regularly burned to provide the right conditions for red grouse. The areas dominated by bracken contain patches of acid grassland and a scattering of trees and low shrubs.

MOOR HOUSE WOODS

– CO. DURHAM –

Location
3 miles northeast of Durham. Map reference 88:NZ305460.

Habitats
Woodland.

Nature conservation features
Moor House Woods lie in the valley of the River Wear. The woods are unusual because they contain beech and hornbeam – two trees that are generally found wild only in southern Britain. In these woods, many specimens of these two species have been coppiced. Oak is the most common tree, but small-leaved lime also grows here in some numbers. Bluebells, wood millet, wood sorrel, sanicle and wood avens grow on the woodland floor, alongside a mixture of shrubs.

ROSEBERRY TOPPING Dead bracken fronds catch the autumn sun.

ALLEN BANKS

– NORTHUMBERLAND –

Location
Near the junction of the River Allen and the South Tyne, 3 miles west of Haydon Bridge. About ¹/₂ mile south of the A69. Map reference 86 and 87: NY799630.

Habitats
Woodland.

Nature conservation features
The steep and sheltered slopes above the River Allen create a favoured environment in the otherwise exposed Northumbrian landscape. Verdant woods of beech, oak, chestnut, sycamore and ash – some species native, others introduced – cling to the sides of the valley, providing food and cover for roe deer and red squirrels. Dippers and grey wagtails live along the river, while the woods above are one of the most northerly places in Britain where the nuthatch can be seen. The small areas of grassland are the home of the devilsbit scabious and lousewort, a semi-parasitic plant that has bright pink flowers.

· · ·

ALNMOUTH

– NORTHUMBERLAND –

Location
On the coast immediately to the south of Alnmouth. Access from the A1068.
Map reference 75:NU241094.

Habitats
Sand dunes, grassland, saltmarsh.

Nature conservation features
Alnmouth's sand dunes and saltmarshes are worth visiting both for their wild flowers and their birds. The dune plants include marram grass and lyme grass, and also the colourful bloody cranesbill, the purple milk vetch and lesser meadow rue. Where grassland has formed over the sand, it is rich in low-growing plants such as birdsfoot trefoil and eyebright. Two kinds of stonecrop – the biting stonecrop or wall pepper and the white stonecrop – flourish here on dry ground. The saltmarsh that borders the River Aln is one of the few large areas of this habitat in northeast England. Alnmouth's extensive mudflats attract large numbers of waterfowl and waders.

· · ·

CRAGSIDE

– NORTHUMBERLAND –

Location
1 mile northeast of Rothbury on the north bank of the River Coquet.
Map reference 81:NU073022.

Habitats
Woodland, heath, lakes, streams.

Nature conservation features
This impressively landscaped estate, with its lakes and woodlands, has many features of great interest to the naturalist. The woodlands harbour woodcock, sparrowhawks, wood warblers, siskins and pied flycatchers, and tree pipits nest beneath them on rough ground. The mammals of the woodlands include red squirrels and roe deer. In the nineteenth century, thousands of trees were planted on the estate, and today mature conifers grow in extensive swathes. Patches of heather, bilberry, purple moorgrass and cross-leaved heath mark the remaining areas of the heathland that originally covered much of this area.

· · ·

DUNSTANBURGH CASTLE

– NORTHUMBERLAND –

Location
On the coast between Alnmouth and Beadnell; just east of Embleton via the B1339.
Map reference 75:NU258220.

Habitats
Cliffs, grassland.

Nature conservation features
Crowned by the dramatic ruins of a fourteenth-century castle, the precipitous cliffs at Dunstanburgh are an important breeding site for seabirds. About 700 pairs of kittiwakes nest here, together with fulmars and shags. Eider ducks breed nearby, nearer to

DUNSTANBURGH *The castle seen from Embleton Bay.*

the shoreline. The castle is surrounded by rich grassland, which in spring and summer becomes a colourful carpet of flowers. Purple milk-vetch, field madder, spring squill, wild thyme, bloody cranesbill and several species of clover all contribute to the display.

· · ·

FARNE ISLANDS

– NORTHUMBERLAND –

Location
Off the coast opposite Bamburgh. Access by boat from Seahouses Harbour.
Map reference 75:NU2337.

Habitats
Cliffs, cliff-tops.

Nature conservation features
The Farne Islands make up one of Britain's most important sites for seabirds. About 20 species breed on the islands, some in huge numbers. At the height of the season in May and June, the cliffs are crowded with nearly 6,000 pairs of kittiwakes, 14,000 pairs of guillemots and a scattering of razorbills. Four species of tern breed on the rocky platforms that top many of the islands. They include not only the common, Arctic and Sandwich terns, but also the roseate tern, a much rarer species. Up to 25,000 pairs of puffins nest on the islands, excavating burrows where the cliff-top soil is deep enough. Eider ducks also nest. Most of the breeding birds depart by late summer. However, the fascination of the Farnes' natural history does not come to a close then because, in the autumn, grey seals use the islands as a breeding site, forming one of the largest colonies in Britain.

FARNE ISLANDS *The low, flat-topped rocks provide one of the few offshore breeding sites for seabirds on Britain's east coast.*

NEWTON LINKS & EMBLETON LINKS

– NORTHUMBERLAND –

Location
On the coast between Beadnell and Alnmouth, stretching from 2 miles north of Low Newton-by-the-Sea to 2 miles south.
Map reference 75:NU236417 and 243235 to 243240.

Habitats
Dunes, grassland, freshwater, beach.

Nature conservation features
The glorious beaches on this part of the Northumbrian coast are backed by extensive dunes, rough grazing and freshwater pools. The dunes are of all ages – some new and easily shifted by the wind, others fixed in place by the roots of marram grass, lyme grass and couch grass. Bloody cranesbill, burnet rose, restharrow and harebell grow around the older dunes, while the slacks between them shelter common butterwort and tufted centaury. A hide overlooking Newton Pool provides good views of the local bird life. Ducks, including the shoveler, waders and seabirds can all be seen, and in spring and

autumn, many more species pause briefly on migration. Black-headed gulls, which have a large breeding colony here, are always much in evidence.

· · ·

THE LEAS & MARSDEN ROCK

– TYNE AND WEAR –

Location
East of the A183 South Shields to Sunderland Road.
Map reference 88:NZ388665.

Habitats
Limestone grassland, cliff, foreshore.

Nature conservation features
These crumbling and eroded limestone cliffs support one of the most important breeding colonies of seabirds on the northeast coast of England. Over 4,000 pairs of kittiwakes breed here, and herring gulls and fulmars abound, with some lesser black-backed gulls. Cormorants nest on the top of Marsden Rock. Divers and guillemots can be seen in the coastal waters, and the shore attracts purple sandpipers and turnstones. In winter, migrant birds such as the Lapland and snow buntings make brief visits, as they fly along the coast.

· · ·

BRIDESTONES MOOR

– NORTH YORKSHIRE –

Location
12 miles south of Whitby, 1 mile east of the A169. Access by toll road through Dalby Forest Drive.
Map reference 94:SE8791.

Habitats
Moorland, woodland, bogs, rocky outcrops, grassland.

Nature conservation features
The Bridestones Moor nature reserve extends over some 120ha (300 acres) and contains many animals and plants typical of the North York Moors. The reserve is most famous for its "bridestones", oddly shaped Jurassic sandstone outcrops. It is also home to a variety of plants that can survive on poor, dry acid soil. Birch and rowan are common on the slopes, while the woodlands contain oak, ash and larch. Although the reserve is not rich in bird life, kestrels and sparrowhawks are commonly seen. Lizards can be spotted on warm days basking in the sun, as can adders and – on occasion – slow-worms.

· · ·

BRIMHAM MOOR & ROCKS

– NORTH YORKSHIRE –

Location
8 miles southwest of Ripon, approached via the B6265 Pateley Bridge road.
Map reference 99:SE2165.

Habitats
Rocky outcrops, moorland, woodland, scrub.

Nature conservation features
The fantastic shapes of its weathered sandstone rocks, together with far-reaching views, attract many visitors to Brimham each year. Those willing to walk a short distance from the famous rocks will discover a range of upland plant life and the animals that feed on them. The drier areas of the moor are covered by

heather. The heather is managed for the benefit of red grouse by regular cutting, and it also provides a home for the common heath and yellow underwing moths. The curlew and snipe breed where the ground is damp.

· · ·

FOUNTAINS ABBEY & STUDLEY ROYAL

– NORTH YORKSHIRE –

Location
4 miles west of Ripon, off the B6265 to Pateley Bridge.
Map reference 99:SE2769.

Habitats
Parkland, woodland, grassland, ponds.

Nature conservation features
The Cistercian abbey ruins near Ripon lie within the eighteenth-century landscaped park and ornamental water gardens of Studley Royal. This property has many features of interest, including parkland trees, woodland, grassland, ponds, deer and at least six species of bat.

The many old parkland trees, with their abundant dead wood, are host to over 30 species of beetle that are found only where there is a long and unbroken history of large, old trees. Nuthatches, redstarts, green and great spotted woodpeckers use the old trees for feeding and nesting. The woodlands have a rich bird life, including hawfinches, and in summer they are good places for seeing butterflies such as the white-letter hairstreak and purple hairstreak. In some parts of the ponds waterplants, including brooklime and skullcap, are plentiful. All the British species of newt have been recorded here.

MALHAM TARN *Winter floods inundating the pasture and drystone walls.*

HAYBURN WYKE

– NORTH YORKSHIRE –

Location
6 miles north of Scarborough, via the A165. Access also by the Cleveland Way long-distance footpath.
Map reference 101:TA010970.

Habitats
Scrub woodland, rocks, fore-shore, cliffs.

Nature conservation features
Hayburn Wyke is coastal scenery at its most varied. It includes a small and beautiful bay with a rocky beach surrounded by cliffs, woodlands and the Hayburn Beck, which cascades over a low cliff in a series of little waterfalls to a pool among the seashore boulders. The woods are broad-leaved – mostly oak – with some holly, ash, hazel, hawthorn, rho-dodendron and sycamore. The slopes immediately above the beach provide a habitat for the common spotted orchid, kidney vetch and butterwort. Warblers are plentiful in the scrub, and Hayburn Wyke's birdlife also includes the great spotted wood-pecker, spotted flycatcher, red-start, woodcock and goldcrest.

· · ·

MALHAM TARN

– NORTH YORKSHIRE –

Location
6 miles northeast of Settle in Upper Craven, midway between Ribblesdale and Wharfedale. Map reference 98:SD8966.

Habitats
Moorland, limestone grassland, lake, bog, fen, rocky crags.

Nature conservation features
Malham Tarn, a high lake lying over a bed of limestone, is not only highly scenic but also of international importance for its plant and animal life. Mallard, tufted duck, coot and great crested grebes all breed on the Tarn, and their numbers swell every winter as more birds arrive to feed in the lime-rich waters. The variety of plants that grow in the bog and fen around the Tarn is quite exceptional, and can be appreciated at close hand from boardwalks that cross it. Away from the Tarn, blue moor-grass, which is confined to limestone areas, grows on rocky ledges, and with it green spleenwort, a species of fern. The "unim-proved" grassland is rich in sedges and plants such as wild thyme, mountain pansy and eye-bright. Birdseye primrose is a highlight of wet areas, and cran-berry, cloudberry and bog rose-mary all grow on the raised peat bog. In autumn, kestrels, pere-grines and, occasionally, merlins can be seen hunting over the estate. Roe deer are recent arriv-als in the area.

· · ·

RAVENSCAR

– NORTH YORKSHIRE –

Location
15 miles north of Scarborough. Access by side-roads from the A171.
Map reference 94:NZ980025.

Habitats
Cliffs, grassland, scrub.

Nature conservation features

The cliffs of this beautiful part of the Yorkshire coast are composed mainly of soft rocks that are easily eroded by the sea. At Ravenscar, the cliffs have slumped to create a contorted landscape higher up. This constant movement of the ground makes life difficult for the majority of plants, but it does not deter herring gulls or cormorants, both of which breed here. The steeper slopes, which are often covered with scree, are generally occupied by heather, bell heather, some bilberry and crowberry. The flatter areas are good places to see harebell, yellow rattle, devilsbit scabious and less common plants such as adder's tongue fern and grass of Parnassus. Meadowsweet, wild angelica, butterwort and sundew grow in the wetter areas. Please note that the cliffs are dangerous, and care should be taken when visiting them.

· · ·

DERWENT ESTATE

– SOUTH YORKSHIRE AND DERBYSHIRE –

Location

13 miles west of Sheffield, approached via the A57 Sheffield to Manchester road.
Map reference 110:SK1994 (Ashopton viaduct).

Habitats

Moorland, streams, woodland.

Nature conservation features

With its wide sweep of open moorland stretching without interruption from horizon to horizon, the Derwent Estate is typical of many Trust holdings in the Peak District. High up on the deeper peat, harestail cottongrass is usually the dominant plant. At lower altitudes, heather takes over to form extensive heather moors, while lower down still, purple moor-grass makes up most of the vegetation. Although exposed, this upland landscape has many breeding birds, including the dunlin, golden plover, snipe, curlew and red grouse. In summer, the ring ouzel can be seen on rocky outcrops. Mountain hares also live on the moorland, as do the emperor and fox moths, both of which feed on heather and other plants as caterpillars.

· · ·

HARDCASTLE CRAGS

– WEST YORKSHIRE –

Location

1½ miles northwest of Hebden Bridge, off the A6033. 5 miles northeast of Todmorden.
Map reference 103:SD973302.

Habitats

Woodland, rivers, rocky crags, moorland.

Nature conservation features

The rocky escarpments known as Hardcastle Crags lie in woods on the north bank of Hebden Water. The National Trust owns a total of 175ha (434 acres) of mixed woodland in this area, some of it ancient. There are old millponds in the valley and the bed of the Crimsworth Beck is designated as a Site of Special Scientific Interest for its unusual geology. Sycamore, oak, ash and beech are the most frequent trees in the broadleaved woods, which are carpeted with bluebells in spring. Grey wagtails and dippers are common along the river, and the great spotted woodpecker, spotted flycatcher, heron, ring ouzel and short-eared owl inhabit the woods and riverbanks. Both the grey and red squirrel live here.

RAVENSCAR The shore, looking northeast across the blue pebbles and shingle.

NORTHWEST

· · ·

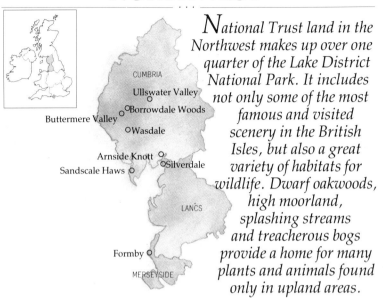

*N*ational Trust land in the Northwest makes up over one quarter of the Lake District National Park. It includes not only some of the most famous and visited scenery in the British Isles, but also a great variety of habitats for wildlife. Dwarf oakwoods, high moorland, splashing streams and treacherous bogs provide a home for many plants and animals found only in upland areas.

ARNSIDE KNOTT & HEATHWAITE

– CUMBRIA –

Location
Overlooking the Kent estuary, about 4 miles west of Milnthorpe on the A6.
Map reference 97:SD456774.

Habitats
Woodland, scrub, grassland, heath, rock.

Nature conservation features
Arnside Knott is a wooded limestone promontory rising above the estuary of the River Kent and Morecambe Bay. The hill gives spectacular views over the bay, the Lakeland fells and the Forest of Bowland. An unusual feature is the fine scree on the south-facing slopes, known locally as the Shilla slopes. The Arnside

area is best known for its wide range of butterflies, which includes large numbers of fritil-laries and the northern brown argus. Glow-worms also live here. Roe deer and red squirrels are numerous, and the varied habitats attract many different birds, some to breed, others to pass the winter. The plant life is particularly rich – at least six species of orchid grow here, along with several species of fern.

· · ·

BORROWDALE WOODS

– CUMBRIA –

Location
3 miles due south of Keswick, extending from the south shore of Keswick Water to Honister

Pass. Access by the B5289.
Map reference 89:NY258147 (head of valley).

Habitats
Woodland.

Nature conservation features
The 29 woods owned by the National Trust in Borrowdale account for over three-quarters of the woodland in this beautiful valley, which has more tree cover than almost any other in the Lake District. The predominant tree is the sessile oak, but ash and birch also find a place, along with cherry, rowan and alder. The composition of each wood is shaped by features such as the position, soil depth and rainfall. As a result woods just a short distance apart can be quite different. All, however, are notable for their abundant growth of lichens, mosses and liverworts, which thrive in the damp air, covering trunks, branches and boulders alike. Red squirrels live in some of the woods. Pied fly-catchers, redstarts, wood warblers, tree pipits and nuthatches feed on insects within them, while the woodcock probes the damp soil for its food.

BUTTERMERE VALLEY *The view towards Honister Pass.*

ULLSWATER VALLEY *Aira Force falls, seen through autumnal woodland.*

SANDSCALE HAWS

– CUMBRIA –

Location
3 miles north of Barrow-in-Furness.
Map reference 96:SA190750.

Habitats
Sand dunes, grassland.

Nature conservation features
Sandscale Haws' large dunes, which give good views northwards into the Lake District and westwards into the Irish Sea, are noted for their plants and insects. The tall, chalk-rich dunes have an extensive covering of marram grass. The dune slacks, some of which flood in winter, have a rich plant life, including perhaps ten species of orchid and rarities such as the yellow vetch. Bloody cranesbill and sea kale also grow here. The area's insects include the uncommon coastal dart and shore wainscot moths, and a number of mining bees and wasps. The slacks between the dunes are also one of the few breeding sites of the natterjack toad.

. . .

BUTTERMERE VALLEY

– CUMBRIA –

Location
9 miles south of Cockermouth. Approached by the B5289 from Cockermouth or Keswick. Map reference 89:NY1815.

Habitats
Woodland, scrub, grassland, rock, freshwater.

Nature conservation features
Framed by the peaks of Grasmoor, High Stile and Buttermere Fell, the Buttermere Valley is an area of classic lakeland landscape. The main valley contains two lakes – Crummock Water and Buttermere itself – and at Ghyll Wood, Long How Wood and Nether How Wood, it has remnants of the sessile oakwood that once covered many hillsides. A broad band of mixed woodland lies at nearby Loweswater, and this contains fine specimens of beech, oak, lime and sweet chestnut. With such a diversity of habitats, the valley's bird life is varied. Mergansers, great crested grebes, coots, mallard and goldeneye live on the lakes, while common sandpipers nest on the shoreline. The birds of the woods and open ground include the pied flycatcher, barn owl, tawny owl, sparrowhawk, goldcrest and peregrine. Buzzards soar overhead, announcing their presence with a distinctive mewing cry.

ULLSWATER VALLEY: GLENCOYNE WOOD & GOWBARROW PARK

– CUMBRIA –

Location
Southwest of Penrith on the A592, which runs along the north shore of the lake.
Map reference 90:NY3819 and

90:NY4020 (Glencoyne Wood, Gowbarrow Park).

Habitats
Lake, woodland.

Nature conservation features
Seen against the backdrop of towering peaks, trees contribute greatly to Lakeland scenery. The trees around Ullswater include many that were planted in the eighteenth and nineteenth centuries for their visual appeal – copper beeches, Wellingtonias, oaks and a number of other species from all over the world. Now fully mature, they offer cover for birds and shelter for red deer. Glencoyne Wood, at the south end of the lake, contains many fine old oak trees. In spring, the ground is carpeted with daffodils, while autumn brings with it a large crop of many different kinds of fungi. Nearby in Gowbarrow Park, the spray generated by Aira Force, one of the most powerful waterfalls in the Lake District, bathes moisture-loving ferns, mosses and liverworts.

. . .

WASDALE & WASTWATER

– CUMBRIA –

Location
9 miles east of Seascale. Approached via side-roads from the A595.
Map reference 89:NY1806 (Wasdale Head).

Habitats
Mountains, moorland, bogs, scree, woodlands, lake.

Nature conservation features
The reflection of Wasdale's screes – steep fans of unstable rocks and boulders – in the calm surface of Wastwater is one of the most dramatic sights in the Lake District. The screes and the associated crags and gullies are famous for their mountain plants, which include species such as the dwarf juniper, alpine lady's mantle and purple saxifrage. The lake itself is deep and its waters acid. Few plants or animals can live in these inhospitable conditions, but the Arctic char, a fish that arrived in the last Ice Age, still survives here.

. . .

SILVERDALE: EAVES & WATERSLACK WOOD

– LANCASHIRE AND CUMBRIA –

Location
4 miles northwest of Carnforth, via the A6.
Map reference 97:SD465758.

Habitats
Limestone pavement, limestone grassland, woodland.

Nature conservation features
These wooded limestone slopes lying across the Lancashire-Cumbria border are rich in plant life and, more particularly, fungi, with over 350 species recorded. The terraced hill of Eaves Wood is covered with sessile oak, ash, small-leaved lime, beech, juniper, wild service tree, wild cherry, Scots pine, larch and wych elm. The plants of the woodland floor include herb Paris, lily-of-the-valley, angular Solomon's seal, mezereon, yellow star of Bethlehem, fingered sedge, mountain melick and the toothwort, a parasite of trees. Green woodpeckers thrive here on the abundant ants, and sparrowhawks, woodcock and wood warblers are among the birds also to be found. The woods' mammals include the red squirrel.

WASDALE *Cotton-grass growing on a high and exposed fellside.*

FORMBY Mature planted pines, home of red squirrels.

FORMBY

– MERSEYSIDE –

Location
On the seaward side of Formby. The main approach by car is from Victoria Road. Also reached by a number of footpaths.
Map reference 108:SD275080.

Habitats
Woodland, scrub, dunes, ponds.

Nature conservation features
Formby's sand dunes are a haven for wildlife on the heavily built-up Merseyside coastline. Famous as one of the few sites in Britain where the natterjack toad breeds, Formby is also of great botanical interest. The meadow-like sandy flats abound with maiden pink, harebell, yellow rattle, restharrow, wild parsnip, yellow bedstraw, yellow-wort and both the Portland and sea spurges. Near the main Victoria Road, Formby boasts another curiosity – a colony of red squirrels. These are not native animals, but descendants of red squirrels introduced from the continent.

WALES

W*ales is a country defined by its mountains. The spectacular massif of Snowdonia and the gentler hills of the South are the closest approach to wilderness that can be found in southern Britain. The National Trust's countryside in Wales includes large areas of upland ground, and also stretches of coastline with outstanding scenery and a wealth of seabirds.*

Cemlyn
Llandona
Graig Fawr
Carneddau
GWYNEDD
CLWYD
Aberglaslyn Pass
Migneint
Braich-y-Pwll
Domelynllyn

POWYS

Abergwesyn Common
Dolaucothi
St. David's Head
DYFED
Brecon Beacons
Whitford Burrows
GWENT
Stackpole
GLAMORGAN
Bishopston Valley
Rhossili Down
Gower Cliffs

GRAIG FAWR: DYSERTH

– CLWYD –

Location
At the north end of the Clwydian Hills, 2 miles south of Prestatyn. Access by side-roads from the A5151.
Map reference 116:SJ060805.

Habitats
Limestone grassland, scrub, woodland.

Nature conservation features
This large, craggy hill is a perfect viewpoint from which to look out over the Vale of Clwyd. It is made of limestone, and is famous for its abundant fossils. The summit of the hill is bare rock with some small trees, mostly hawthorn and black-thorn, stunted by strong salt-laden winds blowing in from the sea. The northeast corner has areas of grassland supporting small lime-loving plants, among them salad burnet, white clover, small scabious, sheep's fescue, birdsfoot trefoil, wild thyme and lady's bedstraw. Hoary rock-rose, a plant found only on a few sites in Wales and England, clings to the western face.

St. David's Head

– Dyfed –

Location
At the seaward end of the B4583, about 2 miles northwest of St. David's.
Map reference 157:SM721278.

Habitats
Cliffs, scrub, heathland, grassland.

Nature conservation features
This spectacular and exposed headland at the northern end of St. Bride's Bay is an excellent place for watching seabirds as they travel along the coast and around the offshore islands. The land birds of St. David's Head are also of interest, with choughs – a local speciality – ravens, buzzards, stock doves and rock pipits. House martins nest on the cliffs, along with several of the more common species of gull and the fulmar. Orpine, wild chives and sea spleenwort grow on the cliff ledges, while wind-clipped heather and bell heather live on the cliff-top near the edge. The ground near the cliff harbours the rare hairy greenweed, as well as kidney vetch and spring squill, while the heath spotted orchid flowers further back from the cliff among the gorse.

· · ·

Dolaucothi

– Dyfed –

Location
Between Llanwrda and Lampeter at Pumpsaint on the A482.
Map reference 146:SN6640.

Habitats
Woodland, heathland, grassland, meadows, rivers, ponds.

Nature conservation features
Famous for its ancient goldmines, the Dolaucothi Estate contains over 1,000 ha (2,500 acres) of farmland and woodland. Paths lead from the village of Pumpsaint up the Cothi valley, past conifer plantations and oak woods to higher ground. For plants, the richest woodland on the estate is the Llandre Carr alder wood, which has an abundance of mosses and lichens. In the valley above Llandre, there are some damp "unimproved" meadows, rich in wild flowers such as whorled caraway, devilsbit scabious, heath spotted orchid, petty whin and ivy-leaved bellflower. Red kites may be seen over the estate.

· · ·

Stackpole

– Dyfed –

Location
4 miles south of Pembroke.
Map reference 158:SR977963.

Habitats
Cliffs, grassland, woodland, farmland, lake, dunes, beaches.

Nature conservation features
Stackpole is a place of contrasts, embracing both the placid shores of an artificial lake and the majestic cliffs of Stackpole Head. Much of the landscape away from the sea has been created by man. Mature woodlands, which were planted in the eighteenth century, offer shelter and food for birds. In summer, parts of the three-pronged lake are covered with waterlily flowers. The coastline is dramatic and varied. The cliffs are made of limestone, and many seabirds, including razorbills and guillemots, nest on their ledges. A few puffins also

DOLAUCOTHI The overgrown entrance to an old gold-mine.

breed in burrows in the turf. Grazing by sheep has maintained the variety of the cliff-top flowers, which thrive on the thin limestone soil. The two beaches at Broad Haven and Barafundle Bay attract quite different birds, such as sandpipers, which feed where the waves lap against the sandy shore.

· · ·

Aberglaslyn Pass

– Gwynedd –

Location
12 miles southeast of Caernafon, on the A4085, extending south for 1½ miles from Beddgelert.
Map reference 115:SH600468.

Habitats
Mountains, moorland, woodland, rough pasture, river.

Nature conservation features
At the bottom end of a spectacular gorge, the swift-flowing waters of the Afon Glaslyn tumble over rapids before filling slow-moving pools. Aberglaslyn Pass is a famous beauty spot, and the view looking north from the stone bridge, Pont Aberglaslyn, is one of the most scenic in Snowdonia. The well-wooded slopes of the gorge, with their oaks, ash trees, birches, beeches and sycamores, are rich in mosses, liverworts and lichens. These simple plants flourish in the moist, clean atmosphere. The mosses and liverworts grow mostly on and between rocks and boulders, while the lichens grow on the trees. The slopes are also an ideal habitat for rhododendrons, which, although delightful when in flower, create problems by spreading rapidly and swamping other plants.

BRAICH-Y-PWLL

– GWYNEDD –

Location
At the extreme tip of the Lleyn Peninsula near Aberdaron, about 18 miles from Pwllheli via the B4413.
Map reference 123:SH140254.

Habitats
Cliffs, heathland, grassland.

Nature conservation features
This rocky promontory, with its commanding views towards Bardsey Island, is one of the few places in Britain where choughs are regularly seen. Large flocks sometimes feed on the upper cliff and, in spring, the birds fly to and from their nests, which they build in inaccessible rocky crevices. Kittiwakes, guillemots, razorbills, ravens and buzzards also use the cliffs as a nest site.

Braich-y-Pwll has good examples of almost all the habitats found along the coast of the Lleyn Peninsula. Close to the sea, golden samphire and sea spleenwort grow among the rocks, as do many lichens. Further up the cliffs, heather, dwarf gorse and bell heather make up a type of vegetation known as western maritime heath, which is only found in a few parts of Britain.

· · ·

CARNEDDAU

– GWYNEDD –

Location
8 miles southeast of Bangor, astride the A5, near Capel Curig.
Map reference 115:SH6760.

Habitats
Rocks, moorland, grassland, woodland, farmland, lakes, streams.

Nature conservation features
Covering 6,420 ha (16,860 acres), Carneddau contains some of the most dramatic scenery in Snowdonia. It includes Cwm Idwal with its mountain lake, Lyn Idwal, 373 m (1,223 feet) above sea level, and the peaks of Carnedd Dafydd and Tryfan. Like the rest of Snowdonia, the landscape of Carneddau was created by glaciers. The high, treeless massif is covered with extensive areas of acid grassland, bilberry heath, blanket bog and scree. Mosses cover most of the bogs, and alongside them grow sedges, cotton-grass, purple moor-grass, heather and cross-leaved heath. Few large animals can be seen on the high tops, but ravens and buzzards are conspicuous overhead as they scan the open ground for food.

STACKPOLE *Barafundle beach, with woodland on the limestone rock.*

CEMLYN

– GWYNEDD –

Location
2 miles west of Camaes Bay on the north coast of Anglesey, reached by side-roads from the A5025.
Map reference 114:SH325933.

Habitats
Farmland, lagoon, beach.

Nature conservation features
This small but varied site, part of which is managed as a nature reserve by the North Wales Wildlife Trust, is of major interest for its bird life. Common and Arctic terns breed on the main shingle bank in spring and summer, and in some years they are joined by Sandwich terns as well. In winter, a number of different species of duck, including the wigeon, teal and mallard, may be seen either offshore, on the brackish lagoon or feeding on the wet meadows. The beach at Trwyn Cemlyn has a good range of plants that thrive on shingle, including sea kale, sea holly and sea radish. Thrift, restharrow, sea campion and spring squill grow on the rocky ground.

· · ·

DOLMELYNLLYN

– GWYNEDD –

Location
5 miles northwest of Dolgellau, on the west side of the A470.
Map reference 124:SH7222.

Habitats
Moorland, heathland, grassland, woodland, rivers.

Nature conservation features
The National Trust's holdings at Dolmelynllyn consist of woods and farmland which rises from the banks of the Afon Mawddach to merge with the high moors of the surrounding mountains. The woodlands, mainly of sessile oak, together with ash, birch and some small-leaved limes, are an important area for wildlife, providing nesting sites for redstarts, nuthatches and buzzards. Above the woods on the high and exposed mountain slopes, *Sphagnum* moss, cross-leaved heath and bog myrtle grow on the thick and boggy peat.

· · ·

LLANDONA: BRYN OFFA

– GWYNEDD –

Location
Overlooking Red Wharf Bay, Anglesey. 2 miles northeast of Beaumaris.
Map reference 114:SH579817.

Habitats
Heathland, grassland.

Nature conservation features
This small site on Anglesey's north coast is notable for its plants. These grow in two distinct habitats – lime-rich heathland and maritime grassland. The heathland is dominated by bell heather and dwarf gorse, but is unusual in having many more plants besides these. Over 30 species have been recorded here, including columbine, creeping willow, sawwort and quaking grass. Some are typical of acid ground, others of alkaline. Its animal life includes a coastal species of ant and a whorl snail. The grassland, which lies towards the coast, contains cowslips, and the sea spleenwort grows in the cliff crevices.

DOLMELYNLLYN *Broadleaved woodland clinging to rocks by the river.*

MIGNEINT

– GWYNEDD –

Location
5 miles east of Ffestiniog on the B4391, between the B4391 and the B4407.
Map reference 124:SH7843.

Habitats
Moorland, heathland, bog, lakes, rivers.

Nature conservation features
This large, isolated area of upland forms part of the National Trust's Ysbyty Estate, and is one of the best examples of blanket bog in Wales. The most notable vegetation on the high, open ground is mature heather heathland, but there are also large tracts of wet bog with *Sphagnum* moss and cotton-grass. The wet heathland has heather and cotton-grass, while the moorland is covered with grasses, sedges and rushes. Crowberry, cowberry, bog rosemary and lesser twayblade all grow on the hilltops and slopes. There are several lakes and rivers, and common sandpipers, which breed by the rocky streams, can be seen feeding at the water's edge. The high moorland is the haunt of the red grouse and the golden plover, both of which nest in the heather and grass.

· · ·

ABERGWESYN COMMON

– POWYS –

Location
In the Cambrian Mountains, west of Llandrindod Wells, and extending from the Irfon Gorge to the Wye Valley.

BRECON BEACONS Ponies grazing on the high hill-tops.

Map reference 127, 128 and 141:SN8359 to 9861.

Habitats
Grassland, moorland, scree, bog, heathland, streams, woodland.

Nature conservation features
Reaching an altitude of over 640 m (2,100 feet), the extensive plateau of Abergwesyn Common gives views northwards as far as Snowdonia. Heavy grazing has done much to shape the vegetation here, something which is noticeable in the places that sheep cannot reach. The sides of the stream valleys have lush ferns and flowering plants, while the crags, rocky outcrops and scree slopes support clubmosses, lichens and mountain melick. Red grouse and waders, such as the golden plovers, live on the moorland.

BRECON BEACONS

– POWYS –

Location
Between Brecon and Merthyr Tydfil, to the east of the main A470 Brecon to Merthyr Tydfil road.
Map reference 160:SO010200.

Habitats
Mountains, crags, moorland, woodland, streams, rivers.

Nature conservation features
The smooth grass-covered slopes of the Brecon Beacons in south-east Wales are in complete contrast to the rock-strewn peaks of Snowdonia further north. As farmers discovered long ago, this terrain is good for sheep, and over the centuries, they and their animals have done much to change the vegetation. At one time, the mountains were covered in broadleaved woodland, and some fine areas of woodland still remain. After most of the woodland was felled, heather and bilberry moorland took its place. Centuries of grazing then turned this into the grassland that exists today. This open country, with its scattered pockets of woodland, is perfect for watching birds of prey. Kestrels, buzzards, merlins, hen harriers, sparrowhawks and the occasional peregrine all hunt over the higher ground.

· · ·

BISHOPSTON VALLEY

– WEST GLAMORGAN –

Location
On the Gower peninsula, 6 miles southwest of Swansea, via the A4067 and B4436.

Map reference 159:SS575894.

Habitats
Woodland, limestone grassland, stream.

Nature conservation features
This deeply incised, winding valley provides sheltered and pleasant walking as well as considerable biological interest. Much of the valley is wooded, and some parts have a particularly wide range of trees. These include oak, ash, small-leaved lime, holly, field maple and the wild service tree. The shrubs growing beneath, among them hazel, spindle and dogwood, were formerly coppiced. The birds that breed in the woods include the blackcap, green woodpecker and buzzard. Many different plants, especially dog's mercury, grow in the areas of older woodland, while meadows in the valley bottom are good places to see wild flowers.

. . .

GOWER CLIFFS

– WEST GLAMORGAN –

Location
On the southwest coast of the Gower peninsula, from Worms Head eastwards.
Map reference 159:SS383878 (Worms Head).

Habitats
Cliffs, limestone grassland, heathland.

Nature conservation features
The tumbling limestone cliffs of the southwest part of the Gower peninsula are fascinating to anyone interested in birds or plants. Fulmars, kittiwakes, shags, cormorants, guillemots and razorbills breed at Worms Head, and smaller numbers of

these birds can be seen along the rest of this rocky shore. But it is not only seabirds that nest on the cliffs. Ravens, barn owls, swifts and stonechats also breed on their rocky ledges. Where the limestone has created an alkaline soil that is safely beyond the reach of the plough, the grass is rich in wild flowers such as kidney vetch, wild thyme and small scabious, and carnation grass also grows here. Juniper is a local speciality.

. . .

RHOSSILI DOWN

– WEST GLAMORGAN –

Location
15 miles west of Swansea, at the end of the Gower peninsula.

Map reference 159:SS420900.

Habitats
Heathland, grassland.

Nature conservation features
Rhossili Down dominates the western end of the Gower peninsula, and has long been a popular place for visitors. From its highest point at over 180 m (600 feet), there are extensive views west along the South Wales coast and out over the Bristol Channel. The down is covered in heathland and grassland, made up of those plants that can survive both the acid soil and the constant buffeting of the wind. In spring and autumn, many migrant birds make a landfall here, either recovering from their flight across the Bristol Channel, or waiting for good conditions before setting out across the sea.

GOWER CLIFFS *The beach and marsh at Three Cliffs Bay in late autumn.*

WHITFORD BURROWS & LLANRHIDIAN MARSH

– WEST GLAMORGAN –

Location
On the north and northwest coast of the Gower peninsula, stretching westwards from the village of Crofty. 6 miles west of Swansea via the B4295.
Map reference 159:SS490932 (Llanrhidian Marsh).

Habitats
Sand dunes, saltmarsh, mudflats, farmland.

Nature conservation features
The tall sand dunes of Whitford Burrows, with their mile-long stretch of golden sand, protect the flat expanse of the Llanrhidian Marsh mudflats from the scouring action of the sea. The dunes, which are managed by the Nature Conservancy Council as a National Nature Reserve, are an excellent example of gradual colonization by plants. The young dunes are dominated by marram grass, while the older, more stable dunes have patches of thyme and yellow-wort growing on them. The slacks between the dunes are rich in wild flowers, including the pyramidal and fen orchids. The marshes to the east are heavily grazed by cattle and sheep, and are dissected by deep creeks, making access difficult. The whole of the estuary area, including the marshes and mudflats, is a very important source of food for birds, especially the oystercatcher, grey plover, redshank, knot and pintail. In winter, a variety of sea-ducks, including eiders, may be seen offshore.

NORTHERN IRELAND
· · ·

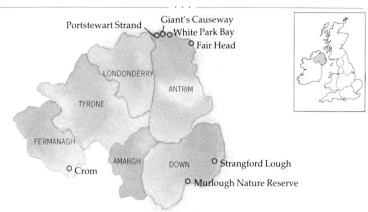

*T*he coastline of Northern Ireland is one of great variety, including not only majestic cliffs and sweeping beaches, but also the extraordinary rock formations of the Giant's Causeway and the great tidal inlet of Strangford Lough. Much of the coastline under the protection of the National Trust is outstanding both for its plant and bird life.

FAIR HEAD & MURLOUGH BAY

– CO. ANTRIM –

Location
3 miles east of Ballycastle.
Map reference D185430 (Fair Head) and D199419 (Murlough Bay).

Habitats
Cliffs, heathland, bog, grassland, woodland, shore.

Nature conservation features
Fair Head overlooks the north channel of the Irish Sea, with Rathlin Island and the Mull of Kintyre in the distance. On its eastern side, the wooded slopes of Murlough Bay contrast with the bleak rocky plateau above. The vegetation above Fair Head consists of a mixture of wet and dry heath, and acid grassland. Creeping willow, crowberry and bog myrtle can be seen, as well as the insect-eating sundew and butterwort. The heath near the cliff edge is a favourite feeding place for choughs, and ravens and peregrines nest on the steep cliff-face. Fair Head is an excellent vantage point for watching pilot and killer whales in the summer and autumn.

· · ·

GIANT'S CAUSEWAY

– CO. ANTRIM –

Location
2 miles east of Bushmills, on the B146 Causeway to Dunseverick road. Access also by the North

Antrim coastal path.
Map reference C952452.

Habitats
Rocks, shore, rockpools, cliffs, marsh, heathland, grassland.

Nature conservation features
Designated as a World Heritage Site, the Giant's Causeway has both spectacular rock formations and abundant wildlife. The cliff-top heathland contains plants such as mountain everlasting, heath spotted orchid, spring squill, heath and gorse. On the sunniest slopes, a mixture of grassland and seashore plants flourishes, with sea campion, thrift and kidney vetch growing alongside devilsbit scabious, red and white campions, harebells and tormentils. Grey seals can be seen offshore, while birds are numerous inshore and on land. Among the many species to be seen here are two rarities – the chough and peregrine.

· · ·

PORTSTEWART STRAND & BAR MOUTH

– CO. ANTRIM AND
CO. LONDONDERRY –

Location
Portstewart Strand: 1 mile west of Portstewart; map reference C720360. Bar Mouth: 3 miles east of Castlerock at the mouth of the River Bann; map reference C782365.

Habitats
Sandy shore, dunes, heath, saltmarsh, mudflats.

Nature conservation features
Portstewart Strand, an attractive and popular beach, is backed by

GIANT'S CAUSEWAY A platform of eroded basalt columns frames the view west across the bay to the grass-covered headland beyond.

an extensive sand-dune spit which diverts the River Bann. The young dunes provide a habitat for marram grass, sea spurge, kidney vetch and birdsfoot trefoil. Sea buckthorn – a plant that is alien to this area – also grows here, forming dense thickets that have to be cut back regularly. Fourteen species of butterfly breed on this part of the coast, including the grayling and dark-green fritillary. Typical birds of the dunes and scrub include the meadow pipit, cuckoo, reed bunting and willow warbler.

· · ·

WHITE PARK BAY

– CO. ANTRIM –

Location
1½ miles west of Ballintoy, 7 miles northwest of Ballycastle via the A2.
Map reference D023440.

Habitats
Chalk grassland, scrub, cliffs, dunes, sandy shore.

Nature conservation features
At White Park Bay, chalk cliffs rich in fossils give way to a sandy beach. Between the beach and the surrounding cliffs is an extensive area of grassland and scrub. The narrow band of sand dunes has dune plants such as fragrant agrimony and both sea and Portland spurge. The site is particularly rich in orchids, with eight species, including pyramidal orchids on the dunes, frog orchid, fragrant orchid and the very rare small white orchid. Butterflies are also plentiful, with the dark green fritillary and wood white being the most notable. Eiders and oystercatchers breed on the shore, and swifts nest on the cliffs.

MURLOUGH NATURE RESERVE

– Co. Down –

Location
2 miles west of Newcastle, 28 miles south of Belfast. Map reference J410350.

Habitats
Beach, sand dunes, heathland, scrub, woodland, saltmarsh.

Nature conservation features
Murlough was the first nature reserve to be created in Ireland. Its sand dunes lie in a superbly scenic position across Dundrum Bay with the Mourne Mountains in the background. The dunes contain a whole spectrum of plants, from those that flourish on young dunes, such as marram grass, sea bindweed and viper's bugloss, to those that favour more stable dunes, such as wild thyme, restharrow and birdsfoot trefoil. Sea buckthorn forms dense and spreading thickets in the youngest dunes to the north, while blackthorn, hazel and spindle grow on the older dunes. Murlough is especially rich in insect life. The rare marsh fritillary breeds in the heathland areas, while blues and burnet moths live in the dunes. The sea buckthorn scrub is very attractive to birds. Large numbers of wildfowl and waders can be seen on the sea and estuary in winter months.

· · ·

STRANGFORD LOUGH

– Co. Down –

Location
In east Co. Down, extending south from Newtownards and Comber in the north to Downpatrick in the southwest, and to Killard Point and Ballyquintin Point in the southeast. Map reference J560615.

Habitats
Grassland, scrub, mudflats, saltmarsh, beaches, rocky shore.

Nature conservation features
Strangford Lough is one of the largest sea loughs in Northern Ireland. The landscape of Co. Down is dominated by rounded hills of boulder clay, called drumlins, which were formed during the last Ice Age. Many drowned drumlins lie in the lough, and form 120 small islands, some large enough to be farmed, others used only by nesting seabirds such as terns, or by loafing seals. With about 50 square km (19 square miles) of ground between high and low water, Strangford Lough is unrivalled in the diversity of its shoreline habitats. It is internationally famous for the plants along its shores and also for its marine life. The lough's waters teem with small plants and over 2,000 species of animal, and these support large numbers of wintering wildfowl and waders. These include over 16,000 pale-bellied Brent geese, which feed on the extensive eel-grass beds on Strangford's northern mudflats, and thousands of other wildfowl, particularly wigeon, teal, mallard and whooper swans. Up to 2,000 shelduck feed on small snails in the mud, while goldeneye and red-breasted merganser feed on fish. The lough is also important for large mammals. It is the most important breeding site in Ireland for the common seal. In summer, porpoises and killer whales can sometimes be seen from the shore.

· · ·

CROM

– Co. Fermanagh –

Location
6 miles southeast of Lisnaskea, 2 miles west of Newtownbutler. Map reference H236324.

Habitats
Woodland, parkland, meadows, fen, lake.

Nature conservation features
This extensive estate on the shores of Upper Lough Erne is of international importance for its wildlife. Many wading birds breed on the estate, and the rare corncrake has nested in the hay meadows. Large numbers of wildfowl spend the winter on the lough, and whooper swans and Greenland white-fronted geese may be seen grazing in the meadows at this time of year.

WHITE PARK BAY *A chalk arch behind the boulder-strewn beach.*

INDEX

Page numbers in *italic* refer to illustrations and captions; those in **bold** refer to gazetteer entries.

A

Aberglaslyn Pass, **180–1**
Abergwesyn Common, **183**
acorns, *54*, *62*
adder, *66*, *67*
Afton Down, **139**
agrimony, *42*, *43*
alder, *12*, *14*, *92*
Alderley Edge, **162**
algae, *86*, *87*, *94*, *117*, *125*
Allen Banks, **171**
Alnmouth, **171**
amphibians, 96–7
ancient woodlands, 10–23
Anglesey, 38
ants, *17*, 48
  black, 73
Arlington, 63
Arnside Knott, **176**
arrowhead, *90*, *93*
ash tree, *11*, *12*, 14, *19*, 23, 41, 58, *63*
Ashridge, **139**
aspen, 20
asphodel, bog, *98*, *98*, *99*, 101, *102*
aster, sea, 116, *119*
avens, water, 32

B

badger, *19*, *19*, 72
Ballard Down, **154–5**
banded agrion, *91*
banded snail, *50*
Bar Mouth, **186**
Barafundle, *181*
barnacle, 125, *125*
basalt, 78
Basildon Park, **135**
bats, 20
bean gall, *107*
Beckland Cliffs, **152**
bedstraw, hedge, *48*, *49*
beech, *12*, *13*, *16*, 19, 37, *56*, 58, 61, *62*
beefsteak fungus, 61
bees, 26, *32*, *43*, *45*, 47, 49–50, *90*
bellflower: clustered, *45*, 47
  ivy-leaved, 33
bent, 79
  common, *38*, *113*

bilberry, 78, *82*
bindweed, sea, *113*
birch, *17*, 22, *106*
birds: in ancient woodlands, 23
  bogs, 105
  chalk grasslands, 50–1
  cliffs, 131–3
  coppices, 18
  estuaries, 120–1
  fens, 108–9
  fields, 34–5
  heathlands, 70–2
  lakes, 94–5
  mountains and moorlands, 82–3
  parkland, 61–2
  saltmarshes, 116
birds of prey, 70, 85
birdsfoot trefoil, *126*, *127*
Birling Gap, **146**
Bishopston Valley, **183–4**
bistort: amphibious, *27*, *108*
  common, 32
bittern, 108
Black Down, **146**
blackbird, 27
blackcap, 18
blackthorn, 37, 129
bladder wrack, *119*
bladderwort, 96
blaeberry, *78*
Blakeney Point, **160**, *160*
Blickling, *27*, *30–1*, *36*, **160**
bloodvein moth, *32*
blue butterflies, 47–8
  Adonis, 48, *48*, *49*, 73
  chalkhill, 48, *48*, *49*, 73
  large, 45
  silver-studded, 73, *73*
bluebell, *16*, *17*
bogs, 98–105, 109
Bookham Commons, **143**
Borrowdale Woods, 23, **176**
Bosherston Lake, 95
box, *44*
Box Hill, *44*, *45*, *50*, **144**
bracken, *56*, 64, 66, 129
bracket fungi, 61, *61*
Bradnor Hill, **165–6**
Braich-y-Pwll, **181**
bramble, 15, *16*
Bramshaw Commons, **136–7**, *136*
Brancaster, **160**, *161*
brandy bottle, *88*
Branscombe, **151–2**
Brean Down, **156–7**
Brecon Beacons, **183**, *183*
Bridestones Moor, **173**
Brimham Moor, 98, **173**
bristletail, *125*
Brockhampton, **166**, *166*
brome, least soft, *129*
Brook Down, **139**
brooklime, *92*
broomrape, thistle, 47

Brown, "Capability", 52, 54
brown argus butterfly, 49
Brownsea Island, **155**
Bryn Offa, **182**
bryony, black, 57
bulrush, *87*
bumble bees, *32*, *43*, *91*
bunting, reed, 35, *108*
bur-reed, 94
burnet: great, 32
  salad, *43*
burnet moth, *46*, *47*
bush-cricket, grey, 131
buttercup: bulbous, *128*
  creeping, *25*, *31*
butterflies: chalkland, 38, 47–9
  cliffs, 131
  fields, 33–4
  heathlands, 72–3
  meadows, 26
  rivers, *90*, *93*
  woodlands, 15
Buttermere Valley, *176*, **177**
butterwort, 104
buzzard, 85

C

caddisfly, 89–90
Caledonian Forest, 12
Calke Abbey, 55, *56–7*, 63, **163**
campion, sea, *126*, *127*
Carneddau, **181**
carnivorous plants, 104
carrot, wild, 46
caterpillars, 20, 23, 48, *59*, *67*, *72*, *109*
catkins, *12*
catsear, common, *112*
cattle, 28, *59*, 72, *133*
caves, 38
cedar of Lebanon, 58
celandine, *16*
  lesser, *17*
Cemlyn, **182**
centaury, common, *45*, *114*
chalk grasslands, 38–51
Chapel Carn Brea, **150**
Chapel Porth, **150**, *150*
charcoal, 22
Charlecote Park, **169**
Charnwood Forest, **167**
The Chase, **138–9**
Cheddar Gorge, 51
Cherhill Down, **147–8**
cherry, wild, *17*, 37
chestnuts: horse, *56*, 58
  sweet, 15, 58, *58*, 62
Chilterns, 48
chough, 133
Churnet Valley, **169**
cinquefoil, marsh, *103*, *107*
cistus forester moth, 49
Cladonia lichen, *60*

Clent Hills, **166**
Cley Hill, **148**, *148*
click beetle, *130*
cliffs, 25, 122–33, *122–3*, *126–7*, *130*
Clitocybe fungus, 57
Clovelly, **152**
clover, 35
  haresfoot, *64*
  red, *25*, *30*
  twin-headed, 129–30
  upright, 130
  white, *31*
clubmosses, *80*, *85*
  Alpine, *81*, *85*
  fir, *81*
Clumber Park, **167–8**
coasts: cliffs and rocky shores, 122–33, *122–3*, *126–7*, *130*
  dunes, saltmarshes and mudflats, 110–21, *116*, *118–19*
cockles, *119*
cockroach, lesser, *114*
Collybia fungus, 57
coltsfoot, 129
comfrey, 33
Compton Down, **139**, *139*
conifers, 51, 75, 104
Coombe Hill, **136**
coot, 94, *95*
coppices, 14–23, *14–17*, *21*, *23*
copses, 12
cord grass, 112
cormorant, *120*
Cornwall, 23, 128, 129–30
Corophium volutator, 120
cotoneaster, 51
Cotswolds, 39
cotton-grass, 101, *101*
couch-grass, sand, 114
cow-wheat, 18
cowberry, *100*, *101*
cowslip, *16*, 26, 50
crabs, *118*, *124*, *128*
crab spider, 74
Cragside, **171**
cramp ball, 23
cranberry, *100*
crane-flies, *130*
cranesbills: bloody, 114
  wood, 32
Craven, 47
crickets, 131
Crickley Hill, **164**
crocus, autumn, 33
Croft Castle, 58, **166–7**
Crom, **187**
crosswort, *43*
crow, 35
crustaceans, 120
cuckoo flower, *25*
cuckoo-spit, *17*
Cumbria, 79
curlew, 35, *83*, 105, *117*
Cwm Idwal, *80–1*

D

daddy-long-legs, *46, 130*
daisies, *25, 30*
  ox-eye, *33*
damselflies, *90, 91, 93*
Danbury Common, **159**, *159*
dance fly, *32*
dandelion, *46*
dead trees, *55*
deer, 18, 52, *52–3*, 53, 59, 72
deer parks, 53
Derbyshire Dales, 47
Derwent Estate, **175**, *175*
devil's coach-horse, *69*
dipper, 88
ditches, 95–7
dock, *29, 32, 46*
dog violet, *14*
dog-whelk, *124*
dog's mercury, *13*
dog's tail, crested, *30*
dogfish, *113*
Dolaucothi, **180**, *180*
Dolebury Warren, **149**
dolerite, 78
Dolmelynllyn, 23, **182**, *182*
Domesday Survey, 53
dor beetle, 28
dormouse, 19
dotterel, 83
Dovedale, 39, *41–3*, 49, **163**, *163*
Dover's Hill, 164
dragonflies, 74, 86, *90, 93*
drainage, 34–5, 97, 109
dryad's saddle, 61
ducks, 86, *94*, 117
  tufted, *102*
duckweed, *91*, 95
dunes, 110–15, *111, 115*
dung, 28
dung-fly, 28, *32*
dunlin, 85, 105
Dunstanburgh Castle, **171–2**, *171*
Dunwich Heath, **161**
dyer's greenweed, 33
Dyserth, **179**

E

eagle, golden, 85
earthworms, 35, 39, 67
earwigs, 47
East Anglia, 98, 107, 122
East Head, **146**, *146*
Eaves Wood, *178*
eelgrass, 117
elder, 37, 79
elm, 61
  wych, *10*
Embleton Links, **172–3**
Enclosure Acts, 36
Enterprise Neptune, 133

epiphytes, 59–60
erosion, *77*, 78
estuaries *see* mudflats;
  saltmarshes
Exe, River, 76
Exmoor, 23, 85, 92
eyebright, *126*

F

Fair Head, 133, **185**
fallow deer, 18, *52–3*, 53
Farne Islands, **172**, *172*
Fatacott Cliffs, **152**
fens, 98, *102–3*, 105–9
ferns, *17, 80*
fertilizers, 24, 28, *35*, 75, 97
fescue, red, *128*
fields, 24–35, *27, 30–1*
Figsbury Ring, **148**
finches, 50
fish, 86, 87, 88, 125
flycatchers: pied, 23
  spotted, 62
Fontmell Down, **155**
forget-me-not, 26
  field, *31, 127*
  water, *24*
Formby, *115*, **179**, *179*
Fountains Abbey, **173**
fox moth, *68, 72*
fox, 19, *34, 63, 72*, 132
Frensham Common, *65, 68–9,
  72, 74*, **144**
fritillary (plant), 32, 33
fritillary butterflies: Duke of
  Burgundy, 50
  Glanville, 123–4, 131
  heath, 15–16
  high brown, 15
  marsh, 33
froghopper, *17*
frog, 96–7, *107*
Fulking Escarpment, **146–7**, *147*
fungi, 23
  chalk and limestone
  grasslands, 39
  on dead wood, *17, 22*, 56, 60,
  61, 63
  on heathlands, *75*
furniture beetle, common, *55*
furze, *70*

G

galls, *13, 16*, 55, *57, 107*
geese, 117, *118*
  brent, *117*
Giant's Causeway, **185–6**, *186*
glasswort, 112, *119*
Glencoyne Wood, **177–8**
Glenthorne, **152**

globeflower, 32
glow-worm, *46, 47*
goats, 25
goatsbeard, *30*
Godlingston Heath, **156**
godwits: bar-tailed, 121
  black-tailed, 121
Golden Cap, **155–6**, *155*
gorse, 64, 66, *68*, 70, 73
  dwarf, *69*, 129
  European, 129
  western, 129
Gowbarrow Park, **177–8**
Gower Cliffs, **184**
Graig Fawr, **179**
grass of Parnassus, 32, *102, 109*
grass snake, 67, 109
grasses, 26, 78
  in bogs, 101
  moorlands, 79–82
  pollen, *24*
  on sand dunes, 114–15
  water, 86, *87*
grasshoppers, *43*, 131
grasslands, chalk and
  limestone, 38–51, *42–3*
grayling butterfly, *33*, 72–3, *73*
grazing: in ancient woodlands,
  22–3
  chalk and limestone
  grasslands, 40, *45*
  cliff-tops, 133
  hay meadows, 29
  heathlands, 66
  meadows, 25–6, 28–9
  moorlands, 82
grebe, great crested, 94–5
green hairstreak butterfly, 50
greenbottle flies, *46*
grouse, red, 85
guillemot, *126*, 131–2, *132*
gulls, 35, *117, 128*
  black-headed, 35, *121*

H

hair-grass, 79
hairstreak, green, 73
hairy stereum, 56
Hale Purlieu, **137**, *137*
Hardcastle Crags, **175**
harebell, *42*, 70
hare, 40
harriers: hen, 70, 109
  marsh, 98, 108–9
harvestman, *46*
Hatfield Forest, **159**
hawkbit, rough, *45*
hawkmoth, privet, *131*
hawthorn, *13*, 37, 57, 58, *59*, 79
hay, 25, 29–32
Hayburn Wyke, **174**
hazel, *11*, 12, *12*, 14, *14, 16–17*,
  19, 37

Headon Warren, **140**
heath, cross-leaved, *64, 102*
heath butterflies: large, 104–5
  small, 84
heather, 64, 66, *68*, 73, 78, 82,
  83–4, *84, 98, 99,
  101–4, 103*, 129
  bell, *68, 112*
heather beetle, 85
heathlands, 64–75, *65, 68–9, 74*
Heathwaite, **176**
Heddon Valley, **152–3**, *152*
hedgehog, 27
hedgerows, 24, 35–7
hemiparasites, *29*
herbicides, 24
heron, *95*
Hindhead Common, **144**
hobby, 70–1
Hod Hill, **156**
Holnicote Estate, 92, **157**, *157*
honey bee, *32, 45*
honey fungus, *62*
honeydew, 48
honeysuckle, *17*
hoopoe, 62
hornbeam, 14
Horner Valley, 23, 92, **157**, *157*
horses, 28
horsetail, *30*
Hottentot fig, 130
hoverflies, *46*
Hydrobia ulvae, 120

IJ

Ice Age, 64
insects, 67
  chalkland, *46*, 47–50
  cliffs, 131
  in dead wood, 55, 63
  heathlands, 74–5
  meadows, 28–9, 33–4
  riverbanks, 93
  saltmarshes, 116
Iron Age, 98
iron industry, 22
ivy, *57*

Jack-go-to-bed-at-noon, *30*
Jacob's ladder, 47, *47*
jay, *54*
juniper, 51

K

kestrel, 51, *51*, 62
Kinder Scout, 100
King Alfred's cakes, *23*
kingcup, *28*
kingfisher, 92, *94*
Kingston Lacy, *89–91, 96*, **156**

Kinver Edge, **169**
kittiwake, *122*, 132, *132*, *133*
knapweed, black, *48*
Knole Park, 63
knot, 121

L

ladybird, *13*, *93*
lady's mantle, 32
lady's smock, *25*
Lake District, 23, 32, 79, 83, 84, 85, 94
lakes, 86, 88, 94–5
Lancashire, 100, *115*
landscaping, 52, 54, 58
Langdon Cliffs, **141**
Lansallos, **151**
Lantic Bay, **151**
Lantivet Bay, **151**
lapwing, *34*, 35
larch, 51
Lardon Chase, **136**, *136*
layered hedges, 37
leaf-beetle, *93*
leafhopper, 85
The Leas, **173**
leatherjackets, *130*
Leigh Woods, **149**
Leith Hill, **144**, *145*
lichens, 60, 85
  on cliffs, 128, *130*, *131*
  heathland, *68–9*, *75*
  on sand dunes, 115
  on trees, 22, 23, 59–60
lime, 39, 45
lime trees, 12, 58
limestone, 38–51, *42–3*, 78
limpet, 125
Littleworth Wood, *11*, *16–17*, *21*, **164**
liver fluke, *26*
liverworts, 22, 23, 76, *80*, *81*, leafy, *81*
The Lizard, 129–30, 133, **150**
lizards, 67
  common, 67
  sand, 67, *67*
Llandona, **182**
Lleyn Peninsula, 133
Llanrhidian Marsh, **185**
Lobaria pulmonaria, 60
Long Mynd, **168**, *168*
loosestrife, yellow, 107
  purple, *91*, 107
Lough Down, **136**
lousewort, marsh, *105*
Low Scrubs, **136**
lowland heaths, 64–75, *65*, *68–9*, *74*
Ludshott Common, 72, **137**
Lulworth skipper, 131
Lundy, **153**, *153*
Lyme Park, **162**, *162*

M

Macroplax preysleri, 49
madder, field, 112
Malham Tarn, 78, *102*, **174**, *174*
mallard, *94*
Malvern Hills, **167**
mandarin duck, 62
maple, field, 37
marjoram, *48*
marram grass, 111–12, *111*, 113, 114, *114*, *115*
Marsden Rock, **173**
marsh marigold, *28*, 86
marsh orchid, *105*
  northern, 32
martin, house, 35, 92
mat grass, 79
May Hill, **164**
mayfly, 89–90
mayweed, scentless, *38*
meadow brown butterfly, *24*
meadow-rue, 33
meadows, 24–35, *27*, *30–1*
meadowsweet, *103*
medick, black, *31*
merganser, 94
merlin, 82–3, 85
mermaid's purse, *113*
Miarus weevil, 47
mice, *19*, 67
  long-tailed, 28
micromoths, 21
Middle Hope, **149–50**
Midsummer Hill, **167**
Migneint, 104, **183**
Milford Common, **145**
milk parsley, 107
milkwort, *127*
millipede, *16*
millstone grit, 78
Minchinhampton Common, **165**
mint, water, *91*, *96*, 97
mites, 33, 85
mole, 39
moor-grass, purple, 79, 101, 107
Moor House Woods, **170**
moorlands, 76–85, 86
Morden Hall Park, **142**
mosquitoes, 98
mosses, 22, *22*, 23, *23*, 59–60, *80*, *84*, 85, *99*, *100*, 101, 115
moths, 20–1, 23, *109*
mountain ash, 79
mountains, 76–85, 86, 100–1
mouse-ear, sea, *128*
mudflats, 110–11, *115*, *116*, 117–21, *118–19*
Murlough Bay, **185**
Murlough Nature Reserve, **187**
mussel, *125*
Mycena fungus, *56*
Mycena galericulata, *62*
myrtle, bog, 101
myxomatosis, 44

N

nectar, 26, 32
The Needles, **140**, *140*
Neolithic deforestation, 13, 100
nettle, 29
New Forest, 12, 72
Newtimber Hill, **146–7**
Newton Links, **172–3**
Newtown Estuary, *110*, 117, *118–119*, **140**, *141*
newts: great crested, 97
  smooth, 97
nightingale, 18
nightjar, *70*, 71
nitrates, 45
Norfolk Broads, 94, 95, 98, 100
Normans, 40–4, 53
North York Moors, 85
northern brown argus, 49
Northey Island, **159–60**
nuthatch, 62

O

oaks: bog, 98
  on cliffs, 128
  coppices, *15*, *16*, 21–3
  holm, 51
  lichens and mosses, 60
  on moorlands, 79
  in parkland, 54–8, *54*, *56*
  pedunculate, *54*
  sessile, *54*
  spangle galls, *55*, *57*
  standards, 19
  woodlands, 10–12, 14
oat grass, downy, *129*
old man's beard, *48*
Oldbury Castle, **147–8**
Omphalina toadstool, *80*
oolitic limestone, 39
orb-web spiders, *109*
orchids, 29, *115*
  early purple, *21*
  green-winged, 32, 33, 46
  heath spotted, 29
  pyramidal, *44*
  southern marsh, 28
orpine, 39, 83
otter shell, *118*
ouzel, ring, 83
owls, *62*, 63
  tawny, 20, 62
oxygen, 87, 99, 112, 116
oyster, *119*
oystercatcher, *116*

P

Padley Woods, **163–4**
pansy, mountain, 32

parasites, *29*, 46, 47
parkland, 15, 52–63, *56–7*
partridge, 28
pasque flower, 46
pastures, 24–35, *27*, *30–1*
peacock butterfly, *90*
Peak District, *41*
peat bogs, 64, 79, 98, *99*, 106, 109
peewit, *34*
Pegwell Bay, **141**
Pencarrow Head, **151**
Pennines, 78, 83, 85
pepper saxifrage, 33
Pepperbox Hill, **148**
peregrine, *82*, 84, 132–3
periwinkle, *118*
pesticides, 24
Petworth Park, 63, **147**
pheasant, *16*, 53
  ring-necked, *53*
phosphates, 45
piddock, *118*
pill-bug, *16*
pimpernel, scarlet, *69*, 72
pine trees, 51, 75
  Scots, *68*, 71
pintail, *121*
pipits: meadow, 84, 85
  rock, 133
  tree, *19*, 23
plantain, 129
  hoary, *47*
  ribwort, *128*
ploughing, 24
plovers: golden, 35, 82–3, 85, 105
  ringed, *111*
pollarded trees, 14–15, 58–9, 63, 66
pollen, *24*, 26, 32, 64, *87*, 99
pollution, water, 97
polypore, many-zoned, 61, *61*
Polytrichum moss, *80*, *81*
ponds, 86, 95–7
ponies, 72
pools, rock, 124–5
Poor's Acre, **167**
Portstewart Strand, **186**
primrose, *14*, *16*, *17*
  birdseye, 32, 47, 78
puffball, *39*, 52, 69
puffin, 132
purple emperor butterfly, 20
pussy willow, 20

QR

quaking grass, *38*, 126
Quantock Hills, **157**
quillwort, land, 130

rabbit, 29, 40–4, *40*, 49, 63, 72
ragged robin, *25*, *31*

ragwort, hoary, *45*
rainfall, 79
Ramalina siliquosa, 128
Ranmore Common, **145**
raven, 85
Ravenscar, 174–5
razorbill, 131–2, *132*
red deer, 84
redshank, 35, 116, *117*
redstart, 23, 62
redwing, 35
reed beetle, *92*
reeds, 108, 109
    common, 93, 95, 106, 107
reptiles, heathland, 66–8
Repton, Humphry, 52, 54
rest-harrow, spiny, 33
Rhossili Down, **184**
rivers, 25, 86, 88–94, *90–1, 96,*
    115
robin, *18*
rock pools, 124–5
rock-rose, *42*
    common, *38, 42,* 46, 49
rocket, sea, 114
rocks: coastal, 122–3
    erosion, *77, 78*
Rodborough Common, **165**, *165*
roe deer, 18
rose-hips, *59*
Roseberry Topping, **170**, *170*
Rough Tor, **151**, *151*
rowan, 21–2, 79
Runnymede, **145**
rushes, 26, 82
    compact, *26*
    dwarf, 130
    hard, *103*
    jointed, *26*
    sharp-flowered, *31*
rye-grass, *27*

S

sage, wood, *42*
St David's Head, 122, **180**
St John's wort: perforate, *49*
    slender, *81*
    trailing, *71*
St Margaret's Bay, **142**, *142*
Salcombe, **154**
Salcombe Regis, **151–2**
sallow, *16,* 20, 106
saltmarshes, 110–11, 112, 113,
    115–17, *118–19*
samphire, rock, 128
sand dunes, 110–15, *111, 115*
Sand Point, **149–50**
sand wasp, 74–5, *114*
sandpiper, purple, 133
Sandscale Haws, **177**
Sandwich Bay, **141**
sawflies, *92, 107*
saxifrage, *82*

mossy, *80, 82*
    rue-leaved, 112
scabious: devilsbit, 33, *102, 105*
    small, *42, 45*
scarlet tiger moth, 33–4
scathophagid flies, *20*
Scolt Head, 115, **161**
Scots pine, *68,* 71
scurvy-grass, 128, *128*
sea anemones, *124,* 125
sea-beet, 128
sea holly, *114, 115*
sea ivory, 128
sea-kale, 128
sea-lavender, 112
sea pink *see* thrift
sea spurrey, *129*
seal, *132*
    common, *132*
    grey, *132*
seaweeds, 125
    red, *118*
sedges, *31,* 101, 105, 106, 109
    distant, *127*
    great fen, 107
    yellow, *79*
sedimentary rocks, 38
Selborne, **138**, *138*
self-heal, *38*
Selsdon Wood, **142**
sessile oak, 21–2
setts, badger, *19*
Sharpenhoe, **135**
sheep, 22, 25, 28, 40, 49, 72, 82,
    85, 109, 133
sheep's fescue, 79
shelduck, *117,* 120–1, *120*
Shippards Chine Cliff, **139**
shrew, *19, 67,* 72
    common, 85
    pygmy, 85
shrimp, 125
shrubs: chalk grassland, 50–1
    moorland, 82
Silverdale, **178**
sitka spruce, 12
skipper butterflies, *33*
skylark, 28, 34–5, *35*
Slindon Woods, 53–4, *147*
slow-worms, 67
slugs, *17, 22, 23,* 26, *75*
small copper butterfly, *129*
smooth snake, 66, 67
snails, *16,* 26, 39, *50,* 105, *115,*
    120
    banded, *126, 130*
    great pond, 86
    water, *86*
snakes, 67, 109
sneezewort, *101*
snipe, 35, 98, 108
Snowdonia, *80–1*
soil, chalk and limestone
    grasslands, 39, 46
soldier beetle, *46*
solitary bees, 49–50

Somerset, 51
Somerset Levels, 100
South Downs, 38, 48, *50*
Southampton Water, 112
spangle galls, *55, 57*
spearwort, lesser, *105*
speedwell, 26
    germander, *31*
    marsh, *37*
Sphagnum moss, 100, 101, *103*
spiders, 26, 29, *46, 67,* 73–4, *85,*
    109, 115, 116
    orb-web, *46*
spindle tree, *12, 56*
spire shell, *17*
spleenwort, maidenhair, *81*
springtail, 85
spurge: sea, *126*
    wood, *16*
squill, spring, *127, 128, 129*
squirrel, *19, 54*
Stackpole, 95, *123, 126–7,* **180**
standard trees, 19
starfish, *125*
starling, 35
Stiffkey Saltmarshes, **161**
stint, little, 121
stitchwort, marsh, *35*
Stockbridge Down, **138**
stonechat, 71
stonecrop, 128
stoneflies, 88
stool, coppice, *15*
Strangford Lough, **187**
strawberries: barren, *18*
    wild, *18*
streams, 86, 87–9
Studland Heath, 72, **156**
Studley Royal, **173**
sundew, 104
    round-leaved, *102*
swallow, 35, 92
swallowtail butterfly, 98, 107
swan, 86, 94
sycamore, 51, *58,* 61

T

Tack Coppice, **167**
tannin, 22
tawny owl, 20, 62
teasel, *96*
Tennyson Down, **140**
tern, little, *111*
thistles, *42,* 47
    creeping, 29
    dwarf, *42*
    marsh, 107
    meadow, 33
    musk, *43*
thrift, 84, 116, *122, 126,* 128
thrips, 26
thrush, 35, 50, *59*
Thuidium moss, *80*

thunderbugs, 26
thyme, 27, *38,* 45, 46
tits, 50
    bearded, 108
    long-tailed, 37
toadflax, bastard, 46
toad, 96–7
    natterjack, *115*
toadstools, *39,* 56, 61, *75, 85*
tormentil, 37
tortoiseshell butterfly, small,
    30, 93
Toy's Hill, **142**
traveller's joy, *48*
tree lungwort, 60
treecreeper, *19,* 62
trees: ancient woodlands, 10–23
    boggy areas, 104
    chalk grasslands, 50–1
    coppices, 14–23, *14–17, 21, 23*
    epiphytes, 59–60
    fungi, *60,* 61
    moorlands, 79
    parkland, 54–61
    pollarded, *14–15, 58–9, 63,* 66
    riverside, *92*
    standards, 19
trout, 88, 92
Turkey oak, 51

UV

Ullswater Valley, **177–8**, *177*
Ulverscroft, **167**

valerian, *104, 108*
Ventnor, **141**
vetch, *126*
    horseshoe, 48
    kidney, 49, *126*
violet, *15*
viper's bugloss, *126, 127*
voles, *19, 67,* 72
    bank, *19*
    short-tailed field, 28
    water, 94

W

waders, 110, *117, 118*
Waggoner's Wells, **137**
wagtail, grey, 88
wall brown butterfly, *48*
warblers, 50
    Dartford, 70–2
    garden, *18*
    grasshopper, 108
    sedge, 35, 108
    wood, 23
Wasdale, **178**, *178*
wasps, 49–50, *55*
Wastwater, 94, **178**

water: erosion, *77, 78*
  lakes and rivers, 86–97, *90–1, 96*
water crowfoot, 89, *89, 93, 96*
water dropwort, *33*
water-parsnip, lesser, *93*
water-plantain, *93*
water-soldier, *95–6*
water speedwell, blue, *91*
water starwort, *90*
watercress, *26, 92, 96*
waterlilies, *89*
  white, *95*
  yellow, *88, 91, 95*
Waterslack Wood, **178**
Watlington Hill, **143**, *143*
wayfaring tree, *12, 37*
weevils, *26, 47, 92*
Wembury Bay, **154**
Wenlock Edge, **168–9**
Westridge Wood, **165**
wheatear, *51*
White Horse Hill, **143**
White Park Bay, **186**, *187*
White Sheet Down, **148**
whitebeam, *44*
Whitford Burrows, **185**
whortleberry, *78*
Wicken Fen, 93, 98, 106, **158**, *158*
wigeon, *121*
"wildwood", *13*
willow, *12*
willowherbs: great, *86*
  New Zealand, *79*
willows, *92, 107*
Windsor Great Park, *62*

winkles, *124*
winter cress, *87*
winter moth, *20*
Witley Common, **145**
wolf spider, *73–4*
wood anemone, *15*
wood blewit, *56*
wood sorrel, *16*
woodlands, 10–23, *25*
woodlouse, *17, 22, 23*
woodmouse, *19*
woodpeckers, *19*
  great spotted, *37, 62*
  green, 27–8, 50–1, *62*
  lesser spotted, *37, 62*
woodworm, *55*
Woody Bay, **154**, *154*
Woolton Hill, **138–9**
worms, *35, 39, 67, 120*
wren, *18, 37*

XY

Xanthoria parietina, 128

Yealm Estuary, **154**
yellow flag, *90, 115*
yellow rattle, *29, 31, 32*
yellowcress, *96*
  marsh, *97*
  yellow, *97*
yew, *12, 44, 51*
Yorkshire Dales, *32, 39*
Yorkshire fog, *87, 128*

SANDRA FERNANDEZ

Born in Bombay, India, Sandra Fernandez came to live in England in 1966 and attended the Harrow College of Art from 1979 to 1983, specializing in natural history in the final year of her Diploma in Illustration course. From 1983 to 1986 she attended the Royal College of Art, where she studied natural history illustration. She obtained her M.A. in June 1986, and also won the Hugh Dunn award. While at the RCA, she worked for the National Trust on their Coast and Country posters and on a series of paintings for their stand at the Chelsea Flower Show in 1985. Since leaving the RCA, she has worked for the London Zoo design unit, and as a freelance artist.

PUBLISHER'S ACKNOWLEDGMENTS
Dorling Kindersley would like to express their gratitude to Vanessa Luff for design assistance and for preparation of the maps. Thanks are also extended to Samantha Wyndham of the National Trust for administrative assistance, to Hilary Bird for preparation of the index and to Tradespools Ltd for prompt and accurate typesetting.

PHOTOGRAPHIC CREDITS
136 (top) NT/Rob Judges; 136 (bottom) NT Library; 137 NT/Martin Dohrn; 138 NT/John Bethell; 139 NT/Jonathan Cass; 140 NT/Martin Trelawny; 141 NT/Mike Williams; 142 NT/Skyfotos; 143 NT/Nick Meers; 145 NT/Derek Forss; 146 NT/Alan North; 147 NT Library; 148 NT/P A Wenham; 150 NT Library; 151 NT/R Westlake; 152 NT/R Westlake; 153 NT/E Clapham; 154 NT Library; 155 NT/Mike Williams; 157 NT/Nick Meers; 158 NT/Jonathan Player; 159 NT/John Hannavy; 160 NT/Mike Williams; 161 NT/W R Davis; 162 NT/Mike Williams; 163 NT/Mike Williams; 165 NT/A Williams; 166 NT/Martin Trelawny; 168 NT Library; 170 NT/Joe Cornish; 171 NT/Mike Williams; 172 NT/Charlie Waite; 174 NT/Alan North; 175 NT/Joe Cornish; 176 NT/Mike Williams; 177 NT/Doris Nicholson; 178 NT Library; 179 NT Library; 180 NT/Alan North; 181 NT/Martin Trelawny; 182 NT/Alan North; 183 NT/C M Radcliffe; 184 NT Library; 186 NT/Alan North; 187 NT/Mike Williams.

AUTHORS

Dr. JOHN HARVEY
Chief Adviser on Nature Conservation

Dr. KEITH ALEXANDER
Leader, Biological Survey Team

DAVID RUSSELL
Forestry Adviser

CONTRIBUTORS

JIM HEMSLEY
Past Adviser on Nature Conservation

VALERIE WENHAM
Editor of Annual Publications

AUTHORS' ACKNOWLEDGMENTS
The authors would like to acknowledge their indebtedness in the preparation of this book to work previously carried out by the Trust's Biological Survey Team and Nature Conservation Advisers. This work, in turn, has drawn widely on the knowledge accumulated by the Nature Conservancy Council, county wildlife trusts, many amateur natural historians and the Trust's regional staff. Their help is gratefully acknowledged. The authors are also most grateful to the publishers, to their editor, and to the Trust's Publisher for their help and guidance, freely and patiently given.